THE DEADLY GAME

THE DEADLY GAME

A BRITISH ARMY SECRET AGENT HANDLER IN THE TROUBLES

WILL BRITTEN

The History Press

Cover illustrations: Close Quarter Battle training in Kent; the author and his inconspicuous ops car.

First published 2024

The History Press
97 St George's Place, Cheltenham,
Gloucestershire, GL50 3QB
www.thehistorypress.co.uk

British Library Cataloguing in Publication Data.
A catalogue record for this book is available from the British Library.

ISBN 978 1 80399 381 2

Typesetting and origination by The History Press
Printed and bound in Great Britain by TJ Books Limited, Padstow, Cornwall.

MIX
Paper from responsible sources
FSC® C013056

Trees for Life

To all handlers and their agents wherever they work.
To comrades passed and present.
To Lieutenant Colonel Tom Carter, who made it happen.
And to my children.

★★★

'Military intelligence: a contradiction in terms.'

A tired age-old adage. May you be the judge.

CONTENTS

PREFACE

It was 16 April 1987, a Thursday morning. I looked at my watch – it was just passed 1115 hours. As I had driven to work that morning, in my dirty, covert Colt Sigma, it had looked like being just another routine day in the office. Bessbrook Mill was the grimy, noisy, decaying ersatz headquarters and nerve centre of the Army's operation in the Bandit Country of south Armagh. The Mill was also *our* home.

I was a 27-year-old captain in the British Army and the Officer Commanding South Detachment, Force Research Unit. I was the youngest officer to have commanded a detachment in the unit when I had taken over the role two years previously. The FRU was the British military's most sensitive undercover unit anywhere in the world. Our job was to target members of the Republican movement, recruit them, then run them as secret, undercover agents. Our mission was to control them and work them against their comrades in the terrorist groups of which they were members. This was a secret, dangerous and unrelenting, sometimes dirty battle, to persuade them to turn their backs on their community, heritage and faith, and risk a horrific death as the most powerful 'weapons' in the fight against the scourge of our modern age – terrorism. We desperately needed them in this struggle to prevent yet more cruel and senseless deaths in this tragic, magic land at the hands of the killers of the Provisional Irish Republican Army and their lunatic cousins in the Irish National Liberation Army.

My stomach rumbled. Breakfast in the house I called home, forty minutes north on the outskirts of Belfast, had been too long ago. My head was beginning to ache pouring over the handwritten agent report spread out on my untidy battered desk.

The first deep, dark, distant detonation resonated with a heavy, suffocating sense of evil, doom's drum heralding flame, molten matter, and stench, intent on snatching more souls into the abyss. It penetrated to the very core of my senses. There went a second, a third, a fourth, a fifth, and a sixth with a rolling, thundering inevitability. It was as if, with a predictability and a regularity, a heavy-footed ogre was steadily, horribly lurching towards us as each round exploded, seemingly closer and closer still. I remember instinctively yelling for my guys in the next-door 'binner', if they needed any encouragement, to 'Take cover!'

I lost count as the explosions hammered our senses, but a further ten 100lb home-made mortar rounds arced their way from their bed in the deviously modified tractor-drawn trawler. It had been abandoned 300m away on the normally quiet backroad into the base. The shells exploded as they impacted the walls, roofs and ceilings of the ancient mill. I dived under the desk and just waited, for some sort of end.

There is always the inevitable question asked of soldiers in situations like this, asked perhaps throughout the history of warfare – 'What did you feel? Did you feel fear?' I guess the rehearsed answer is to admit to the terror, and to that feeling of expectation and suspense, waiting for the worst to happen. I knew what was happening; my brain was able to rationally process what could happen, but what I felt was only a supreme emotion of detachment. This was something touching the life of someone else, somewhere else, but bizarrely not me. I was a spectator. It was not my time and not my place. I somehow knew that all of this was not for me. I was to experience this again in the years to come, in other places, more than a handful of times.

By now the devil's alarm had been replaced by another more terrestrial, and the air filled with the ear-splitting fire bells of man.

I got up from under the table, opened my door, and moved into our open plan office. We were lucky – this part of the Mill had not been hit. No damage, no fire, no smoke. Everyone was OK. We six smiled a little shakily at each other as Alistair D, my Field Source Controller and Det 2IC, emerged from his adjacent office – FSC was, I think, an old Secret Intelligence Service label. As we metaphorically shook ourselves off, I made a mental list ticking off everyone who was absent from the office. Certainly no dubious red badge of courage for them, but no doubt instead some black, no-prisoners, Army humour would be raining down on them over the next few days.

I sniffed involuntarily. The dense sweet, cloying, sickly aroma of marzipan had begun seeping under the main locked security door into our office space – way worse than any cake shop at Christmas. Unmistakably the aroma of home-made explosive. Another IRA attack. And none of our agents had reported in – there had been no intelligence to warn of its coming.

'Time to get back to it, boys. Looks like we've got some work to do.'

INTRODUCTION

My name is not Will. Neither am I a Britten, but I am proud to be a Briton. This, however, is not important.

I have always been in two minds, since an old colleague first suggested I put my experiences down on paper, whether to write this account.

Now I have. My reality is that it has now been twenty-one years since the Iraq War, my last operational deployment, and nearly thirty-seven since that April day in Bessbrook. It may feel to me like yesterday, but it is not. Since then the world has changed, the British Army has changed, massively, and with it too the world of military intelligence.

Looking introspectively, I have never described those events on that day in 1987 to family, and certainly not to friends. In fact, I have told very few tales. Those I have, have been fleeting, have been short, vague and probably not very gripping in my telling. My generation – I think I have reached that stage in life when I can point to generational differences – was brought up, regarding things military, to be tight-lipped. And as members of the intelligence 'brotherhood', we have been guided, and constrained, by the catechism 'Need to Know'. More practically, frankly, I've always found it a chore, and a challenge, to match the starkly real pictures in my mind's eye with words that deliver anything near a representative picture that either informs or entertains. Being essentially a lazy person, I could never summon the energy to construct the sentences to match and convey the vivid sounds, smells, colours, dialogue and, above all, images imprinted on those memories. I think there was also a sub-cultural element to this reticence – we found 'swinging the lamp' inappropriate and lacking in relevance – distinctly lacking in modesty and all actually rather tedious and remote for anyone who hadn't been there too.

But those times have changed – and enough time has passed.

When I first sat down, I worried that I would have difficulties. Firstly, in remembering with sufficient clarity and detail to make this 'project' feasible. Twenty-seven years of service is a long time. I was absolutely adamant that I did not want things to be vague recollections supporting a tapestry of, at best, unintentionally blurred, and at worst, out of necessity, 'artistic' invention. But I vividly recall a conversation on the roof of one of our safe houses on the outskirts of Basra in southern Iraq, soon after the conventional war fighting had stopped. Mark D was a member of one of my in-country HUMINT collection teams. They were deployed and tasked primarily to identify human sources who could report on the whole Weapons of Mass Destruction fairy tale. Mark had been a very talented agent handler, I would say one of the best, without any reservation, back in FRU days. In the late 1980s he was running the unit's best agent, acknowledged as the crown jewel in the government's fight against Republican terrorism. Within fifteen minutes I was amazed, and appalled in equal measure, at just how many of the experiences that we had shared in the unit I had been unable to readily recall. Talking with him, so much came tumbling back, however, that I knew in fact that I had in reality forgotten very little. The memories were just somehow trapped waiting to be freed like a miner in a collapsed shaft. They have subsequently continued to reappear, like long-lost relatives at the reading of a will, one memory triggering another and another and another, the trail of breadcrumbs leading steadily and resolutely back into the dim recesses of my memory. It has proved to be both a fun and cathartic exercise.

My second concern was that I was not confident I had done enough to fill a book – there are no short story biographies in the library. But as I started to follow the breadcrumbs, I quickly realised that the FRU, collectively, could write dozens. What we took for granted, our day-to-day work, challenges and successes, were actually not ordinary.

Why did I feel that now is the right time, or rather perhaps no longer the wrong time, to put pen to paper?

The first reason is that everything I will write about happened a long time ago. In professional terms, several generations ago. The campaign in Northern Ireland is a closed book militarily, and politically the Province is relatively stable, though continuing to change and evolve. Nothing I write can prejeudice this. But I do feel strongly that it is healthy to remind ourselves of this chapter in our history, if only to confirm that the tragedy and waste it represents should never be allowed to be repeated.

The second driver for me has been the desire to address and redress a certain imbalance. There is a torrent of Special Forces 'tell-alls'. The war in Iraq, post-stabilisation, and in Afghanistan, have required allied SF to make a monumental commitment, both in terms of sheer operational pace and output, and in terms of personal cost. It takes only the most cursory read of books like Stanley McCrystal's *Team of Teams* or *Task Force Black* by Marc Urban – both limited to Iraq – to get a barometric flavour. In terms of their skill sets, their personal bravery and their sheer motivation, there are no higher-calibre troops in uniform anywhere in the world. But despite the obvious glamour and the appeal of kinetic solutions to our very visual and action-orientated society that they epitomise, they are not the lone standard bearers of the way we bring war to our modern-day enemies.

I want to use this book to shine light on, and pay tribute to, the members of other agencies, other units, and other 'cap badges', who were vitally engaged in our offensive and defensive successes, in this case in Northern Ireland. Then, by abstract extrapolation, to those more contemporary operational theatres beyond. Not least among these are members of the intelligence community – specifically the HUMINT community. They will always play a crucial role in the low-intensity, asymmetric conflicts that may likely continue to leverage military assets into the middle future. No other intelligence source gets inside the enemy's head, into his thought, planning and decision-making processes like human source handling, and I am confident that this will not change with the continuing fight against Islamic extremist terror of today and tomorrow, the threats posed by other 'isms', and the eco-terrorism that I am sure will blight the near future.

Not so many years ago a documentary was made providing a detailed and 'up close' insight into the activities of the Australian Special Air Service. The then Director of Special Forces in Canberra was interviewed and, when asked why the veil of secrecy was being lifted, stated that he felt it right that the time had come to pay homage to the men of the unit and inform the Australian taxpayer of the successes that they, the soldiers, had fought for, and they, the taxpayer, had funded. That resonates with me.

It's not easy, particularly in a counterterrorist scenario, to portray HUMINT's contribution in a way that will excite or enthuse readers. An intelligence success may well be the prevention of something rather than the execution of something: aborting a move of explosives, the disruption of an abduction or an ambush, or the foiling of a full-blown terror attack. Difficult to dramatise something that does not happen. On the other hand, of course, graphically, a helicopter assault on a compound in northern Pakistan and the subsequent shooting of the free world's most wanted man, virtually live on TV, hits every conceivable base. There are books to read, films to watch, TV interviews to sit back and applaud. And truly, a brilliant military operation in every sense, measured against every parameter and metric. But let's be clear. It is less readily apparent and is less readily acknowledged that the success, the very genesis of the operation, like *any* operation, was predicated on painstaking intelligence work at an analytical level, and then by courageous human intelligence operatives on the ground. Ultimately, it was their operational work that confirmed the location and the validity of the target premises. No amount of skill inserting into a target area, no breaching skill, no target clearance skill, no close quarter marksmanship will get the job done if the expertise of others has not generated a job to do in the first place. I want to give taxpayers some sense and insight that their hard-earned contributions can, and have been used, in other effective and, particularly, cost-efficient approaches.

Third and lastly, it is for the families and friends of these other 'hard-hitters', those I served alongside, directly and indirectly, that I want to raise a pennant in recognition of their contribution to our country and our wider alliances.

What I write now is the story of my time across the water in a Special Duties unit, another generation of 'English' soldier fighting on the island of Ireland – and hopefully one of the last. If it also conveys some sense of what it was to be a soldier during these times, then I will be happy. What I write is not an adventure story, nor is it meant to be a history book. The task I have set myself is to create a written documentary that will serve to provide a snapshot of life in a highly specialist unit in British military intelligence.

That stated, it is a matter of enduring trust that as members of the security forces, whether we are military, police, or civilian agency, we bear an inalienable duty to refrain from any act or word that could identify and potentially endanger the life and well-being of those who trusted us – with their lives. Our agents. Despite the passing of so many years, I have gone to great lengths to protect the identities of all sources, and others, and the more sensitive aspects of tactics, tradecraft and some operational capabilities – not already exposed in other intelligence related books, in podcasts, or on our big and small screens – that might impinge on the security of future HUMINT operations. I think we cut deepest with the blade of self-censorship but I also submitted the manuscript to the MOD for clearance and made the relatively few changes that they required. I have to say that this process was conducted with the utmost professionalism.

As a final footnote, all names of military personnel in the text below are not the real ones of those involved in this story, regardless of whether they are alive or no longer with us. Where I have used real identities, they are historical figures and are in the public domain. This is to prevent any likelihood of them being identified, potentially threatening their personal security and that of their families, and encroaching upon their personal privacy. Of course, those directly involved or close to those who feature in the events I relate will likely make the connection. I hope the response is positive.

Despite taking the opportunity to pay tribute to these 'unsung heroes', reveal more of our collective history, and to allow the public a glimpse of the secret world that they have funded, this collection of experiences is recorded first and foremost for my children. Hopefully these words might help them understand more, both about me as their father – I am aware that I am a product of these experiences, good and bad – and perhaps aspects and traits of themselves. Above all, I hope that these pages will make them feel a sense of pride, in me, perhaps in the UK as their country, and maybe help instil in them a sense that it is not a bad thing to pursue and share ideals, nor to work to try to make the homes of others, safer places.

1

FROM LITTLE ACORNS ...

In my earliest coherent memory I am 2½ years old. It's the middle of winter, cold and damp, in a small village on the outskirts of Maidstone in Kent, the Garden of England. I puzzle my mother by absolutely refusing to wear a coat.

But getting to the front door of my nursery school, it is clear to anyone that I am driven by purpose. There is no delaying formality of stopping to hang up a coat, or anything else, as I rush inside. It is equally clear that I have assessed situations, evaluated risks, and formulated a plan of action.

I have accepted that I must brave the cold, clearly negate the time wasted in dealing with a coat, so that I can rush straight to the toy pedal car and grab it before any potential 'enemy'.

Just the actions of an egotistical, self-centred child with sharing issues? I prefer to take a different and more hermeneutic view. With the luxury and perspective of hindsight, I interpret early indicators and precursors, partially formed glimpses of my future as a clandestine military intelligence operator. It's plain to see that I recognised the requirement for bold, cunning planning; a suitable and credible cover story for my mother; the need for the acceptance of physical discomfort; and an overridingly clear appreciation of the interest and value of the car, one of the covert intelligence officer's most precious tools.

Whatever the subsequent analysis, this fleeting episode in my personal development provided a snatched view of formative times that begins to throw light on, and illuminate, some of the early twists and turns in the path life led me down.

2

A MATTER OF LIFE AND DEATH

Two months until the Christmas break and the end of 1983. It was the year the CD player was developed, and pound coins were introduced into circulation. The race horse Shergar was horse-napped, the wearing of seat belts in the front of British cars was made mandatory, and Michael Jackson's 'Thriller' went to Number One in the US. On the world stage, Korean Airlines Flight 007 was shot down by a Soviet interceptor and the Cold War became another degree warmer. At home on the mainland, PIRA exploded a bomb outside Harrods in Knightsbridge, killing six, and in the Province thirty-eight IRA prisoners escaped from the Maze Prison, killing three Prison Service guards. The second anniversary of the death of the hunger striker Bobby Sands had passed in May.

Things in life can and do move quickly when you least expect them to, never less so than in the world of covert operations.

I had only been back from the course a few weeks. As the youngest qualified agent handler in the Det, I was now also the newest. I was still finding my feet but gaining confidence with each new day. More than this, I couldn't wait to get down the road each morning from the safe house I lived in, half an hour up the road, to start work and see what the new day would bring.

I had just finished the Contact Form from my agent meet the night before and had been checking a point of detail in the source file, leaning against one of the filing cabinets in the Det office.

My lasting memory of the office space was that it was without character. It neither excited nor vexed. Our infrequent visitors departed with two shared common impressions. They were invariably impressed with whatever briefing or update they had received, but they would struggle to provide a clear description of the physical space that they had just vacated. It was fundamentally low key, low intensity, and bland.

There was an odour of something, neither attractive nor unpleasant but impossible to name. The temperature was neither warm nor cold. The few windows set into the outer wall were above head height, barred and sealed tightly shut. The penetrating strip lighting compensated for the lack of natural light and generated a battery-farm-like sense of perpetual brightness. Both the heavily painted walls and ceiling – an ageless yellowy cream reflected back the artificial lighting, enhancing the nicotine pallor – and the worn cardboard-thin tattered brown carpet were a study in neutrality. Fixtures and fittings were Army issue utilitarian with absolutely no concession to style or decoration.

The handlers worked in the 'binner', the largest single office. TC occupied his own small room, and I was standing in the ops space where the unit collators worked and from which Det operations were run from the ops desk, dominated by a massive perspex-covered map of our TAOR, our patch. At the far end was a small kitchenette, a small equipment store, and our most secure debriefing facilty decked out as a comfortable but artistically neglected sitting room. This was where we sat with our agents and conducted most of our covert agent meets. A secure door led out discreetly to where our ops cars were parked at the rear of the Mill complex and through which our agents were 'smuggled' into the debriefing room.

The whole place was a triumph of function over form.

TC grabbed me. He was the Warrant Officer running this forward office, FRO Bessbrook – based in an old linen mill in a small village on the outskirts of Newry and a stone's throw from the lawlessness of South Armagh's Bandit Country – reporting back to the OC of E Det in Belfast. And he was my boss even though I was a young officer and he was an older WO2.

He was a legend in the handling world, his easy charm and the soft burr of his West Country drawl were instant draws. His boyish face, belying his forty years, was invariably creased by, at the very least, an infectious twinkling half smile. He sported a full midriff and stood below average height, certainly not a sportsman, but there was a compelling vitality about his easy movements. He projected calm, effortlessly, metaphorically, drawing people towards him with the magnetic quality of a Svengali. He was a natural-born handler.

He asked me to help him out on one of his cases that evening, if I had nothing else planned. I, of course, without a moment's contemplation, jumped at this opportunity to work with him and see him in action, even if it would have meant cancelling a date with Miss Northern Ireland.

The case was one of the first recruitments to be made in south Armagh and had in fact been pulled off by Captain Bob, as Robert Nairac was still openly referred to, with some affection and awe, by people living along the border. Source 1001 was a criminal, loosely affiliated to a Republican organisation south of the border in the Irish Republic.

He knew Dominic 'Mad Dog' McGlinchey. 'Mad Dog' was not a local south Armagh man, nor was he from the border area, south, but he was a devout and ardent Republican from a devout and ardent family. He had been born up in County Londonderry and been interned in Long Kesh in 1971, and the security situation in the Province escalated and began its downward spiral. He was subsequently imprisoned, again, after his release on arms charges. It was then, while incarcerated, that he married Mary. She was to become as ruthless a terrorist as Dominic until she was shot dead, while bathing her young children, in 1987, another victim singled out for retribution at the height of the INLA internal feud. 'Mad Dog' continued to bounce between acts of terror and resultant jail time. While in Portlaoise in the Republic, he became progressively more and more 'radicalised', clashing with the PIRA hierarchy. The relationship fractured and he threw in his hand with the newly formed Irish National Liberation Army. By 1982, he had rocketed up their ranks, combining intelligence and ruthlessness, to become the Chief of Staff. His leadership turned the faction from being a disorganised rump into a finely tuned and feared terror grouping mounting individual targeted assassinations, and the higher-profile Droppin Well disco bombing that killed eleven soldiers and six civilians. He was murdered in 1994 after being released from yet another jail term, probably by members of PIRA in retaliation for a local blood feud, seven years after his fellow terrorist wife Mary.

I provided TC with cover for the pick-up and drop-off phases of the operation and sat in as the acting co-handler. The meet itself was, in the event, uneventful, but continued to raise the prospect of positive case development with increased access centred on McGlinchey. This was tantalisingly upbeat. I expected that I would co-handle the next meet and thought no more about it, next day, as I resumed my own routine that week.

Fact being stranger than fiction is one of life's lamer clichés, but when a few days later TC grabbed me, its validity as a truism never appeared more solid. He hurriedly told me that there had been unplanned developments in the case and bustled off into his office to the secure green phone. Always light of touch and never far from humour, on this occasion his demeanour was far less laid back and considerably more pointed and focussed. TC's comments turned out to be an understatement of dramatic proportions.

Another of our agents had reported the shocking news that our source had been compromised – in less clinical language, blown. Inexperienced as I was, this news sent a cold, icy chill running up and down my spine. That in its own right was inexplicable and fantastic. Even more shocking was the revelation reported back from our other agent that he believed McGlinchey was intending to use the prospect of a meet with the agent to lure us, his handlers, into a deadly ambush. This is the agent handler's worst nightmare – bad enough to be shot dead, but to be taken alive did not bear consideration. Without our warning we were blindly staring in the face a situation that had the potential to be the most far-reaching disaster in the intelligence war since 1969, given the combined weight of our knowledge, especially TC's, of FRU and other agency activities. We would have blindly deployed on the next routine meet with the agent and found ourselves confronted by a likely maelstrom of events that we would have had to fight for our lives to extricate ourselves from.

The shock waves were to roll on. Unbelievably, no other word would do, the compromise had occurred because INLA had in their possession a draft, handwritten copy of the Contact Form TC had written detailing our last meeting – a real FRU document. They now had in their possession TC's and my real identities, how and where the source was met, the vehicles we had used, how much the agent had been paid and all the other operational details pertaining to the meeting.

But still worse was to come. From analysing the contents of the Contact Form, they, INLA, had successfully deduced the agent's identity. While the contents of the CF did not represent a breach of security, the fact that a terrorist grouping, and one so ruthless as McGlinchey's INLA, had a copy of one of our most sensitive outputs was a devastatingly serious lapse of almost inexplicable proportions. But even the most cursory damage limitation assessment was able to identify how the unthinkable had happened.

Tracing and analysing the paper trail, it quickly became apparent that the Det clerk, relatively new, young and inexperienced, had dutifully typed up TC's handwritten draft CF. Upon completion of this routine task he had duly booked the finished document into our secure registry and put the now superfluous draft into the bin. Sensitive waste was placed in the 'burn bag' for proper, thorough regulation destruction by burning, along with all other classified waste from that day. In his haste to have his tea, finish for the day, or whatever else had depressed or distracted his attention span, he had placed the draft in the wrong container. The one he had selected in error held non-classified 'household' rubbish. This was not routinely incinerated. Instead, it was collected internally within the Mill, by whatever internal process the Armagh Roulement Battalion employed, and centralised for collection by the local authority. No one had spotted the document as it sat surrounded by far less valuable detritus either in the Det, not least the man who put it there, or as it was moved around the Mill to the central collection point. Before reaching that point in the process it was truly lost.

Domestic refuse from Bessbrook village, including from all residents of the Mill, was transported to the civic tip in neighbouring Camlough, a hard Republican village, for landfill. Unbeknown to the Army, everything arriving at the tip was sorted through by local volunteers and anything of interest passed on to the Provos. They would have sorted through this delivery as it lay stinking on top of years of other refuse, non-classified papers, crisp packets, teabags, soiled paper towels, empty cans, bottles and all the other unwanted spoils of modern life, and no doubt to their incredulity found an intelligence document, each page stamped 'SECRET' in vivid red top and bottom – our draft Contact Form. PIRA, perhaps half wondering whether this was a ruse and part of some black deception operation, had passed a copy of it onwards to their cousins in INLA.

That is the chilling and freak anatomy of an agent compromise – perhaps the most bizarre and incredible in the history of the Irish troubles.

Regardless of right or wrong, blame or anything else, we had to take action and take it rapidly. Our lives were not now in any current danger, as we now knew the full scope and scale of the situation, but the life of our agent was unquestionably suspended by a thin and, as each minute passed, an ever-thinning thread. We confronted, in the most literal and serious terms, a race against time.

If he had not been grabbed by 'Mad Dog' already, a team could, at this very moment, having been made aware of the traitor, be en route, with fury and retribution in their hearts. His end could be imminent. The worst-case mental image of him sitting on a ring of an electric cooker somewhere in Drogheda or Dundalk was not an appealing one, nor was that of his final moment, hands tied and eyes blindfolded as 'Mad Dog' or one of his henchmen squeezed the trigger.

The Top had already sanctioned an extraction plan and ordered TC to get moving and quickly. For their part they would have notified the Security Service through the Assistant Security Political in Headquarters Northern Ireland, HQNI, in Lisburn, and invoked the required liaison to activate planning for a resettlement somewhere on the mainland – work for London.

Back in Bessbrook, we needed no push to get us into action. We sat down as a detachment and hastily identified and drew together the various hard and fast factors and potential variables, putting together an operation to get the source out of immediate danger, over the border from his home in the Republic, and into the North and away. If the gods were not with us, it was clear to everyone that there were a lot of things that could go wrong and a lot of 'what ifs' that might not break our way. These could make shaping some sort of happy ending much less likely and considerably more dangerous in the trying. Things were simplified because the agent did not have to vector this potential complication into our planning or have the problem on the ground of trying to persuade a wife to accompany her husband on his extraction in order to minimise potential leverage that could be exerted on him once the terrorists realised he had escaped them – in the case of a high-level agent compromised, through no fault of our own, and successfully pulled out of the Province, without his family, that was to break open not too many years from now, it was graphically exemplified that it is imperative that once resettled, an agent must cut all physical and emotional ties with home, or his life will never be free from the prospect of danger. Failing to make this break cost this highly placed and courageous FRU agent his life. We also had to ensure that on his sprint north, 1001 brought with him as much relevant documentation as he could feasibly grab: passports; proof of investments and deeds, if any; and bank books. All the paperwork that defines and regulates a modern life, and cash and valuables.

Phase One of the operation that we crafted was to reverse contact the source, give him an overview of his predicament, and brief him on what actions we now needed him to take. TC made the telephone call to the agent's home. Thank God he happened to be there and answered the phone. TC reported that, so far, he was safe, that all appeared calm and normal, and that he appeared to understand the update he was given, and its gravity. He appeared calm and ready to accede to his quick-fire, immediate tasking.

We readied ourselves to make the extraction.

We had already made the decision that to cross the border into the south was not only dangerous – we could handle that – but could potentially cause a major diplomatic incident. Members of the SAS had already been arrested by the Garda several years before in totally 'innocuous' circumstances. Just the presence of two covert vehicles equipped with communications gear carrying heavily armed British soldiers would be the catalyst for a ringing, stinging demarche. A firefight on southern soil would likely bring down the walls of Dublin Castle, even without the reality of casualties.

Instead, the source was instructed to drive north, and at the point where he crossed the border from the Republic into the United Kingdom, we would be waiting for him. As the driver of the lead car, I was ordered, if he attempted at any time, once we had RV'd, to re-cross the border southwards, to ram him off the road – this did seem unlikely but had to be planned for. We planned the contingency that he might wish to stop by his parents' home in Camlough to say his farewell. With this quick visit over, we would lead his car to a location and transfer him into another of our vehicles, rather than continuing in his own, in order to protect him, and take him to the security of the East Det secure debriefing location, inside the safety of Palace Barracks on the edge of east Belfast. Tommy W, one of our collators, and myself would take the source's car in a two-car convoy and leave it in Thiepval Barracks in Lisburn. We would then join the rest of the team at the Palace safe house. A simple but effective plan? We could only hope and pray that it would be so, and ensure that we were as professional and operationally flexible as we could be on the ground.

The atmosphere in the Det was tense. This was the most serious job the office had ever mounted. We were facing our most challenging demons with no clear expectation as to who would triumph. Everyone was inwardly focussed not just on their individual roles in the forthcoming operation, but on the stakes if things went wrong, as we prepared our personal and support weapons, readied the cars, and ensured we had comms to the ops desk. As I readied myself, I thought back to our meeting those few short days ago. Although, as I had witnessed, not the sharpest knife in the kitchen drawer, he certainly was a credible street animal, having sufficient savvy, guile and courage to mix with his terrorist-affiliated confederates.

This gave me confidence he could do his bit. I was not, however, convinced in my own mind that he had grasped the true implications of what TC had hurriedly imparted to him, but it sounded encouraging that he was at least reacting to them. Above all else, I felt a great weight pressuring me with the appreciation that a lot could change very rapidly and that the situation intrinsically held a raft of variables that could rapidly turn against us, and ultimately sink us.

There were eight of us now on the road south from Bessbrook and we looked anything but covert. A male/female mix in a car draws not a second glance – in both a covert surveillance and an agent-handling scenario. Two men in a car can look incongruous, and in the heart of south Armagh would get 'the look'. Four rough-looking, relatively unkempt gents will be eyeballed all the way down the street – the car is either being driven by terrorists en route to commit a murder, or by likely covert policemen in pursuit of the terrorists to prevent that murder. This was not, however, the time for introspection, or for tradecraft niceties. The cars would be changed after the operation and if need be we could alter our appearances with little effort: a shave here, the growth of some facial hair, or even just a haircut.

We headed towards the border at speed. This was no time to dally. It was imperative that we were in position first, in order to monitor the situation from a security standpoint. We needed to make sure that the immediate area was clear and that the source's progress would be unimpeded as he entered the North.

We got to the RV point with no sighting of the source's car and prepared to await his arrival. Conversation was light and constrained. I don't know what the atmosphere was like in the second car, but in mine it was serious with none of the usual banter and joking. We were fully wound and coiled spring-like, but collectively calm and controlled. Nothing appeared untoward, certainly at this stage of the operation. We sat in our vehicles, providing cover to each other from the 50 yards that separated us. Of course, time began to drag as the seconds turned to minutes. It was not feasible, conducting the most rudimentary time and distance calculation, that we had missed him. Either he had decided not to show, had been grabbed at this final, fateful last minute, or, following his instructions, he was on his way as planned. How long does it take to grab your life, stuff it into a battered suitcase and flee? It's probably not quick, even though he did not have any explaining to do to a Mrs Agent as to what an earth was going on. In an ideally run case, neither a wife nor children, nor any other relative or friend, would have any inkling of the agent's secret life with us, or potentially little earthly idea of the types of terrorist thug our agent had been fraternising with.

We strained our eyes, looking as far as we could down the road and into the Free State. We kept checking all our arcs of view ensuring we were alone, hoping that they would not become 'arcs of fire'. Left, right, right, left and back again, all the time willing his car to come into view and for it to be alone. And then there he was! I recognised his car. His tail appeared to be clear. There was no one following, at least in close attendance. He got closer. All seemed to be OK. As he drove past us he clearly had seen us. He was alone in the car, behind the wheel. We pulled past him and the cover car slipped in behind his. There was an almost audible momentary release of tension like the air escaping from a bicycle tyre as the valve of the pump is disconnected.

Once we had cleared the immediate border area, and ascertained that we were still not being followed, we pulled over to enable TC to have a quick update chat with the source and establish that all was well, that there were the minimum of issues from the source's perspective, and that we could continue north and to safety. TC nodded – the lighter feeling among us grew perceptibly lighter yet. It looked like we had done it, and disaster had been averted. Back to my rule of thumb that an operation that starts well usually ends well. But we were not yet in the clear, and fortune has its ruthless and unforgiving way to punish over-confidence.

When he got back into the car, TC confirmed the suspicion that we needed to make a quick diversion to the parents' home in Camlough. We alerted the cover car and the ops room and moved off again. By now it was definitively clear that neither we nor the source were being followed. However, the parents' place represented a potential known location that could be exploited by the terrorists in any last-ditch hot pursuit attempt to grab their traitor and maybe take us on. It seemed an unlikely contingency but by no means to be glibly shrugged off. We had assessed that it was unlikely a terrorist ASU would directly assault a group of covert soldiers – that would be poor and dangerous risk management on their behalf. PIRA were more predictable but in the case of INLA any ground rules, or conventional wisdoms, were always pitched at a different and less predictable level. They had some crazies who might not be constrained by the established etiquette and operational niceties of terror.

We pulled into the parents' quiet street and parked up, still in tight formation. TC got out again and briefed the source to be as quick as he could – he did mention the continued possibility of some sort of contact with the bad guys. For his part, our man, at least outwardly, remained calm and unhurried. If he did truly understand all the ramifications of his current situation, he did not display any overt concern. I felt a sudden wave of affection towards this brave, brave man – it was a relief that at this stage, as he confronted family, that we were not having to deal with some sort of outburst or fight that could trigger a return home. That would have complicated things exponentially. Perhaps this would come later, but by then we might be able to contain and direct the emotion in more convivial surroundings than here on a hard Nationalist street.

As the agent, now effectively an ex-agent, entered the house, we resumed our anxious wait in the cars, continuing to feel a little easier that things looked like they were going to play out to our play book. The street remained quiet. I am sure curtains were twitching, but if they were, they were in the hands of experts. We felt we were provoking no undue attention even though we continued to look like a sectarian death squad on a break. At least in a Nationalist area no one was likely to call the police. As the clock ticked on, I for one started to get twitchier, but this was more a symptom of inactivity than the fear of action to come. We continued our vigil for some forty minutes. The street remained empty and completely devoid of any activity – it was almost as if the neighbours felt something was afoot and that they should play their part accordingly and remain inactive as sequestered observers in the wings. Finally, he re-emerged. TC intercepted him and briefed him on the next phase of this surreal morning – literally the next phase of his life, although at this juncture I am positive he had no inkling that his life was about to be so drastically reshaped and relocated, never to be the same again.

North of Bainbridge, on a parallel country lane, we RV'd with the rest of the team, with another Det vehicle driven by the other collator and another cover car, driven by Tommy W, the last of the Det's deployable manpower, just as had been detailed in our orders. Source was swiftly transferred into it and the three vehicles continued on their journey up the A1 towards Belfast, ultimately to safety and a time and place to take stock and rationalise the activity and meaning of the few last hours. Tommy's role was now to accompany me to Lisburn. We surveyed the wreck that up until that moment had been our man's car – it would never be so again, but for an additional reason that was yet to play out.

I decided I would drive the source's car. I scrutinised it as I walked around it conducting a brief cursory inspection, like a potential buyer at a dodgy car auction. If it was roadworthy it was certainly borderline. The bodywork was rusted, the paintwork faded, scratched and marked. It was indeed a bucket. It struck me as perverse how in the different world I felt I lived in, a car was, if not an extension of one's personality, then certainly an important visual signal as to how one wanted the rest of the world to see and judge one. Clearly in the world our agent had up to this very moment inhabited, his car bore no more importance to him than a hobbling old donkey. The driver's door creaked with terminal arthritis. The interior was even worse. I had my doubts that the seat belts provided any degree of security or that the heater worked, but noted that the ashtrays were still definitively fully functional. The stench of stale cigarettes, to a non-smoker like me, was overpowering. Every pore of the car's internal fabric must have been clogged and choked by nicotine and tar residue. I climbed reluctantly in, turned over the engine, got the gear lever and clutch to function in unison selecting first gear, and, seemingly defying the laws of auto engineering, moved off cautiously. I was relieved not to stall it. It felt strange driving the car of a man who had so courageously lived and risked his life helping us make this land a safer place, and at this moment, through no fault of his own, was being forced to abandon friends, family, heritage, lifestyle and this car as he fled northwards towards an unknown and uncharted new life.

But before we had gone too many miles, my reverie and our luck ran out as the engine, without drama or warning, died and we coasted to a halt. There was fuel in the tank, if indeed the gauge was functioning properly, but something beyond my technical expertise had clearly failed. Thankfully here, a few miles from the Loyalist stronghold of Hillsborough, rather than on the outskirts of Dundalk, a wild-west town and refuge for northern on-the-run gunmen, sitting menacingly just over the border. If the car had broken down in the south we would have been facing the challenges of a very different morning.

All FRU cars had emergency kit in the boot, so we fitted the tow rope and crawled the rest of the way to Lisburn, four-way hazard warning lights on, amazingly seemingly functioning normally, and the main gate of Thiepval Barracks – really covert. At the time I was glad we did not have to negotiate the traffic around Belfast. I was to change that opinion by the early hours. Tommy cleared us into the HQ and we lurched to one of the internal car parks, disconnected the rope, switched off the four-ways, locked up, and left for Palace Barracks, Tommy at the wheel of his works Peugeot.

By the time we arrived, our guest was already settled into the Palace safe house and TC had begun the process of explaining the new realities and ramifications that would now be steering his life, and reassuring him of the support and help that he was going to receive. Beyond this, more pressingly to us, a babysitting rota had been drawn up to cover the week as it unfolded while arrangements were confirmed for his future. He would not be alone for a single minute, day or night, but reassuringly fully engaged and occupied to keep his mind focussed from being distracted.

Later that evening, as we continued settling into our new routine, as we were finishing the first of a host of takeaway meals, we got a call from a very unhappy FRU Commanding Officer. A car parked on one of the Thiepval car parks had been reported to the main Guard Room. Its hazard warning lights had been blinking away furiously, and that and the whole dilapidated state of the car had provoked the suspicions of an onlooker. A roving guard force had moved to check the vehicle and on radioing through the car's VRN, all involved were rocked by the trace that came back – the car was registered to a known INLA associate from South Armagh, yet, unbelievably, it was sitting parked up in the middle of the headquarters responsible for directing all military operations throughout the Province. Naturally the proverbial hit the proverbial. A monstrously major foul-up had somehow conspired to admit a terrorist car bomb into the holy of holies. ATO, the bomb squad, had been tasked to deal with this threat and the immediate area was cordoned off to contain any resulting damage.

At this point someone with a keener brain had thought it could be useful to run the facts, as they appeared, past the FRU for any inside steer or comment. As this conversation was taking place, there was a dull explosion as ATO conducted a controlled explosion to disrupt the suspected vehicle-born device and neutralise the threat. Our agent's car had now definitively and without debate made its last journey for sure and was irrefutably an insurance write-off, if indeed it had ever been insured – an unlikely proposition for a car garaged in Bandit Country.

What obviously had transpired was that after I had switched off the four-way flashers on parking the car, an electrical fault had, at some point later, reactivated the circuit and they had begun flashing merrily away again with Christmas-tree regularity, until an observant military passer-by had reported them. It was an embarrassment for the unit but just one of those blameless quirks of life once an untoward chain of events begins to uncoil – Murphy's Law. Ultimately, we had to remain sanguine. That this was the worst that fate had dealt us in this freakish disaster should have left us massively relieved. But we cursed yet more bad luck – the incident with the bins should have satisfied the gods and persuaded them to move another unit or organisation into their sights.

The ensuing week was uneventful. The time passed quickly for us as we had the distractions of Det life to contend with outside of the constraints of our babysitting duties. I'm not so sure that the clock hands spun with the same dexterity for the source. He remained upbeat but I think was still recoiling from the 'shock of capture' and unable in these early days to fully process the full implications of the whole event. The real reality and the real implications were only abstract. He was, however, slowly but surely starting to come to terms with that new reality and was beginning to paint tentative mental pictures of how things might be. For him, his past was over and his future not yet begun. How the two phases were to weld into one was something too alien and too opaque to fully comprehend.

We continued to distract and entertain him to the best of our ability, consciously attempting to repay him now as best we could for his sacrifice. At one stage we escorted him out shopping, not in the circumstances the dangerous, risky enterprise that it might sound, as up here in the safety of Prodland the risk was strictly minimal and controllable. We conducted more debriefs to ensure we had sucked out every last drop of juice from the case, and then our agent was scooped up and taken on his way to his new life across the Irish Sea.

In the post-mortem that inevitably followed the whole sorry chain of events, it was confirmed beyond doubt how the draft CF had ended up on Camlough tip. I am pleased to say that the young clerk was of course disciplined but not sacked from the unit. He was stunned and shaken, for the first time confronting the serious reality he was professionally immersed in. He had not followed procedure but it was an honest stupid mistake.

It was also confirmed that when the terrorists were handed the draft CF, they very quickly identified their mole and made the decision to attempt to set up the handlers. Maybe there was some discussion as to whether so blatant a piece of good fortune constituted some sort of black operation on the part of the 'SAS', as all covert agencies were labelled. We did not know, nor did we find out the answer to that one. There could well have been, because certainly McGlinchey, for his part, was not stupid, nor were PIRA. We didn't know whether the plan to hit TC and me included turning our man, or whether they aimed to put him under surveillance so that he unwittingly led them to us. We were fortunate enough to get inside their decision-making cycle thanks to the timely reporting of our other agent – whatever the bad luck we had courted, this piece of stunningly good fortune had more than compensated for it. Of course, it could be argued that we had made our luck, but being so close to the potentially awful outcome I did not underestimate or underplay my good fortune. It had been a positive fluke that our other agent had not been down with flu, at his parents' home, off on a tryst with his girlfriend, shopping in Dublin, or the dozens of other innocuous everyday events that could have prevented him getting sight of the CF when it was discovered. Thankfully he was able to appreciate its significance and call through his warning to us before it was too late.

In conclusion, the Det's handling of, and reaction to, events was assessed as having been beyond reproach and a model hot extraction. We bemoaned the loss of an asset who had not yet achieved his full potential, but could be content that strategically we had not positively affected the collective psyche. We had not allowed the forces of terror to dump yet another mutilated body on some desolate border crossing point, hands bound, eyes blindfolded. Every dead agent reinforced the imperative and Republican mantra that informing would end in death, serving graphically and chillingly as the ultimate deterrent dissuading targets from agreeing to work. Instead, it demonstrated that the Army would look after its people, and if the time should ever come, get them out to safety rather than deserting them and leaving them for dead.

As a postscript, the source rapidly slipped into drugs and crime. Perhaps this was only an extrapolation of the way he had already lived life and was inevitable. I have not heard whether he has since married and settled down, or whether he returned home, with or without new family – that would not be unthinkable, as the bond with soil is a very tough link to break for the Irish – or whether he is still living in his adopted but enforced new homeland. Whatever, he still had his life, and at least it did not end with a bullet in the back of his neck. The closing of this case brought focus to some of the wider subjects that intrigued me as a handler, but of course were not topics one could ever openly discuss with an agent. Did they ever dwell on the prospect of compromise? How effective were our words of reassurance and the example of our tradecraft and the tacit protection that they implied? How did they feel their own motivation developing and broadening – did their commitment harden and negate some of the fears that would assail any normal person brought into this world? How did they ever envisage the end coming if they speculated about it? Did they believe that we could and would protect them? Did they ponder the prospect of a new life away from the pressures of life in the Province – might they even subliminally welcome it? In this case, did our source become resentful of his commitment to us? How much blame did he apportion to us for the dramatic and far-reaching effect on his personal and family life, or did he accept his fate stoically? Compromises were very, very rare for us as an organisation – I can say unreservedly that the FRU did not lose a single working agent during its existence – so most of these mental meanderings were moot, but I think we would be less than human or professional to ignore them.

For our part, we had been loyal to the very robust and ethical philosophy that the FRU preached – no agent's life would be sacrificed for any 'greater good'. If the life of a FRU agent was threatened, and exposure was assessed as imminent, he or she would be hauled from out of the jaws of danger, 'smuggled' across the Irish Sea, and provided with a new identity and a new life.

Whatever, we had been very, very lucky – it ended as a matter of life, not death. But it had been a close-run thing.

3

ONE STEP AT A TIME

It was the early spring of 1983 and I had not yet met TC or journeyed down to Bessbrook Mill, passed the course, let alone played my part in so crucial a covert operation as the previous pages detail.

I unpacked my kit, preparing to settle into the busy cosmopolitan Headquarters Northern Ireland Officers' Mess, situated within Thiepval Barracks, after taking possession of my jerry-built room in one of the overflow portacabins. Someone had obviously rated my potential to alter the balance of power in the Province as low to non-existent and allocated me accommodation to match. I didn't care. I was here to work not sleep, and as far as I was concerned a bed was a bed – the pragmatism of youth.

I had just finished, a mere fortnight ago, my first job in the Army attached to the Royal Scots, an infantry battalion on a so-called eighteen-month 'residential tour'. We had been based not far away down on the south Down coast in Ballykinlar, where, in the words of the song, the Mourne Mountains sweep down to the sea. Despite my simple relocation a mere forty-five-minute drive north to the HQ in Lisburn on the southern outskirts of Belfast, as a young Intelligence Corps officer, my professional life was about to start for real as I collected myself, poised to commence my first intelligence job.

The previous twelve months had been fun but challenging, leading infantry soldiers on live operations in the border country where this part of County Armagh rubbed up against the southern county of Monaghan. The war against the ruthless terrorists tearing this beautiful land apart was not quite as intense here as the one being waged further south in the Bandit Country of the south of the county, but it was nonetheless no picnic. I had learnt a lot about soldiering, about soldiers, about the Troubles, and about myself.

I was 23, and not so long out of university, where I had spent my three years as a young Second Lieutenant on a Cadetship. We were fully sponsored and paid by Her Majesty, identified, supposedly, as the most promising twenty or so officers of our year of entry. Tomorrow would be my first day as a professional intelligence officer on the path that, as I stood gazing reflectively out of my single badly fitted window, would lead me on the adventure that was to befall me.

I was privileged. I was being posted, again, to the British Army's only live operational theatre, worldwide, as the rest of my colleagues 'fought' their phoney battles as part of the wider Cold War. No matter how the government chose to package it, war was raging in the Province, we were fighting it, and it was a hot and dangerous one.

123 Intelligence Section was unlikely to find itself directly in the firing line, but it was an operational intelligence unit. It was the professional intelligence cell responsible for pulling together all incoming, accessible intelligence reporting, collating it, and producing written, and where pressure of time dictated, verbal briefs, for the pair of Brigade G2 intelligence staff officers. The Brigade in Londonderry was supported by 122 Int Sect, and Headquarters Northern Ireland, where the generals sat commanding the campaign, by 121 Int Sect. 120 Security Section provided protective security cover for all units on a Province-wide basis. The Brigade G2 officers, paradoxically non-intelligence professionals, as captains and majors fulfilling career-advancement-dictated staff posts, were responsible for producing intelligence assessments to inform their brigadier's operational planning.

My role was to command the twelve-man section. I was to be responsible for maintaining the quality of its product and managing the welfare of its soldiers, male and female. On my arrival in Lisburn, the unit was about to be relocated from the Headquarters to the outlying 7/10 UDR company location in Ladas Drive, literally directly adjacent to the infamous RUC Castlereagh police headquarters/holding centre. Coincidentally, and fatefully as it transpired, Ladas Drive was also home to another lodger unit, East Det FRU, the base from which the unit's agent handling operations in Belfast were mounted.

I arrived, thankfully, on the back of my predecessor's logistical work to move the unit. He was a big bear of a man, later moving on to work for Barclays Bank. It was very quickly brought to my attention that his claim to fame in the Brigade HQ, co-located next to HQNI in Thiepval Barracks, however, was inadvertently to have fired his 9mm Browning pistol into a radiator in the main corridor – the hole was pointed out to me with relish, but certainly none was felt on my part. So-called negligent discharges, or NDs, totally negated any claim that an incident like this could be accidental. They were consistently attributed to a disregard of safe weapon handling drills, which in reality was always invariably the case, and ruthlessly punished under military law by loss of a month's salary. I figured any perception of my professional image was already in credit.*

* At the very end of my career, I served as the Senior Member, as a Lieutenant Colonel, on a Board of Enquiry convened to review the evidence surrounding a serious incident during the Iraq War. The unit involved was the Black Watch. They had served in the conflict as a Warrior armoured infantry battalion. The Warrior Armoured Personnel Carrier mounted a 7.62mm chain gun alongside its main armament, a 30mm RARDEN cannon. During the incident in question, it was claimed that the commander of one of the battalion's Warriors, himself an extremely experienced and senior NCO, had initiated an ND with his chain gun, resulting in the life-changing amputation of another senior NCO's leg – he had happened to be in the line of fire. Myself, a Junior Member (a Major), and a civilian judge advocate reviewed all the evidence, much of it relatively technical but understandable, including personal witness testimony, and the evidence of technical experts, most slanted towards the Ministry of Defence perspective, over several days of deliberation. We concluded without hesitation or doubt, much to the surprise of those in the courtroom, and to the consternation of the MOD, that on that tragic evening there had been no compromise of safe weapon handling drills, and that there had been no negligent discharge by the SNCO 'in the dock'. →

Time passed slowly and without incident – or any excitement. I learned plenty more about the background to the Troubles, increased my personal knowledge of the main terrorist personalities and the various groupings' modus operandi, and a little about the secret units engaged at the forefront of our war on terror.

I returned to the mainland, to Ashford, to tuck a couple of professional career int courses under my belt, including an NI-related int staff course. Not very interesting or testing. As OC of the int section, I was also the Brigade Screening Officer. I did the short Screening Course at the Joint Service Interrogation Organisation in Templer just before the concept of Screening was abandoned. Screening was a hangover from the days when, exploiting their powers of arrest, the Army could hold targets for a maximum of seven hours and question them before being obligated to release them. In the 'good old days', it had proved to be an excellent means to generate the 'point of contact' to initiate dialogue with a target who was assessed as having the potential for cultivation, and ultimately recruitment, as a human source. As a tool, it had played some role in the early careers of a number of FRU assets.

I was fortunate to have a very talented and able WO2 as my deputy. He was not only good company but proved a generous and informed tutor. His excellence left little for me to do. So I would often catch myself watching the comings and goings of the East Det guys, and a couple of girls, through the window of our shared office. They seemed forever on the go. Untidily dressed in innocuous jackets and jeans, hair longer, one or two with overly tightly curled locks, a few beards and moustaches, swinging duffel bags into and out of their cars, and mysteriously leaning over into

---

Rather, the firing of the chain gun had been precipitated by a technical design fault in the Warrior's electronic firing circuit resulting in this 'un-demanded firing'. Frightening. The 'verdict' vindicated the Black Watch Warrant Officer Class 1 (WO1), but sadly did not prevent the premature ending of his career. The exposure of the technical fault cost the MOD a large compensation claim, and required extensive and costly modifications to all Warrior APCs. The last I heard, the unjustly accused WO1, instead of enjoying the commission he could have expected in recognition of twenty-two years of exemplary service, was running a pub on a Scottish island. Altogether, a sad tale.

car boots before unobtrusively heading out the main gate. I was soon to learn the explanation for these rituals, and indeed practise them myself. This seeming degree of variety and implied excitement looked like representing the vague, shadowy roles alluded to in those Int Corps recruiting pamphlets that had impressed me as a very young potential officer trying to decide on the direction of my future, just six short years before.

As part of my professional development as OC 123, I was scheduled to go to Hereford, to the SAS depot, to undergo a Close Quarter Battle – CQB – range course. An exciting enough prospect, but with even greater anticipation I was also booked to attend, through the ministrations of Colonel Tom Ford, the very course from which all FRU operators had to graduate, the misnomered Northern Ireland Research Course. The term 'Research' used in the context to denote agent handling, rather than some analytical role or process, was another old throwback tipping the hat in recognition of the pedigree of SIS in this discipline. As I daydreamed, my mind most definitely began to wander and focus on what could and might be – one day.

Then lo – never doubt or dismiss the power of positive thought or underplay the sheer imagination behind the hands that fate stores up and deals our way. The decision was taken, ostensibly out of the blue, to dis-establish the officer post commanding 123, no doubt based on my assessment of its value being shared by bigger boys with greater influence. Still, a bit of a shock and slightly disconcerting. But I could hear the muted conversations in the corridors inhabited by other big boys that this bold initiative precipitated. What, then, to do with the young me? No NDs, no RTAs or car accidents, no premature marriages, positive feedback from a few good performances on the recent courses, no real dramas at all – he must be a fairly OK young guy. Seems pretty mature, maybe he has potential.

The FRU, like all the Special Duties units, was always under-recruited with desks sitting vacant in all six of its operational locations. I suspect that at some point the hierarchy entered at least one of the aforementioned discussions. 'Why not give him to us for the experience – he is already at Ladas, why not send him across the car park to our side?'

4

BIG BOYS' RULES

So, incredibly, cross it I did. I had now become, ostensibly out of nowhere, a member of E Det FRU, currently without portfolio, but with my foot very firmly in the door. To say that I was the happiest soldier in the box was an understatement. I was unable to believe the scale of my good fortune and an accruing sense that some bigger force may just have been set in motion.

Like the other FRU detachments, then two, with an additional four forward offices, plus a HQ team, manpower in E Det was split roughly down the middle. Half were Int Corps volunteers, and half from other arms and corps within the Army. Most of these were infanteers. Later, under what became OP MAXIMISE, recruitment was widened to all three services and the FRU began competing with the recruiting machine of the Army's surveillance unit, 14 Coy, on an equal footing, looking, however, for fundamentally different character traits and skill sets, despite necessary operationally related skills overlap. All handlers within the FRU had to be volunteers and had to have successfully passed the Research Course at SIW in Templer Barracks, Ashford. Later, under the OP MAXIMISE umbrella, recruitment would become more formalised and structured, and all volunteers, responding to 'the call to arms' on unit routine orders, would have to attend and pass a testing pre-selection phase, also run at SIW, as their ticket to the training course.

All officers in the FRU were cap-badged Int Corps, and of course also had to pass the Research course – to an enhanced but uncodified additional standard. In these relatively early days of the unit's existence, most were commissioned Warrant Officers, not Regular Sandhurst-trained officers like myself. Approximately half the Corps' officer cadre were these so-called Late Entry officers. This guaranteed them bringing to the job, in most cases, a tremendous amount of experience in the HUMINT business. Support staff within the unit, clerks, motor mechanics, later radio techs and our own organic logistics quartermaster sergeant, were all posted in on 'normal' routine postings and did not have to receive any specialist training, as their roles were non-operational. (We did, however, take them out on the range periodically with us so they could practise anti-ambush drills and maintain their basic skill at arms.)

When I joined the Det, I have to say that I felt my welcome was not universally open-armed. 'Who is this sprog and what's he doing here?' I could discern some reticence on the part of some of the E2s, the non-Int Corps operators, but the Corps handlers were generally much more open, or hid their contempt more professionally. It did not, however, take long before all ice was broken and I felt completely at home and accepted.

The OC at the time was Peter, a senior captain. We had daily contact; always, without fail, open, warm and professional. When we both returned to the unit, he as the Ops Offr, sitting in HQ FRU located nice and discreetly on the edge of the HQNI compound, me as OC S Det, we did not always agree on everything, but nothing changed – he was always one of the good guys.

Peter took me under his wing during my time in Ladas and certainly played a role in schooling me for my now rapidly unfolding future. His Field Source Controller, known as the FSC, and 2IC, Harry T, was a Warrant Officer who had, unusually, transferred to the Int Corps from the RAF. He was tough and strict, but not without a very dry sense of humour. While not always popular, he was unequivocally respected – much more important in his position. I think, had he been in post a few years later, problems that arose then would not have done so. I liked Harry and always felt that we had a positive relationship. We later attended the same Long

Surveillance Course. We were paired together on exercise on the rural covert Observation Post, OP, phase of the course. Somewhere on the outskirts of Ashford, we were covertly ensconced in some scrub watching the target farmhouse. You know you have a fairly good relationship when you can happily crap into a plastic bag – for strict operational security reasons, nothing else – in front of each other. Actually, I don't, in point of fact, thinking about it, remember him taking a dump! Never mind. Another story involving Harry showed a more ruthless side to his character. I hope, if he reads this, he will forgive me for recounting it, but it quickly became common knowledge within the unit. One of the handlers in the Det was Gary Nightingale. He was also Int Corps, cheerful, easy company, but I think not a favourite of Harry's. On one occasion they were driving together up the hill in Lisburn on the main drag to the HQ in Thiepval Barracks. On the right side of the road there was an extensive warren of married quarters for both officers and NCOs, as there was very little family accommodation situated inside the wire. All the housing was readily accessible by a busy network of access roads. Just passing the junction of one of these side roads, the car drew level with a woman weighed down by shopping, and struggling up the hill. As an observant and situationally aware covert operator, Gary checked the woman. "Look at the state of that pig," he retorted, passing on the invitation to Harry, who was at the wheel. Without breaking step, Harry accepted Gary's kind rejoinder, and, responding in his dour Geordie accent, stated, without any hint of expression, "That's my wife." Whether it was or not, Gary left the unit not long after. He sadly died a few years later, suffering a heart attack while watching *Grandstand* on an otherwise uneventful Saturday afternoon.

Peter made it clear to me that, as an untrained member of the unit, there would be no opportunity for me to get out on the ground on operations until I had passed the course. I had no quibble with this – my lack of tradecraft knowledge and CQB skills at that stage would represent a risk to the security of both handlers and agents on any pick-up or drop-off. I was mollified by the prospect of heading off on the course in a matter of weeks. Then things would be different.

Until the course in October, I was therefore set to work reading-in on case files, extracting as much useful knowledge as I could from them, listening in on ops briefings, the formal orders group led by the lead handler formally briefing his cover team(s) prior to deploying on a job, and generally mixing with the handlers and Det collators. I was able to dig into a mine of wisdom and valuable advice. As I began reading, with intense anticipation, through the Contact Forms, the agent meeting reports from which the case files were constructed, I sought primarily to get an understanding of the lives of these unbelievably brave and courageous people who daily risked their lives in the struggle for peace and normality. I wanted to get a feel for how they lived, what they thought, but primarily what drove them to put themselves in harm's way and daily confront the reality of an awful death at the hands of the terrorist internal security teams. Somehow, however, I found the reality of these written words, instead of trumpeting the high nobility of self-sacrifice and ideological intoxication, was all rather ordinary and mundane.

Of course, the identities of all our agents were scrupulously and very tightly controlled and never revealed outside the FRU, beyond the tight circle of the upper echelons of the Special Branch and the small Security Service presence on the island, but beyond one or two surprises they provoked no seismic gasp of awe. To clarify, although in the nomenclature of covert operations we ran 'agents', the FRU rarely used the term, and certainly not in our day-to-day conversation. We referred to our assets as 'sources', which of course they were – human sources. I will use the two terms freely and interchangeably. In the Nationalist/Republican lexicon, they were, and would only ever be, 'touts'. I have to say we regularly used that term too, despite its obvious negative connotations.

Everything I began to witness bore that semblance of established, unflappable, routine 'ordinariness', epitomising and mirroring the quiet, confident professionalism a visitor would see in any British Army unit. Naïve, really, to have expected anything to the contrary. It was true without doubt that the FRU's role was highly classified, its function and purpose well protected from any casual observer, both inside and outside the military, its work critical to the fight against terror, and its daily routine hazardous – and further, I would contest that it was the most fascinating, valuable and rewarding work any of us would do in our working lives. It was all of these things in spades but, at the same time, to most of those of us inside the unit, it was just a job on which we daily and modestly embarked, in an even-handed and no-nonsense way.

In parallel to building a strong base of tradecraft-related knowledge, I researched the main PIRA personalities active in the various ASUs within the Belfast Brigade structure, and those faces we knew who were part of PIRA's strategic level Northern Command staff. At the operational level there were, of course, the 'shooters', but there were also bomb makers, PIRA's own intelligence 'staff', quartermasters marshalling the group's guns and explosives, couriers, the much-feared internal security team members, their counter-intelligence operatives, and other supporting 'players'. INLA had its own structure and so too did the Loyalist gangs – arguably, the Protestant gangs were more ruthless and indiscriminate than their erstwhile Republican 'colleagues'. There were also the higher-profile politicos in Provisional Sinn Fein. A sound knowledge of the who's who of all the various functional and geographic areas was not just nice to know but essential in tasking our agents and making sense of their reporting. I put together photo books, pulling the latest images, taken from a variety of overt sources – green patrol photography, RUC mugshots, etc. Each handler had his or her own editions and used them as aids during face-to-face meets to help agents identify personalities of whose names they were unsure.

Recalling how the green army addressed the important issue of 'terrorist recognition' demonstrates graphically just how many times the planet has spun in these intervening thirty-odd years. Patrol members would regularly be sat down by the company intelligence NCO and treated to slideshows of Ireland's most wanted, in order to keep their features in the forefront of the young soldiers' minds. I can hear the collective intake of breath expressing concern about big brother, the means by which the pictures had been procured, and the egregious infringement of people's rights to privacy. But the bold, brutal reality was that this was a country ablaze with civil war and this stern rogues gallery was restricted to unsmiling rogues, only to law breakers and fanatics who viciously fanned the flames. In short, killers. Except that it was not, and they were not. To keep the minds of the captive audience focussed, alert and receptive, additional pictures of grinning, 'improperly dressed' young ladies were ingeniously slipped in, at very regular intervals, to bolster the impact of the running order. A contemporary take on the subliminal images of the 1950s pushing Coke and hot dogs, only now less subtle and more pointed. If 'now' was 'then', imagine the social media frenzy.

I also destroyed large-scale Ordnance Survey map sheets of the city, cutting them up to construct fantastically detailed A4 map books as the first, drier and less-tiring step in getting to know the hard Republican 'ghettoes' of the west and north of Belfast. Every new member in the unit, regardless of Det, would spend their initial days and weeks mirroring this less glamorous, but essential, foundational work, as they found their feet and began consolidating the practical lessons they had learned on the course. As the staff at the Manor back in SIW always stressed, the real training began on arrival in the Unit.

To consolidate my own self-taught geography lessons, I organised to blister onto regular green army patrols deploying in the hard estates to the west of us. These all passed off without too much incident, and served to put very vivid and valuable 'faces' to the infamous names that have now passed out of common parlance – unless you still happen to live there. Every 'parish' had its own unique character and its own chronology of violence. New Lodge and the Ardoyne to the north; the Beechmounts; the Divis flats, now long since pulled down, a nightmare urban planning catastrophe, right next to the famous Royal Victoria Hospital; Clonard; Turf Lodge; the more genteel Andersonstown; Ballymurphy and Gerry Adams's home turf; and the new housing of Twinbrook on the back door of our hometown, Lisburn, to name but some.

I'm not sure which unit was babysitting me but it wasn't the Royal Highland Fusiliers, tough little men from Glasgow – they were working north Belfast. I spent a few days with them later and had a useful time. Somehow the uniforms of the RHF looked as though they had been borrowed from a bigger cousin or a friend – too baggy and too big. Pretty sure it was a less-renowned English county regiment. Anyway, not relevant to the event I relate. We were patrolling on the edge of the Beechmount estate mid-evening. A small crowd had gathered and words were spoken. A small localised fracas erupted. As I looked on, a girl of about 18 marched over, pointedly and directly, to me, spat in my face, and punched me. Not very hard and not much spit, but sufficiently irritating. I did not retaliate. At this juncture a slightly younger lad had, I think, tried to pull one of the patrol members' rifles away from him. He failed, I think punching the soldier in his frustration, and hightailed it with us hard on his heels. He crashed through the front door of one of the dilapidated Victorian terraces down the street. We followed in hot pursuit, bursting through the same door. We were met, incredibly, by a settled family scene as mum, dad, an older sister, a younger brother and the lad we were chasing sat as composed as you like watching a game show on the TV in the corner of the front room. It almost looked as if we had somehow mistakenly charged into the wrong house, but I recognised the runner without doubt. I moved and reached across to him as four or five other young infantrymen crowded into the small parlour. I put my hand on his chest. It was still heaving like a Munro fell runner's – no doubt our man. But with that the whole room erupted as Ma and Pa, little brother and sister launched themselves at the patrol members. All a bit one-sided. Alas, the TV was the first casualty, but happily the only lasting one. In very quick time a couple of RUC officers who had been accompanying the patrol arrived on the scene and took charge. All a great waste of time and energy, perversely humorous, but sadly indicative of the poor relations that generally existed between the Nationalist community and the Army in the west of the city.

Later that week we were the targets of more street violence, and we had to take an injured patrol member to the casualty department of the nearby Royal Victoria Hospital for some stitches and a quick examination of his head. It was a touch bizarre seeing a nurse, who I was then going out with, on the scene and having to ignore each other – the RVH was not a safe place for a soldier or the friends of soldiers.

The most spectacular feature common across the city, in both Loyalist and Nationalist heartlands, were the ubiquitous heavily politicised oversized murals. These were the wasted work of truly gifted artists and brought a splash of sectarian colour and form to the otherwise depressing monotony of endless terraces and semis. I always thought that here was a brilliant project in waiting, to capture these spectacular wall images, and produce a glossy coffee table book – an effective and poignant historical source.

I don't remember how the invitation came about but I also rode for a week of night duty with B Div's Divisional Mobile Support Unit, the DMSU. B Div was the police area covering the most notorious parts of west Belfast. The DMSU's role roughly mirrored the Army's QRF concept. They toured the patch in their light grey armoured Hotspur Land Rovers, providing an instant manpower surge and enhanced capability to colleagues in trouble.

The whole crew was great company. They were very professional and 100 per cent dedicated to their role and to their profession. Bouncing around in the back of the Hotspur for most of the hours of darkness was tiring but never for a moment boring – in fact, I would weight these moments as some of the most physically exciting in all my years out on the streets. And in the fields and lanes. On returning to their base at shift's end we would relax with a quick drink and a laugh before driving home. The tiredness did begin to pile up in the office as the mornings after unfolded, as I worked normally for most of the working day as the quid pro quo for my nights of fun – definitely a good trade.

During my week, I was able to answer a very specific question from one of the handlers regarding an address in the Clonard, and had a short but sympathetic chat with Anne Donegan, a well-known female journalist with the *Irish News* whose father, Joseph, had been savagely and unmercilessly beaten to death by members of the Shankill Butchers gang in retaliation for the kidnapping of Sgt Thomas Cochraine by the IRA in County Armagh.* Joseph

* It was October 1982, and during my year's attachment to the Royal Scots, after leaving university. We had been part of the massive search operation launched to find the UDR man. He was tragically found dead a week later. It was an incredibly poignant experience – I have never forgotten the feelings and thoughts that coursed through my mind as we searched for him in vain.

Donegan's life was forfeited for no other motive than that he was born a Roman Catholic. She struck me as a brave young woman.

The highlight of my busman's holiday, however, was the quick reaction follow-up to a PIRA attack on a mobile patrol using a new and novel, but dated, Swedish-made anti-tank weapon. We had been cruising literally a few streets away when the contact report came over the air. We raced into action, screeching around corners, braced for possible action. I was dressed for the occasion as usual in NI patrol boots – fragile but incredibly light high-ankled boots, perfect for urban work, and designed to fall apart at the end of four months' constant use – nondescript green army lightweight trousers, standard combat jacket and black beret, minus cap badge, and armed with a 7.62 SLR, just in case.**

No sign of the gunmen on the street, but we quickly located their burning getaway car on a small square of waste ground surrounded by a growing and excitable crowd, drawn moth-like to the flames. Missiles began raining down in our direction, then a few petrol bombs to add some back-lighting. I fired off a few plastic bullets from our Federal Riot Gun, on the instruction of the vehicle commander, a super, big, burly sergeant, firing through the ports in the side of the rover. The plastic, not rubber, bullets of the FRG are designed to be a non-lethal weapon to encourage rioters to disperse. They should be aimed and fired at the target's lower body, because at closer range if they strike the head they can, and will, kill. A Molotov burst on the bonnet and petrol-fed flames started licking up towards the windscreen. We reversed at speed, out of trouble, to extinguish the fire. We called in the location of the car for forensic follow-up, and continued sectioning the immediate area. Predictably still no sign of the terrorist team. Eventually, we knocked it on the head. A 0–0 draw.

**The Belgian-made FN SLR was much too heavy, too long, and used overly powerful and weighty ammunition. Eventually, not too far in the distant future, the MOD saw the light and we followed the US precedence of dropping to a smaller, lighter 5.56 calibre weapon. However, instead of adopting their tried and tested Armalite family, we went for our home-grown 1950s bullpup-styled SA80. Better now, but initially a liability loathed by our troops.

Later that same week, I was out again with the same crew. We were mobile on the edge of the famous Milltown cemetery, last Republican resting place, sandwiched between the Falls Road and the M1 motorway. The cemetery has become synonymous with Republican terror; a total of seventy-seven PIRA volunteers are buried here, including the hunger-striker Bobby Sands and three of his comrades. The site filled TV screens on the back of the Gibraltar SAS shootings when UVF terrorist Michael Stone launched a one-man attack on mourners at the funeral of the dead IRA bombers, killing three. In the seemingly endless cycle, the terrifying, graphic 'Army Corporals' incident unfolded with an unstoppable, heartrending inevitability as they unwittingly drove into this funeral procession.

Our sharp-eyed driver had spotted movement on the edge of the cemetery plots. Clearly highlighted by the moonlight were three men. We stopped and piled out to follow up. The three spotted us and made haste further into the cemetery. Two escaped, but one was not so fleet of foot and he was grabbed. He was a youngster. And a glue sniffer. The gaggle had taken cover among the gravestones, not engaging in any terror-related act, but to chase the UHU dragon. He was pretty wasted but was able to remember that he lived in the Divis flats.

He joined me in the back of the Hotspur as we made to take him home. We climbed to the second floor of one of the spines. It was not unheard of for furniture, old TV sets and anything else bulky to be let loose from the ramparts onto troops or police below. As we ascended, we enjoyed the confidence that we were being covered by the permanent OP on top of the taller Divis Tower. At his door, the sergeant knocked, his other hand grasping the miscreant. We could hear movement and sounds from the TV inside, and the door dully opened. Like a crouching tigress, the lad's elder sister listened at the open door to the tale of his wrongdoing, then grabbed him and pulled him inside the closing door. We could clearly hear the blows and kicks she inflicted as she vented her honest, working-class fury on the poor lad. From my perspective, I was greatly impressed at the even-handed manner in which these tough, hardened DMSU guys policed a very ordinary policing matter – for them a rare instance of 'ordinary decent crime' in the NI lexicon. They took the matter seriously, but instead of turning the issue into a criminal statistic as they could very easily have done, they let family assume their traditional role of judge, jury and enforcer. I have never forgotten the comic ending to this episode of drug squad meets community policing. As for the glue, I suspect it was confiscated and played an important role in some weekend DIY project.

Back at my desk, I watched and listened as the wheel of normal activity in an agent-handling unit continued turning. Meeting sources, debriefing sources, report writing, intelligence dissemination, and most importantly, ever pushing and questing to identify and recruit new blood – new agents, new intelligence streams.

Most meets were 'ordinary' and routine. They would produce a steady but ever-changing and growing wealth of background intelligence, depending on the agent's degree of access and their personal motivation and capability, from which our understanding and knowledge of the terrorist groupings and the environment within which they operated continued to accumulate.

Occasionally this rhythm and tempo would be energised by the report of something directly exploitable. Agents with direct access would phone in and pass on to us details of terror attacks about to be mounted. On these days, the handling team would invariably be forced to organise a rapid, responsive 'emergency meet', the ultimate test of tradecraft and training. This is the ultimate pay dirt that underpins the very existence of an agent-handling unit – all the training, infrastructure, expense … This is the one moment that exercises, to the full, every ounce of agent runners' professional expertise. The whole question of exploitation is at the core of the FRU's raison d'être. If it is handled right, the agent lives to report another day, the terror groups receive a hard knock, and it's 'tea and medals'. If it goes wrong, it might ultimately mean death, but hopefully potentially the extraction and resettlement abroad of the agent before then. Enormous disruption and, in a word, failure.

I recall one of these days when the whole organisation slipped imperceptibly up into overdrive. It illustrates with perfection the anatomy of a perfect case study. The poignancy of direct access on the part of the agent, with none of the supreme complications of being too close to the execution of the operation, the flawless illustration of good operational and security SOPs demonstrated by the handlers, and the epitome of unbreakable trust and collective teamwork on the part of both source and operators.

All was quiet, another routine day had already begun as handlers busied themselves preparing for the day's meets, writing up yesterday's reports, the collators and clerks at their desks processing paperwork, names, addresses, typing and filing. The E Det ops desk source phone began its shrill call that something abnormal was about to reset the day's agenda. It jolted the duty operator into action, that instantaneous burst of adrenaline unsteadying her hand as she lifted the receiver. The message was short, crisp and clear. She acknowledged it with equal but confident brevity and replaced the receiver. She checked the emergency meet folder on the console, closed it, and moved to Peter's door to brief the boss that the Det had an emergency meet to execute in just ninety minutes' time.

The handling team slipped into fast-ball mode, rapidly going through the pre-planned emergency meet drill for this agent. The cover team and ops desk were briefed with a practised rhythm covering all the salient points of the pick-up, meet location and drop-off. Actions on unplanned contingencies were confirmed and the team moved briskly to prepare meet gear, weapons and comms.

The source who had called in using the oft-rehearsed code words was a reliable, tried and tested asset with a good track record reporting quality intelligence. For him to phone in and request a non-scheduled meet signified something important and time sensitive – he wasn't calling because he was short and needed a tenner because the fridge was empty, or that his wife was expecting again. The team deployed through the Ladas main gate towards its pick-up locations.

They returned an hour later and moved without break to de-kit, foregoing the normal post-meet coffee and laugh with the duty op, straight to Peter's door. Drawing interested and pointed glances from Det members at their desks, it was obvious something big was about to blow.

The agent had picked up from an associate within one of the main Loyalist terror gangs that they planned to 'assassinate' a leading mover and shaker in the Republican movement. Their plan was to follow his car from a known start point in Belfast city centre that their own intelligence team had identified. At a suitable junction, halted at traffic lights, the attack team's motorcycle would pull up alongside the stationary car and attach a home-made explosive device to the roof of the car. As the motorcycle and its two riders pulled away, a short-duration timer would wind quickly down and the bomb would explode, killing the target vehicle's occupants. The brilliantly simple plan would likely have killed all aboard. Including Gerry Adams!

Let me turn the tables on you for a minute. With the opportunity to let one wild dog kill another and embrace the death of your, and arguably the government's, number one enemy, what would you do with this pre-emptive intelligence? Ponder for a minute. I'll tell you what the FRU did. Peter reported the threat straight to the Ops Officer in HQ FRU. He briefed the Commanding Officer, who in turn alerted the Security Service via its co-located Assistant Secretary Political, and the Head of the RUC Special Branch. Adams was warned, as any off-duty member of the RUC or UDR, or ordinary member of the public, and his life saved. This, ironically, was not the last occasion on which he received redemption thanks to his number one enemies in the Force Research Unit.

Returning to the source, he received a bonus, and resumed both his life and his role as an agent. There was no complicating security issue for the handlers to manage. From the perspective of the Loyalist killers, it was just another operation that had to be aborted when the intended target just failed to show.

Another case illustrates what can be done holistically by a well-coordinated intelligence machine, directed by the Tasking and Coordination Groups, at the top of their game.* A source reported

* The three regional TCGs, one each in Belfast, Londonderry, and one for the sticks, were a vitally important initiative providing a fusion centre in which intelligence reports from all sources, human and technical, could be merged, assessed and used to key operational tasking to exploit it. They were →

on the location of a shop being used by senior members of PIRA's local brigade as a location to meet to discuss operational agendas. As a stand-alone piece of intelligence this was interesting, but unlikely to bring peace nearer or lead to the military defeat of Republican terror. However, from the perspective of professional intelligence officers, begin to scrutinise the report through a wider angle lens. Two readily identifiable operational paths emerge to explore, not necessarily mutually exclusively. Firstly, assess the viability of inserting a covert OP, manned or technical, to impose surveillance on the premises to identify who enters, and by implication who may attend meetings staged there. A second, better option: install a covert remote listening device, potentially with an additional visual capability, into the shop to record the meetings. If during their course future operational matters were discussed, then bingo, exploitable intelligence. This is what happened, and over the duration, produced extremely valuable intelligence.

During this period I got a bizarre call from Justin, the OC of 12 Int & Sy Coy, the holding unit that provided administrative support to all the intelligence sections and, at this juncture in time, also to the FRU. We would later go weekly to sit on, or by, a topographical feature in the pretty and undulating County Down countryside to look at operational scenarios that could face the armoured formations of 1BR Corps sitting looking at the Inner German Border assessing their Soviet rivals in 3 Shock Army. Perverse, yes, but very practical in my preparation for my upcoming captain's promotion exams. His background as a Royal Green Jackets officer, a smart and professional infantry regiment, was absolutely appropriate.

---

also responsible for imposing and managing operationally restricted areas. These areas would be requested to sanitise the location of a covert operation, mounted either by FRU, 14 Coy, SAS, or the Close Observation Platoons. The area placed out of bounds could be very localised or cover a number of grid squares. Once imposed, the restricted area gave confidence to the covert operators that no overt green army unit, or routine police patrol, would be operating in their operational area and thus preclude the chance of a blue on blue gunfight – covert troops and overt troops do not happily mix. Big boys' thinking informing big boys' rules. The FRU did not use OOB areas to protect its meet operations.

On this occasion, however, he made reference to a very sad incident that had recently occurred in far-away Berlin. In the depths of whatever black place he had found himself in, the senior Warrant Officer of 3 Int & Sy Coy had signed out one of the unit Brownings and shot himself in the head in the unit toilets. Justin asked me to visit his estranged widow, living in her native Bangor, and deliver to her a two-fold message. Firstly, to inform her that, currently, her deceased husband's ashes had been misplaced but would be found. And secondly, just as soon as they had been located, they would be en route to her in the post. I was frankly shocked at the Pythonesque nature of his tasking, and wondered how on earth I would be able to find the right words to mollify her dismay, distress, and no doubt disgust, and ease her continuing sense of loss. If nothing else, the blend of character and talents that mark the British Army officer ensures our infinite adaptability, and having located her address in one of my map books, I drove across the city to deliver my messages.

I found her house on one of the innumerable suburban streets of the seaside town, and parked up a couple of hundred yards down the quiet road in front of an identical red-bricked semi. As I opened the garden gate to cross to the front door, it promptly fell off in my hand. I hastily wedged it back into place, speculating on what other disasters awaited me. In the event, things unfolded calmly and straightforwardly. She was a sympathetic and understanding woman who received my shocking, and frankly unacceptable, news with grace and composure. There was little more that a 24-year-old, with scant life experience, could say in the circumstances. I had not really known her husband, nor, at that stage of my life, suffered any close personal loss myself. I quietly left, successfully negotiating the broken gate.*

Back at my desk, I looked on with interest as the time of the Province's 'Supergrass Trials' unfolded. The phenomenon was a

---

* I had met him when I made my one-month attachment to the Berlin Security Company during my final summer break at the end of my degree, but had had little to do with him. As part of my commitment as a Cadetship officer, I was required to attend a one-month attachment during the long summer breaks. At the end of my first year, I spent it learning German in Mulheim on the banks of the Ruhr; during my second, with the security company in Cyprus.

runaway train that looked to have the potential for removing a whole generation of Republican terrorists in one surgical 'name-and-tell' swoop. As they were taken into custody, one after another, these panicked hard men rushed to turn Queen's evidence, implicating the next man, and the next, and the next, each in turn assuming the mantle of the newest supergrass, in return for immunity from prosecution. It looked like the last man standing would be crushed under the weight of bearing judicial responsibility for every terrorist outrage perpetrated during the sick life of the Troubles. The raft of arrested terrorists, technically 'assisting offenders', were positively gushing with evidence of compatriots' complicity in a whole multitude of terrorist crime – a hysterical pyramid scheme of gigantic scope and scale. In one of the ensuing trials, twenty-two IRA suspects, named by PIRA member Christopher Black, the first of this crop of supergrasses, were convicted and sentenced to over 4,000 years in prison. From my limited and relatively uninformed perspective, this potential revolution looked capable of bringing the end of the war a very considerable step nearer. What was the future for highly specialist agencies like the FRU if the volume of violence substantially reduced? Could things begin winding down before I had had the opportunity and time to even 'wind up'? By the end of the year, over 600 terror suspects from all groups, from both sides of the sectarian divide, had been named in the testimony of a further twenty-five supergrasses – an unbelievable development. In the end, however, most of these convictions were overturned, and by 1985 the brief era of the supergrass had run its judicial course. Its collapse saw a return to business as usual with the killings and maimings tragically continuing apace, and with them a continued raison d'être for units like the FRU.

As I alluded to, the covert agencies were perpetually undermanned. Too few volunteers volunteered. Too few volunteers successfully passed the courses. The Det in Belfast did not have enough handlers, but the situation in Bessbrook, from where the FRU mounted operations in south Armagh, was even more chronic. My personal fate was about to take that far-reaching twist, and all my preparatory work in Belfast go for the proverbial 'ball of chalk'.

At the time, the office located in the Mill was a Forward Research Office, or FRO as they were labelled, commanded from Belfast by Peter. Day-to-day command was in the hands of one of the unit's legends, an infantry WO known to everyone as TC. He and Tony D were the duo whose hands, by implication, had saved the lives of dozens and dozens of innocents, when they recruited our top source. North Det, based in Londonderry, commanded three FROs amidst the lakes of Fermanagh, and there was a further HQ Det, that worked directly from HQNI running the unit's best agent.

I had already met TC – of course, I got to know him even better, and very quickly learned to respect and admire him. TC is one of a very small group of former colleagues with whom I attempted, and succeeded, in remaining in touch with all these years. On a trip up to see his boss, with or without any prior discussion, TC formally requested that I be 'detached' and accompany him south to swell the ranks of his small band. Maybe Peter had to first gain approval from the CO, but regardless, the proposal was sanctioned. I now found myself officially detached from 123 Int Sect to E Det FRU, and from E Det to FRO Bessbrook. I felt like I was being money-laundered, but well and truly a million dollars. I was elated because I fully appreciated the challenges against which TC and his team battled, and sensed that the frontier spirit of life on the border was definitely and absolutely for me.

So, I travelled down to the outskirts of Newry in TC's car and became the newest member of the team working the toughest patch in the Province against the hardest target, and the most deadly of PIRA's groupings. I had no conception then, but I would spend somewhere in the region of four years there, returning to the office once it had been 'spun off' into an independent South Det. These were to be the most challenging, rewarding and happiest days of my career.

5

INTO THE MILL

I have always felt happier in big cities, but the prospect of moving to the wild country of south Armagh felt right. I could sense the magnetic draw of the almost mystical rolling hills biting strongly, and the beckoning challenge of facing off against the most feared and formidable group of terrorists in the Province, and perhaps without exaggeration in the history of asymmetric warfare, irresistibly.

The Det occupied a small of suite of office space at the rear of Bessbrook's mill. Since 1845, when work began on its construction, it had been a linen mill, but was now better known as the British Army's headquarters closest to the border with the Irish Republic in this corner of the Province chistened by, and known to, all as Bandit Country. A small, insignificant part of the aging edifice was still operational, in the industrial sense, producing machine-woven carpets, but like the building, the industry was slowly but surely dying as supply moved east to low-cost producers in Pakistan, India and China. The former workforce, a harmonious mix of Loyalist and Nationalist residents from the village, now served the needs of the so-called resident battalion, and its sundry specialist lodgers, as it rotated in and then out every six months.

I very quickly settled into the small office. It was certainly the home of some real characters and a hardcore of seasoned operators – Andy M, who very sadly died a few years later, Gerry A, Martin C, and Phil P. I learnt from TC right from day one that circumstances dictated I would take a much more active and progressive role than my armchair-bound one in East. Springboarding off the course, the plan was that I would return as a fully enrolled member of the handling team, working my own caseload; provided, of course, I made the grade. Until then, though, I would be an active member of targeting patrols and would ride shotgun on cover jobs where a third gun was required. Of course, in quieter moments, I would also need to prep my maps, terrorist recognition aids, and work to learn the patch, but imagine how energised and privileged I felt now that chasing down these mundane tasks was not the only reason for my daily 'commute' to the Mill.

Unlike the other offices in the unit, our role was limited to targeting Republican terror groups – PIRA and INLA. The reality was that the Loyalist organisations had zero presence in the Nationalist heartland of Bandit Country, so were 'ping-less' on our sonar scope. There was a fallacious attitude held generally within the military that the Protestant groups were not really our problem – this was a mistaken attitude not shared by the FRU. Especially in E Det, considerable effort was consistently devoted, successfully, to frustrating the insanity of their savage murderous intent.

Any agent-handling organisation is ultimately only as good as the new assets it recruits and brings online. Relying solely on historic recruitments, without the transfusion of new blood, it will atrophy. To be successful, it therefore has to balance its operational output between running existing cases and targeting new sources. New targets for exploitation are identified by a combination of research and active agent reporting. On a rural battlefield like south Armagh, the quest to recruit them necessitates the systematic, regular and time-hungry exploitation of the only effective way to engineer those initial contacts. That meant handlers had to deploy in uniform and devote tremendous amounts of time and energy blistering onto the regular patrols mounted by the resident infantry unit, the ARB. Targeted patrolling was invariably the only guaranteed way the FRU could get alongside people to begin the courtship that might ultimately lead to a covert recruitment attempt.

Time passed quickly. I jumped at every opportunity to work and gobbled down as much experience as the team tempo could heap on my plate. My apprenticeship provided me with invaluable experience, and served as a tremendous confidence boost as the days counted down to my return to Templer and the Northern Ireland Research Course.

6

TO THE MANOR BORN

Basic training in 'mil-speak' refers to the initial course a soldier, or for that matter any member of all three services, attends during which the essential generic and foundational skills of his or her profession are learnt. For infanteers, or gunners, or engineers, or tankees, attendance will be at their depot. For Army officers, training is at Sandhurst, in the town of Camberley to the south-west of London.

That said, I do not consider my own personal basic training to have taken place at the Royal Military Academy. I do acknowledge that my courses there were key because I did become an officer in the British Army, and to do so an understanding of leadership as a concept and certain practical skills are essential. As young officers, it was essential that we trained to lead. It was a fundamental 'trade' skill, and beyond that it is also an essential life skill. Wider than this, the courses provided an understanding of the institution I would become a member of, what the British Army did, how it did it, and the wider conceptual framework it served. But while fully accepting this, I have always considered myself first and foremost an intelligence officer and, within this broader church, a human intelligence officer – a HUMINTer. So, for me, the skills and lessons I needed to acquire – my basic training – was the Northern Ireland Research course at Specialist Intelligence Wing's Repton Manor.

The Research course distilled and showcased the collective learning and experience of military intelligence collection exploiting human sources in low intensity, asymmetric, counterterrorist warfare, drawing together the British military's lessons since the end of the Second World War. This is a rich background to draw from. It created a course that could not be bettered, I would contest, anywhere in the world by any military or any other agency.

The Manor was how we 'insiders' referred to the institution. It was rarely afforded its full formal name verbally or on paper – in fact, it is slightly embarrassing to admit that I struggled to remember whether it was in fact 'Special' or 'Specialist'. It was always, at its most formal, SIW. It was here that I received the practical grounding and the shaping of my professional outlook that were to underpin everything I was to undertake, and achieve, over the next twenty-three years. With hindsight and without doubt, it was the single most formative experience of my career. I certainly enjoyed other courses and unquestionably learnt valuable lessons, whether it was Military Attache training, Psychological Warfare, the BRIXMIS Special Duties course, or the National Hostage Negotiation Course run by the Met police, but I will always acknowledge the debt I owe to SIW's trainers for the down-to-earth, no-nonsense, no bullshit, professional way in which they directed the training and, critically, passed on their treasure trove of knowledge and experience to me and to everyone else. I think, like the vast majority of handlers who have passed through the course and gone on to dedicate themselves to the operational task, that the staff regarded their job as agent handlers as a near-sacred mission, to be carried like a torch, burning brightly, to be handed on to the next generation following them. I certainly feel, particularly in terms of the FRU handlers of both their and my generation, that we form a small and tightly knit club.

SIW was divided into three functional 'schools' – Surveillance, Agent Handling, and E Branch – a distinct 'need to know' function, plus a small stand-alone team known as Liaison Branch. The Northern Ireland Research course was Agent Handling Branch's baby – the handling branch for short. They also taught a pared-down, tradecraft-centric package to prepare handlers for operations in other more permissive theatres, grandly known as the Rest of the World Course – all theatres outside of Northern Ireland, including diverse and challenging environments like Hong Kong and Belize.

Surveillance Branch taught the covert art of observing and following targets – covert passive surveillance – to Int Corps personnel, and others, who served in surveillance teams deployed across the Int Corps Order of Battle. The objective of this training was to provide the static Observation Post, OP, and mobile skills, on foot and vehicle-borne, with which to obtain intelligence on a target, or targets, maintaining control of them in a completely covert manner. In other words, passively and defensively to avoid detection. Int Corps personnel who served in these intelligence-gathering units, and subsequently volunteered and served with 14 Coy in NI, led the training for the surveillance phase of their course.

The handling branch directing staff who made the greatest contribution, and left the most indelible mark on me, were Nick, Graham, Tim and the OC of the branch, Pete Giddy. I would work with Pete briefly the following year. Having retired from the Army, he perished in a tragic accident while working for another agency.

So what was the course about? As was explained to us in our introductory lecture in one of the Manor's bare bones syndicate rooms, its syllabus would turn us into agent handlers. Above that, into agent handlers working in the least permissive, most dangerous environment anywhere on the globe, against the most formidable and ruthless enemy anywhere in the world.

We would learn everything we needed to know to run agents covertly and securely while inflicting maximum harm to the terror networks. We would learn fundamentally how to talk to them; how to build and maintain relationships that would have the strength and robustness to survive against the corrosive, all-embracing terror of operating against, and among, the terrorists; how to debrief our agents effectively, drawing out every last gem of intelligence that they knowingly, or unwittingly, collected; how to write the reports documenting each and every covert meeting and contact; how to disseminate the relevant intelligence, governed by the sometimes conflicting criteria of maximising both security and utility; how to task our agents while minimising risk but maximising effect; the subtleties of exploitation in terms of steering an agent to increase their direct access et al.

We would learn how to meet agents – all the operational techniques and phases of an agent operation, from pick up, safe debrief, to drop off. And all the contingencies, all the uncertainties, that an agent handler must plan for – the 'what ifs' that can and will intrude on the best-made plans.

We would learn how to identify new targets for recruitment; how to initiate and develop a relationship with a target, in all environments, urban and rural; and how eventually to 'pitch' that target in a planned recruitment operation exploiting the holy trinity of agent recruitment. I would further add the factor of 'capability', assessing if the contact possessed the basic make-up to perform the function.

Because, as agent handlers, we represented PIRA and INLA's most hated number one enemy, it was critical that we learn how to defend ourselves, and our agents, should we come into direct, kinetic contact with our enemies. On the ground this would either occur in a deliberate ambush, the worst-case scenario of all, or through the vagaries of being in the wrong place at the wrong time, running inadvertently into someone else's problem. The shocking news footage of the death of 'The Two Corporals' in Belfast in March 1988 graphically underlined this imperative. This meant close-quarter battle skills, more close-quarter battle skills, range work, range work and more range work. We were re-taught to use the Browning 9mm pistol until every aspect of its operation became more than second nature and more than instinctive – later the unit would adopt the Sig Sauer range of pistols. Safe handling drills became unthinking, smooth and reflexive. Despite the reality, that there had never been a gun battle in the Province when a pistol magazine change had been necessary, we exhaustively practiced the instinctive and smooth reloading of our 9mms. As our only permanent companion, our pistols had to become an extension of our bodies and our marksmanship skills unconscious, automatic, but above all else effective. Hand and eye were synced to work together effortlessly and seemlessly; muscle memory became more than a trite buzz word. This was the period just prior to the introduction of the Heckler Koch family of support weapons, so these were weapons we became familiar with, later, across the water. We had to make do with the bulky Sterling sub-machine gun and its awkward banana-shaped magazine protruding sideways, and pump-action shotguns. Certainly once in Bessbrook Mill operators could grab an Armalite or an SLR for the back seat of the car. We also learnt how to operate a range of weapons that were regularly used by the terror groups, including, naturally, the AK 47.

That was the physical, hands-on aspect of our weapons training, but just as important was the fundamental realignment of our attitude to our personal weapon and the whole ethos of its carriage as we departed the conventional military world and prepared to enter the unconventional world of Special Duties.

The first readjustment was not difficult, being more an issue of relativity, and a distinct matter of differing priorities. We learnt very quickly that it was not only necessary but essential that we became used to dramatically increasing the 'poundage' of ammunition that we fired on the range – as the Army calls it, 'turning live ammunition into empty cases'. Volunteers from the 'teeth arms', the majority from the infantry – making up about half of the FRU's strength at any one time – were more used to spending time on the range. Marksmanship skills were an important part of their job description but their 'special to arm' expertise was still way below the immersive level demanded by the Special Duties world. Volunteers from the rest of the military did little more than launch a few handfuls of ammunition at targets fixed opposite them on their very limited Annual Personal Weapons Test. The APWT provided the same tick in the box, attesting to a base level of competence in terms of safety and weapons handling skills, as the timed three-mile Basic Fitness Test run satisfied a very basic fitness requirement – frankly inadequate. The enhanced standard we trained to on the course applied to our Brownings and all the longer-barrelled support weapons we would carry on operations. We had to master and maintain that degree of instinctive hand–eye coordination and muscle memory that ensured that if we were ever required to engage our enemies, our response would be instinctive and deadly. At Ashford, on the course, this was easy to achieve, and of course necessary, both to teach skills and then to assess whether potential operators had the required physical aptitude and mental focus and aggression. Once deployed in the Province, it became harder to carve out time from the relentless operational pace and isolate the space to keep our skill levels up, but we succeeded with regular range days where we practised not just straight shooting but critically our applied anti-ambush drills – those explosive tactics that we would deploy with a split second's consideration if challenged knowingly or unwittingly by our enemy.. Complementary to putting rounds down the range, it was important that operators adopted the regime of personal visualisation, mentally going through the various actions, reactions and drills appropriate to the scenarios that we might be confronted with. This applied to all our defensive tradecraft, whether it included situations that required kinetic armed responses, or the application of some focussed unarmed combat techniques.

The second readjustment was getting used to the practical and psychological reality of permanently carrying a concealed weapon on our persons. Once over the water we very rarely went anywhere without, at the very least, a concealed, usually holstered, pistol. During the course, this adjustment to our daily lives and daily movements began. We were probably not the only armed lot wandering around the less attractive parts of Ashford town, but we definitely very quickly became the most dangerous! Whatever unease or sense of awkwardness that some may have encountered at this refinement to our dress code was very quickly dispelled, and in very short order I am quite sure all we volunteers adapted readily to the point where not carrying provoked a sense of abnormality and unease.

The final realignment required was undoubtedly the most radical and counter-cultural for the Army boys and girls, and members of the other two services. The British Army stresses safety, especially in all aspects of of weapon handling. Accidents can, and do, occur too easily. To that end, loading and then cocking a weapon, whereby it is live and potentially lethal, are very conscious and deliberate actions governed by very precise and intensively drilled procedures. Weapons are not routinely 'made ready' in the green army until they are required to be fired. A consequence of this strict weapon handling regime is that young soldiers especially can become cautious almost to the point of paranoia about cocking their sidearms and putting a round into the chamber. Firing a weapon accidentally – what the military ruthlerssly labels as a negligent discharge – is punished by a heavy fine. However, by contrast, the weapons that we carried were always cocked and ready to fire, always with 'one in the pipe'. In the operational scenarios within which we worked, and the potential compromises that we faced in the Province, whereby we might be ambushed by Republican terrorists, an uncocked pistol or support weapon was a dead man's weapon. Quite simply, in such an extreme situation, where reaction times would be infinitesimally limited and the need to take aggressive, positive and ultimately deadly control absolutely paramount, in the case of reacting with our pistols, the requirement of drawing them from wherever they were holstered, moving the slide to chamber a round and cock the hammer, then releasing the safety catch, all before discharging the initial double tap, would almost certainly lead to the operator's death. Only draw, point and sweep the safety off, then squeeze the trigger in one fluid movement would offer us the fighting chance we needed.

But as in all other areas of our new business, we adapted and this became just more second nature. To outsiders our conduct might have looked distinctly unconventional, and to the cynics and frustrated wannabees, bordering on the cowboy, but it worked for us and our safety was certainly not compromised, only enhanced.

We were also schooled in unarmed combat skills and techniques, always useful for a night out in the pubs and clubs of Ashford. The rationale was to understand and recognise the concept of 'threat', avoid it if practicable, but possess the personal arsenal to be able to react proportionally and with flexibility to escalate a response as appropriate. As trained operators, we would be capable of extracting ourselves from, or neutralising, a threat with a measured response, deploying any option from a blow or a kick to a double-tapping squeeze of the trigger. It was crucial that we were able to move from calm rational normality to delivering lethal force, employing this focussed aggression in a fraction of a second, then to personally de-escalate to effectively handle the aftermath of an incident professionally. No easy requirement. The techniques we adopted were an amalgam of simple moves drawn from other self-defence 'systems', largely based around Second World War commando training. Being quick, pared-down blows, a degree of preparedness could be maintained, even without regular practice, by rehearsing them mentally – visualisation is a great life skill relevant to so many things we take on in everyday life. Anything more complicated and technical requires constant training or else, come the critical moment, you will fail to create the time and space to extricate yourself from the danger that you are reacting to.

Crucially, we would also be schooled extensively in every facet of the Troubles. It was imperative that we understood why we, the British Army, were in the Province, why we were engaged in the fight against terror, and why, crucially, the various terrorist groups were engaged in their fight against us. All too often, documentaries of modern conflict have conducted interviews with the young combatants to record their expressions of complete lack of understanding as to why they are thousands of miles away from home risking life and limb. History in Ireland, on all sides, is all important, and we had to be able to understand all interpretations of it. We had to learn and appreciate the realities of political and social history, the grievances fuelling the struggle, on the one hand for a united Ireland, and on the other to preserve the Union. This slanted the telling of these stories more towards understanding the perception of Nationalist injustice, but this was necessary because ultimately, to be credible in the eyes of our Nationalist sources, we would have to learn to understand the grudges and prejudices of their folklore and their identity as a minority community. This was not difficult, because the reality of discrimination against the Nationalist population, certainly in 1969, was graphic. I am confident that a majority of handlers very quickly began to identify and sympathise with the Nationalist sources we met regularly and the targets we worked to get to know. There is something that runs deep in the Celtic Irish psyche that draws one in. There is a deep melancholy and mysticism, a sense of saga, of loss, and yet a vibrant love of life and fun and music and family, and a ready expression of emotion.

All these skills began gestation in the classroom, were then exercised practically, then built into increasingly complex exercises until the climatic final exercise. Then, with the end of the course in plain sight, we formed our own Research Office and reacted to a full scenario'd three-day exercise, living, breathing, but above all, handling.

A lot to learn, a lot to assimilate, a lot to practise and perfect, but not a lot of time. The pace was fast and unrelenting, but conducted with a calm, predominantly guiding, rather than testing, hand. Of course, those unable to build the necessary agent rapport, extract the necessary agent intelligence and disseminate it with sufficient clarity, and cope with the physical demands, were dealt with summarily, but never arbitrarily, and always fairly with a degree of humanity. Is it reasonable to expect any other approach from professionals whose forté was managing the ultimate, most intense human relationships?

Whoever passed through the front door of the Manor, whatever their professional and personal backgrounds and experience, the person who emerged at the end of the course and re-crossed that threshold was an agent handler. This modern professional soldier was, however, much more than the sum of the constituent elements of their training. He, or she, without doubt, represented to me the military Renaissance man. Their role as an agent handler demanded honed practical and personal skills, and the confidence and knowledge to apply them in often highly charged and stressful situations – the ability to engage with other human beings, from potentially widely different backgrounds with widely different dreams and expectations of life, and motivations, and to target, to recruit and to run them as agents. As agent runners, they would not survive without the intellectual ability to marshal often complicated information, and question agents comprehensively with logic and sometimes guile, asking searching and incisive questions to ensure that no nuances of a 'story' were missed. As agent runners, they would not survive without the 'smarts' to present the output from covert agent meetings in extensive reports that were often read outside of the unit by other highly professional and demanding specialists – sometimes senior civil servants or political leaders – who might then plan and mount exploitative operations based on their words. Deployed on all the various phases and stages of agent operations, right from the targeting, the recruitment, to the routine meeting stage of a fully-fledged human source, they had to possess the covert tradecraft skills to be able to conceptualise, then plan and operate, covertly and securely, executing sometimes complex and multi-phased operations, in both urban and rural environments, with detailed contingency options incorporated into that planning. And finally, they had to possess the hard-edged combat skills to react, in worst case, to the most hostile enemy action. These skills included those unarmed combat techniques, and of course the ability to ultimately extricate themselves from a gunfight with seasoned terrorists, the most proficient and ruthless on the planet, using a potential mini-arsenal of weapons to kill them.

This was the courageous, incisive, broad, rounded, multi-faceted soldier that the Northern Ireland Research course crafted. I firmly contend that our handlers sat uncontested at the pinnacle of the covert special duties hierarchy. He or she existed nowhere else in our armed services.

I find it odd and puzzling, but the memory of who I joined on the course evades me. I cannot even remember how many of us were there at the start, but it must have totalled a round or baker's dozen at least. There must have been a course photo but I can't place my copy. I do remember two course-mates, not because we later served in the unit together, but perversely because they did not serve in the FRU at all. They had no operational requirement to be trained as agent handlers because they were deploying as Field Intelligence NCOs or FINCOs. FINCOs have been a feature of numerous British operations from Hong Kong to Belize, each demanding its own spin on the concept. In the NI model, they supported the Military Intelligence Officers, MIOs, who represented the military in a vital G2 liaison bridge between the Brigades and ultimately the Regional Heads of Special Branch. I am struggling to recall the exact number, but I think there were five or six FINCOs working across the Province. I later worked with the brother of one of the two on my course, in Bosnia. He was an RAF Reserve officer who served as a Serbo-Croat linguist in my Field Intelligence Team. I will always remember him because he wanted to buy my PX-sourced Leatherman multi-tool and insisted on paying more than the dollar price I had paid for it in Berlin's US military families shopping complex. I think we reached some form of compromise. Certainly in S Det we had a really and positive close working relationship with the MIO and FINCO working out of Newry – Tom C was a truly excellent officer who went on to make his name as a civilian adviser in Afghanistan.

What I do remember very starkly about the course was the whole psychology underpinning the training, and the relationship with the trainers. I was to experience something very different many times in the future on other courses I attended. In most training establishments, and on most courses, it was usual to experience a very tangible 'us' and 'them' divide between the two sides. It was invariably a conscious and deliberate policy; load as much psychological pressure as possible onto students, especially in the early phases of any training. This approach rested, I think, on an institutional outlook – they the staff had 'done it' and were therefore a cut above the 'mere' student, who had to learn to have any chance of being as good. How refreshing that there was absolutely none of this bull in the Manor. Tim, Nick and Graham treated their protégées as equals and sought only to encourage us, and to pass on their knowledge to ensure the greatest chance that we passed the training and joined the unit. The aim at SIW was to do everything to push volunteers to succeed. When I returned ten years later as the SIW Training Major, running all three training cadres within the Manor, I was saddened to see that this openness and plain down-to-earth attitude no longer represented the working face of the handling branch. It sported too many prima donnas for my taste. I did everything I could to kick down pedestals whenever I could and refocus on humility while, of course, maintaining the highest professional standards. I remember it was not easy.

The Manor epitomised the perfect setting for a clandestine training course like the NI agent handling course. It evoked the spirit of a le Carré SIS safe house or, more aptly, a country house requisitioned during the last war by the Special Operations Executive, the SOE, as the secluded base in which to train its people before their drops into occupied Europe and beyond. When I was a member of the Special Forces Club in Knightsbridge, before I let my membership lapse, one would see these old lions in the bar or the restaurant – sad to reflect upon their infirmity, contrasting so graphically against images of them, strong and vital, in their heroic prime. The Manor unquestionably projected a powerful psychological image. In the realm of agent handling there is nothing more important, no driver more powerful, than psychology. I do not know of any other military facility that subliminally set such an apposite backdrop against which to learn our new, novel and deadly serious approach to the world.

Templer Barracks, now sadly disappeared Atlantis-like under the tarmac, hurriedly mowed lawns, crazy paving driveways, gnomes, and semis of suburban development, was small but always projected a real feeling of intimacy. As far as I am concerned, but I am biased, the architectural and functional jewel was unquestionably the intriguing Elizabethan-looking manor house, Repton Manor – written records date occupation on this site back beyond Edward IV to the Domesday Book – inappropriately suffocating in its own undersized grounds, the other side of a screen of trees and a long, low barn building, behind the back of the pedestrian 1960s block-like officers' mess.

Architecturally, one's eye was drawn to the eight-fluted chimney breast dominating its silhouette. It was not a large building but its proportions were pleasing to the eye, its L-shape comprising a three-storey 'foot' with a single, large, white-framed, multi-paned sash window on each floor facing the gravel forecourt. The long side of the L was a storey lower, with an identical single window on the ground floor and a rectangular bricked-up window on the first. The tiled roof was steeply sloping, protecting the warm, rich red brown brickwork. While the Manor was an imposing structure outwardly, it boasted none of the charms or treasures of a National Trust jewel when we ventured through its great green-panelled front door. With the true philistinism of the Ministry, any vestige of a grand past had been long since gutted – as if a coach party of Taliban had visited on their return journey to the port at Dover.

The two upper floors had been converted to bare bones functional syndicate classrooms furnished with battered utilitarian desks and chairs. They were bright and well-lit, and while they projected little character, they were 'positive' places to sit, work and learn. All were fitted with CCTV camera and microphones. The ground floor was dominated by the staff-only monitoring room where all activity taking place anywhere in the building, except in the branch offices, was monitored. The cellar had been converted into cell-like exercise rooms, where practical debrief and recruitment scenarios played out. They were also fitted for sound and vision. The cells were dank, damp and dark. Not positive places to be. White paint peeled and black mould fed and thrived in this subterranean dungeon-like atmosphere. If one was looking to store one's leather or chintz three-piece, an advisory call to one's insurance company would be an initial smart move – your furniture was doomed. Patrick, a FRU CO-designate, joining the course, and sitting in on some of the serials, was struck down by a lung infection and put on sick leave. No concern for health and safety guidelines, or of course their absence, however, had any practical effect on the ghost who roamed the corridors at night.

The CO of SIW, the Training Major/2IC, admin support, and Surveillance Branch were housed in less grandiose portable buildings on the far side of the old wall at the rear of the manor house. E Branch was luckier and enjoyed a more permanent home in what I think was a former stables annex. The only other feature of the school was the unit bar in the old barn set between the officers' mess and the Manor. It was a useful venue in which course students could on occasion work, but more importantly relax, during the few and infrequent moments of downtime, with discretion and privacy – no scope for prying eyes and flapping ears. I remember one evening sitting at the long bar, on a high bar stool. I felt a fairly emphatic tap on my shoulder and guessed whoever was behind me needed my attention. I looked round, and there on the threadbare, grubby carpet was the massive spider that had dropped down from a gap in the ceiling. Lovely.

All in all it was a tight, compact facility perfectly suited for the tasks in hand. With the demise of Templer Barracks the whole establishment moved lock, stock and barrel to the old USAF base at Chicksands on the outskirts of Bedford. With the move and the guiding philosophy of tri-service jointery, I personally feel more was lost than gained – there was certainly a distinct psychological sacrifice with the absence of a new Manor to carry forward tradition.

So what did an agent handler need to know in 1983? Before looking at some more of my operational experiences in the unit, a useful prelude might be to open the box and take a look inside. Putting a few concepts under the microscope, expounding on the lexicon of agent operations, exploring some principles and tactical techniques will generate some context and perspective for the pages that follow.

We will be talking about what I and others consider to be the 'golden age' of agent handling. It was a golden age in tactical operational terms, a golden age in terms of the quality of intelligence the unit disseminated, but also golden from the perspective of leading and commanding agent operations. These were the days preceding the contemporary overregulated, risk-averse society that has progressively induced, in my opinion, the feeling of being systematically smothered. Agent handling operations were, of necessity and rightly so, regulated and tightly controlled, but there was still more than enough freedom and scope for initiative and aggressive lateral thinking to get the job done – this suited someone like me with a reputation and personal propensity for cutting through, and steering around, red tape. These days were, however, numbered and by the early 1990s (post-Stevens), the FRU had its obligatory resident lawyer sitting up in the HQ.*

* I vividly remember, on my return to SIW, the decision to put the unit's first lawyer, Peter T, both an excellent, sound guy and a gifted professional, through the NI Course so that he fully understood and appreciated the nuts, bolts and potential warts of agent operations in the Province. He was working hard one wintry and wet day down on the ranges on the coast, going through the extremely realistic scenario'd CQB-related exercises that involved a host of character players whose role was to ensure that the various situations captured the confusion, stress and violence of real life, on a bad day, out on the streets. In this particular scenario, shots were fired and the crowd, excited and agitated, turned towards the two covert operators who had exited the car before them. Peter was the second of these. He levelled his HK 53 and emptied the magazine into the bus queue standing waiting on the other side of the road. I can still see the blank but manically focussed expression on his face. Valuable lessons.

Against the backdrop of 'just enough' technology to enhance operational efficiency, and security of the agent and the handler – encrypted personal radios, and reliable and effectively intercept-safe telephone communications, to highlight two key factors – running an agent then still fundamentally relied upon regular face-to-face meets. This was the bread-and-butter bones of the job. At these meets, intelligence and tasking were passed both ways across the table.

So, the lessons we learnt.

But first, an observation and health warning – there is so much nonsense and lack of understanding in the public domain concerning covert operations in general during the Troubles, about agent handling in the Province, and specifically about the FRU. A veritable mélange of half-truth, conspiracy theory, outright invention, confusion and crossed wire. I hope to restore some balance and counter the misinformation, whether it stems from understandable lack of appreciation or insidious malice.

7

WHO'S WHO

So what is a human source – what makes an agent an agent?

A human source is any person who provides information, either knowingly or unwittingly. Information is the raw currency of the world of intelligence, like aluminium ore before it is processed into the wing of an Airbus. Analysts – or in the language of the FRU and other military intelligence units, collators – turn or process information into intelligence. An agent is the ultimate human source and intelligence is the finished product of an agent operation. An agent may well obtain this information from sub-sources who might be conscious or, more likely, unconscious, meaning that they are passing on information without realising that their words are subsequently being quoted by our agent. Human source operations are widely referred to as HUMINT, including other 'people-intensive' intelligence activities – information collected and provided by human sources – such as covert surveillance and interrogation.

The staff at SIW expanded on this simple definition, drilling down to expose categories of human source that we had to be mindful of: casual contacts, referred to as CASCONs; official contacts, or OFCONs; and, at the top of the tree, full-blown accredited agents. This was our new language.

In the street language of Northern Ireland, agents, indeed all human sources, are 'touts'. Across the whole breadth of Irish history there is no worse crime than 'touting', no worse sin than passing information about your own to the 'Brits'. This was equally true in the days of Cromwell, the 1916 Rebellion, or the Troubles. The universally accepted fate of the tout is death. Against this societal bedrock and culturally unnegotiable reality, how could anyone consider betrayal? Yet Irish history is so redolent with informers that the Nationalist psyche has mutated into a constant state of paranoia. With regard to PIRA, from the early 1980s onwards, this state of psychosis was fully justified. This proved to be a significant undercurrent that contributed to the peace for which the Good Friday accords have been the enduring catalyst – PIRA realised that its structure was so riven with informers that it could no longer prosecute an effective military campaign.

CASCONs are human sources that have not been formally recruited – in due course they could be recruited, and many were. A CASCON might pass on information in full knowledge of the consequences of their action, or with little or no understanding that they are playing an active role in the intelligence game. Information gathered from a CASCON will likely be of a lower order of importance but this is not to say that they might not be privy to high-grade potential intelligence. The intrinsic value of most CASCONs is their ability to pass background 'eyes and ears' information – still pieces of the jigsaw, but invariably the less interesting blue bits of the background sky. The important distinction is that CASCONs are not under control. To use an inadequate analogy, they are casual labour working without a contract and without remuneration. As such, they are not formally taskable. The conversational flow is essentially one way.

In a rural environment, CASCONs would be typically met informally while the handler conducted a standard regular-looking Army patrol, in uniform. This was an effective and secure method of managing contact. The reality was, however, that from the terrorist perspective these informal relationships still constituted touting. Perception is all. The reality was that CASCONs still required to be protected and their information logged and recorded – sometimes it would also be formally reported.

As I will elaborate on later, all FRU agent recruitment targets had to be formally cleared by the Regional Head of Special Branch. This convention, in line with the policy of police supremacy, accorded tremendous power to the RUC. It meant that they could effectively prevent our, the FRU's, efforts to expand and bring in new blood. The policy also ultimately revealed targets that, by implication, we assessed as 'turnable' and thereby rendered an opportunity for the SB to poach them before the event. The beauty of the casual contact was that no prior approval had to be requested, or received, before developing them. In the days of Hamish Norries's tenure as CO FRU, we debated running all potential recruitment targets as CASCONs to counter what we assessed as a deliberate and systematic policy in the Southern Region, especially, to thwart our attempts to bring in new assets.

Norries's days, after he took over command of the FRU in 1987, were truly the golden days – he was the best officer I have ever worked for and, in my opinion, the best commanding officer of all the unit's COs. He led us with courage, vision, and above all, a messianic dynamism. He also led us with care, concern, interest and fairness. No one was more motivated to strive to drive operations that would make a difference – he was never afraid to risk putting his career on the line in pursuing this goal.

As an agent handler, I don't have much to say about OFCONs. They hold little interest for me and, at the risk of sounding arrogant, require little professional skill to exploit them. They played no real role in the Province. They are, as the name accurately portrays, contacts who represent some third-party organisation and, in meeting in the course of official business, knowingly or unwittingly provide information. Because their official status confers on them some degree of access to useful information, either concerning their own organisation or another third party, they have the potential to fulfil intelligence requirements. Exploitation of OFCONs is particularly applicable to the cocktail party circuit frequented by SIS officers working out of embassies or consulates. It was our understanding, within the wider Army HUMINT community, that they (SIS) regularly reported information derived from OFCONs, according it the status of secret intelligence. What the hell, though; their opposite numbers in the then KGB and GRU routinely passed off open source media stories as agent intelligence during the height of the Cold War. As an aside, this is actually not a flawed approach, as journalists are skilled professionals and frequent the same pond as intelligence officers, trading in the identical currency of information. I suppose, with hindsight, all our liaison contacts were, in reality, OFCONs; but, crucially, we did not recycle the information they passed to us in our MISRs, the name we gave to our intelligence reports. It amused me to see in Northern Ireland that from time to time FRU product was recycled in intelligence reports disseminated by the national agencies in the form of RIRACs – I remember on one particular occasion verbatim. I suppose, though, that this is maybe the highest compliment one agency can pay to another, so it's silly to resent it.

An agent is controlled by an agent handler. An agent is not a member of the armed forces. We religiously ensured that no target was a serving member of the UDR, or police – that does need stressing in order to counter some of the nonsense that has been printed out there. The handler is the serving soldier. The agent, male or female, can be tasked to provide specific intelligence and is rewarded for its provision. An agent is formally registered somewhere within the security apparatus, in the NI context with the Security Service and the Special Branch Source Units. Agents are given code names or numbers to protect their identities. The tightest control and discipline is maintained with regard to the agent's true identity. Despite this, or perhaps because of it, it is also a very unhelpful reality that everyone, even peripherally connected to the intelligence world, plays 'hunt the tout', attempting to guess the identity of sources – it's inevitable, and with regard to trying to work out who was working for the Special Branch, I am as guilty as the next man.

In the FRU we used four-digit numbers, the second digit identifying the detachment handling the agent. Double-name code names – 'Mail Box', or 'Spring Bean', to give two fictitious examples – were a prevalent feature of the 'old days' and would appear in old case paperwork but were otherwise very 'unmodern' and redolent with 'another era' connotations.*

* As a footnote, the Regulation of Investigatory Powers Act 2000, the RIPA legislation, made it de rigueur, and contemporary, to refer to agents as CHIS – Covert Human Intelligence Sources. I have to say that I am not a fan of jargonese, but the Act was an inevitable rush by government to create some moral high ground, occupy it, and confront the whole Pandora's box of using agents to provide intelligence when, in doing so, those agents may have already stepped firmly onto the other side of the law. It's always been an existential dilemma facing the good guys fighting the bad guys. The best-quality intelligence that gives the security forces – any security force, anywhere in the world – any chance of frustrating acts of terror, will invariably only ultimately be supplied by other terrorists who tautologically, to be in such a position, must have broken, or are continuing to break, the law. In the late 1980s, Raymond White, then a very senior RUC Special Branch officer, later to head the Special Branch, raised the spectre of this conflicting reality with the PM, Margaret Thatcher, on a visit she made to the Province. Her response: keep his collective head down and muddle on! See the BBC's *Spotlight on the Troubles*, Episode 4. I don't want to sound trite, but the whole issue is a moral minefield. It is one of the toughest conundrums to address and reconcile a workable equilibrium against the precept of respecting the underlying philosophy of a Western liberal democracy. I prefer to avoid being drawn into a legalistic and philosophical debate, because what I describe is a case of what happened; it is not a case of what could or should have been. As I have already highlighted, a military lawyer was inserted into the FRU establishment on the back of the Stevens Inquiry. His role was to review operational initiatives from a legal standpoint. This undoubtedly had a serious impact and increased the practical difficulties of an already complex task. I understand now that the current UK government's intention is to steer a bill, the Covert Human Intelligence Sources Bill, onto the legislative books to provide some wiggle room for aggressive and effective exploitation of agents, resurrecting some of the scope of the bad good old days.

8

KEY LESSONS

The most fascinating inside track on agent handling is always to try to understand the highly complex and multi-faceted motivation for the agent's recruitment in the first place. Whether or not monetary reward was an initial motivating factor, it was always introduced into the relationship, unless absolutely impossible to do so – in reality, money was always a motivator. Despite this bold statement, however, in S Det we certainly had one agent who would refuse all forms of remuneration. Every agent-handling organisation will try to use money to reinforce the psychology of hierarchy – "I pay you, therefore I am the boss; you take the money, therefore you are my employee, and do what I say!" Money is always a tricky commodity in life to deal with, no less so in agent operations. Fixing the right level of reward is not easy. Partly, it must be predicated on the amount of cash an agent can cover within the circumstances and constraints of their lifestyle. An unemployed agent on the dole can hardly readily explain to an inquisitor, idle or otherwise, how he can afford to buy designer clothes for his wife and kids and drive an Audi Q7.

Shifting focus to the US for a brief moment, it was widely appreciated that Aldrich Ames** had no prospect of funding his

** Aldrich Ames was a CIA officer and long-running Soviet agent right in the heart of the Agency. He was eventually arrested by the FBI after →

extravagant lifestyle on a government salary. Where were these additional funds coming from? The SVR had got it wrong, but fortunately for them no one initially challenged the anomaly.

It was a little easier in the border areas of south Armagh, where smuggling and other criminal activity was and is a systemic reality; but the driving imperative should be to minimise any factors in lifestyle or behaviour that provoke interest or questions in the first place. Various tactics were used to try and reward agents in such a way that would not result in these noticeable lifestyle changes. Some of these were quite innovative. I have always fully endorsed and tried to live by the maxim that one is limited only by the bounds of one's own imagination – this, to me, has always been one of the attractions of intelligence work, especially HUMINT operations where there is always room for innovation and for thoughts focussed well and truly outside of that box. Thus agents would receive a regular weekly or monthly 'retainer', the phraseology we used, depending on the frequency of meets, and a bonus for work carried out particularly well. We did periodically reward our best agents in kind. Because agent mobility was so critical in generating the capability to drive to meets, and often to pursue tasking, we did on occasion provide the cash to enable a few of our assets to purchase affordable second-hand cars. Another agent received the money to pay for his car insurance.

This whole issue of rewards for results is potentially fraught, because it openly lays the ground for, and potentially encourages, embellishment, if not out-and-out invention. It's a difficult balance. I saw this in the aftermath of the Iraq War when every likely lad very quickly cottoned on to the reality that the allied G2 effort, pre-insurrection, was directed at finding Saddam's weapons of mass destruction – a potential bonus bonanza and driver for every far-fetched story imaginable.

Regarding the different categories of human source, what of the double agent? Double agents are a very popular feature of film and novel. They were definitely a major, unforeseen, and negative

---

compromising numerous allied agents, including Oleg Gordievsky, and found guilty of working for Moscow.

feature of Allied efforts to penetrate the East German regime – if you believe Markus Wolf's* memoirs, all agents run from the West were doubled. Within the confines of operations in NI, I have heard of initiatives by PIRA to mount their own covert counter-surveillance against security force surveillance operators, and I have heard stories of PIRA running serving members of the RUC as agents. But I am aware of only one attempt, which failed, of any of the terror groups successfully targeting or running a double agent against the security forces. I suspect they lacked the confidence, and probably the volunteers, to try. It could have been very interesting.

All agents are valuable. An intelligence unit can never have too many, although there are certainly resource implications to running them and it is a time-intensive occupation if it is done professionally. But it is also true that not all agents are of equal value. The immediate value of an asset is based on his or her access – essentially what they are able to find out and report to their handlers. This is a matrix based on who they know and their ability to covertly collect intelligence. But value can also be assessed longer term by identifying a realistic end state to which an agent can be steered. This is a factor of capability and opportunity. A good handling team will exploit their agents to the maximum, ensuring that they milk every drop of information. A good handling team will, in parallel, maintain a continual watch as to where their agents can be steered to increase their access.

In the NI context, clearly agents who were fully sworn-in green-booked PIRA members were potential diamond mines. They guaranteed associate access in that they mixed with other terrorists, even within the narrow confines of small cell structures. Depending on their role within the organisation, they may also have enjoyed exploitable direct access – a bomb maker will be able to inform his handler about the bombs he has, or will make. He will likely pass intelligence about forthcoming operations, the scale and scope of this information being dependent upon the security posture of his unit. A tightly controlled ASU following tight security protocols

* Markus Wolf was the long-time head of the DDR's foreign intelligence service, the HVA, right up until the Berlin Wall fell.

may not pass any operational details to the bomb maker about the operations his weapons will be deployed upon. But he would likely be briefed as to how the ASU members planting his bomb would take delivery of it. Intelligence of this grade, fed from the handler into the TCG, could trigger covert surveillance that could target an operation with the aim of disrupting the planned attack, or killing, or capturing the bombers. This is a perfect scenario, because in any follow-up investigation by PIRA's security team, the agent, who is at least one step removed from the compromised operation, would not be implicated as the potential source of the compromise.

An agent, let's say a gunman, who has a direct and central operational role is very hard to handle. Exploiting his intelligence longer term is very near impossible. Direct access of this quality is regrettably a two-edged sword and invariably cannot, as I said, be maintained for long. Each successive move by the security forces in response to the agent's pre-emptive reporting brings the finger of suspicion nearer to him as the 'squealer'. This is the case even with careful and varied responses – disrupting attacks by removing the target; forcing PIRA to abort an operation by having some form of military or police presence at a key geographic choke point; the agent calling in sick on the day of the attack, or even as has happened, ingesting medication to provoke a violent reaction, even if he is allowed the luxury of not being 'quarantined' in the run-up to the operation's execution. Eventually, a pattern of failed operations emerges and the name of the agent consistently features at some point in the chain of failure. He will find himself very quickly under suspicion and at some key tipping point, unless he has already been pulled out by his handling team, sitting on a chair in a cold, darkened room being questioned by the ruthless and skilled interrogators of the security unit. At this point he is one word away from death.

Much better then to control a player with a supporting role, rather than running an ops man as one's agent. Someone on the brigade intelligence staff with access to the targeting information upon which operations are mounted. A player on the quartermaster side of operations who was responsible for equipment. Or someone on the political side, a member of Sinn Fein, with access to intelligence on strategy and the key question that determined the IRA's campaign – more ballot box or more Armalite. In the case of the former, it is far easier to use their intelligence as start points for other covert operations and ensure their (the agent's) insulation from operational failure.

At the other extreme of the reporting scale are the low-level bread-and-butter 'eyes and ears' agents. They are still accredited and recruited agents but they have no direct, regular access. Their mission and utility is 'barometric'. They may infrequently 'bump' into a player directly involved, perhaps a family member, a family friend, an old school chum, classified as associate access, and be able to recount a conversation or pass on some de visu intelligence, but this will very much be regarded as a bonus. They provide the background sightings information that helps keep track of persons of interest, including unconsciously providing pattern-of-life detail for potential targets for recruitment, and the gossip and scandal that might hold some exploitation potential – they build the scenery against which the main actors play out their parts. These low-level agents might have the ability or opportunity to suddenly move into a position of direct access, or indeed, be deliberately steered into such. A 25-year-old lad living in the right part of town could be steered towards known terror activists and eventually be green-booked and brought into the group – bingo!

Reiterating what I have already stated, crucially an agent handling unit must constantly be on the lookout for new agents. This means there is an unceasing imperative to identify new targets, plan operations to get alongside them to further assess their potential, and ultimately to establish enough of a relationship to stand before them at some point and 'pop the question' – "Will you work for me?" This can, and often will, be a very long, frustrating and twisting road. However, it can, on the other hand, come to fruition very rapidly and without any protracted 'courtship'. Context and situation are the key driving factors. In the former scenario, the process will eat massively into a Det's human capital, requiring manpower and man-hours, with realistically small chance of success.

By 1983, the Army could no longer rely on Screening to engineer a calm, quiet chat with a target. All targeting operations had to be mounted without the luxury of a stage-managed controlled environment, although latterly in my time we began to more aggressively utilise so-called Intermediate Search Centres, ISCs, like the one adjacent to the Maze Prison, to which a target could be brought. Under the pretext of a thorough vehicle search, they could be sat down and an extended chat engineered. But this tactic had to be used sparingly.

The rural handler increasingly had to rely on green patrol activity to bump into the target at their home, work, or at random Vehicle Check Points, to have three or four minutes to talk while searching them and their car. Not ideal. In the city, operators had to be more creative. For the RUC, making contact could be remarkably simple – arrest the target and bring them in to the secure locations of Gough Barracks or the Castlereagh interrogation centre for 'questioning'. A luxury. I'm getting a little ahead of myself, but reassuring to have recourse to a solid tried-and-tested targeting option – help the police or risk falling foul of them.

Before I get into the convoluted nature of recruitment operational planning, I want to admit that, in fact, some of the best agents anywhere in the world, including in NI, have not been recruited by the efforts of agent handlers religiously following doctrine and furiously beavering away to engineer success – they have recruited themselves. They are what are referred to as 'walk-ins' – they invert the process and present themselves to the handler, directly or indirectly, offering their services. Walk-ins are a recurring feature of the history of intelligence, and when they work well they are peerless. The agent has to be trained, and naturally their reliability tested, but the struggle to isolate their motivation and figure out points of contact are essentially done jobs. Again, citing well-publicised examples outside of the Ireland experience, both Gordievsky (kudos for SIS), and Robert Hanssen (one up for the SVR), were both walk-ins (as was Ames), all wreaking tremendous damage on their respective sides.

The imperative to recruit drove operations more aggressively in the rural Dets, especially in south Armagh, because we ran fewer quality sources – we were always behind the curve. This fact did not draw any implied or direct criticism – it was simply the consequence of the reality of working in a harder operational area. Urban environments are easier places to operate within – the hustle and bustle provide perfect cover for covert activity. If the covert operator makes the effort to conform visibly and react naturally to these surroundings, he is virtually invisible. One serious limitation was always the absolute requirement to remain closed-mouthed out on the ground when deployed covertly unless hiding behind a very credible cover story. An English accent automatically meant Army to the Nationalist listener, and that would mean problems. For this reason, native operators from the Province were always welcomed by Det bosses, and were never more valuable than in the flexibility they brought to recruitment operations. In contrast, in rural areas every outsider drew interested and pointed attention and every action of the interloper was 'recorded'. More relevantly, the clannish secular bonds wedding the townspeople of Belfast or Londonderry to their communities, although solid and cohesive, possessed none of the fierceness of the unifying sense of loyalty that Bandit Country commanded, and demanded. South Armagh was, and is, devoutly Nationalist and Republican in its view of the world. These country folk were simply both tougher people, brought up against a history and cuture of non-compliance, independence, and disregard for the law, and were harder targets to cultivate and recruit.

The key teaching points of agent recruitment revolved around four critical, pivotal factors – the holy trinity plus one that I have already alluded to. If the course inculcated no other dogma in its students, they were to dream Access, Motivation, Point of Contact, and Capability. Beyond the words of the Lord's Prayer, and 'I'm Forever Blowing Bubbles', there are no other words that spring more readily to my mind. These guiding principles remained key considerations during the working life of the agent and were reflected in the second part of every post-meet Contact Form, the crucial document produced by the handler and co-handler after each meet. Access, Motivation and Point of Contact details were always assessed and reassessed and religiously updated as circumstances changed and developed.

When considering any target for cultivation, a handler of course must research all the practicalities of the target's day-to-day life, constructing a so-called pattern of life study. But his plan only attains focus and relevance if he organises his recruitment strategy around the pillars – to quote Lawrence out of context, 'The Four Pillars of Wisdom'. Unless the handler can scratch off each pillar with sufficient positive conviction, he should move on to consideration of his next target. To qualify this, as I hinted above, Access is perhaps the only feast affected by any significant degree of mobility – agents can be steered and access increased and developed, but only against the criteria of positive Capability.

From the perspective of the handler, when making his plans, the key point is to use one's imagination. Think laterally, be innovative. Think unconventionally, exploit the lessons of life, disregard red tape and the day-to-day conventions of life – while remaining within the law. This was why the FRU demanded that volunteers generally were very senior corporals or sergeants, or above – they had some life experience and credibility, and gravitas as individuals. It's a cliché, and I've used it before, but I always asserted that handlers are only limited by the limitations of their own imaginations. It really is the key guiding principle – think broad, be bold, be unconventional and inventive, and don't be afraid to contravene rules and expected codes and modes of behaviour.

So, Access. Little point targeting an individual who is a merchant seaman and returns to Crossmaglen for a month once a year. He might be able to report on happenings in the port of Mumbai or Montevideo, but is unlikely to have much to say about PIRA operations in Mullaghbane. Never say never, though. Likewise, there's little point targeting an 85-year-old pensioner if she is hospitalised or in a care home. Extreme cases, but the point is that a target has to have an entry point into some circle or grouping, small or larger. Whatever the underpinning relationship, it must be practically able to generate operational, or operationally related, information, or hold the clear potential to be able to do so effectively and securely in due course. Therefore we sub-delineate access into 'direct', 'indirect' or 'associate', and 'potential'.

Clearly, targets who are 'traced' (identified as members or affiliated to a group) and corroborated by other intelligence reporting, as active supporters, maybe performing low-key supporting operational roles, and active members of terrorist organisations, are the most obvious and will generally be considered first as targets. Second-tier targets might be family members, friends, work colleagues, or boyfriends or girlfriends of supporters or active players who might have the necessary potential. It's not necessary to labour the point.

Just as it was vital to maintain a forward-looking focus, it was always just as important to look to the past. A constant review of assets who had been 'stood down', or dropped out of contact of their own accord, usually for reasons of limited access or less likely, operational considerations, constituted a parallel workstream. The heavy lifting had already been done, probably by a previous generation of handler – they had been recruited. As circumstances ebbed and flowed, it was always conceivable that a quirk of fate could suddenly present access that had previously eluded the case. Equally, I would always religiously seek out old target reports and review old target lists to evaluate if circumstances had changed significantly enough to merit another go.

Motivation: for me, consistently the key factor and the most fascinating, and puzzling. Not the who, not the how, but the 'why'. In the Irish context, against all the history, against all the religious and cultural imperatives, why would someone agree to work as a secret agent? With the sure knowledge that failed spies will meet a horrendous and foul death, why would anyone risk their own lives, and risk the lives and futures of family members? Why embrace the potential shame of being marked by history as a tout? I have said on many occasions, knowing what I know, that I would never, ever allow myself, willingly or unwillingly, to be drawn into so precarious a situation. I would, categorically, never become an agent. The degree of trust that 'crossing the house' demands, trust essentially of total strangers representing ideals essentially foreign to one's own heritage, is not human. I know what, and how, things can go wrong, even if the handling team is the most professional, conscientious and lucky – think back to the

CF in the bin. All agents live their lives just one heartbeat away from compromise. This requires either the most awe-inspiring courage, the most blatant stupidity, or a completely unnatural faith or degree of arrogance or invincibility, to keep going. In the Cold War context, most agents were compromised not by breakdowns in tradecraft or through the skill of opposing counter-intelligence teams, but by defectors or other agents betraying them – they themselves were ultimately powerless and impotent actors in their own unfolding destinies.

Motivation is never simple, never straightforward, and never a unitary entity. It is always a blend and mix of a number of factors. It is always highly personal. Motivation is not an immutable concept – it can change, it can ultimately be developed and steered, and it must be reinforced and strengthened incrementally by a good handler. The absolute in any recruitment plan is that the agent handler understands, or at least thinks he has identified, what will motivate his target, what psychological imperatives will drive that target into agreeing to work. The handler is required to identify the buttons that, if he manipulates circumstances effectively, will position him so that he can press them. This is real world applied psychology. This is why I consider that recruiters are unassailable in occupying the pinnacle of not just the agent-handling profession, but of the art of intelligence as a whole. Recruiters are rare animals and they are definitely born and not made, no matter how good a training course and how much practice one gets. Humans are animals and we 'sense' and 'feel'. If that animal communication and draw is not there, we, as animals, will not respond.

Spy fiction informs us that money is the strongest and surest motivator. I would agree with this – after all, good fiction is usually the mirror to reality. But it is not the sole motivating influence. Once recognised as a motivating tactic, money has to be exploited carefully and cautiously as I explained above. As a means to keep an agent hooked once recruited, it is the most enduring and straightforward tool – and important in reinforcing the psychology of control. Very quickly and readily a dynamic of dependency will be created that the agent, even if they wish to, will find hard to break. Just think about our own financial situations.

But because, as human beings, we are by nature and by culture complicated, the love of money does not always exert the strongest pull, or provide the weightiest push. In our syndicate rooms we were instructed to look for other levers, and provided with illustrative case studies.

These are some other buttons that can be activated. Would-be agents might seek revenge to right the perception of a wrong done to them – resentment after a PIRA punishment beating or knee-capping for so-called 'antisocial' behaviour, potentially to a loved one. Resentment for injustice meted out to someone they care for. Resentment for the damage caused to someone during the execution of a terrorist operation. They could be motivated, as a member of an organisation, by a sense of resentment at having been overlooked or bypassed for 'promotion' or advancement. Issues of ideology always have potentiality. In NI, fatigue or revulsion in response to the seemingly endless cycle of atrocity and violence exerted a powerful incentive to alter people's outlooks. The conviction that the political and economic future lay with a government based in London not Dublin was real. More base drivers to bring meaning to mundane lives can be a desire for excitement; a psychological need to feel special and different; the kick and buzz of walking among peers in the knowledge that they were secret agents. With some agents, there always lurked in the background the suspicion that Walter Mitty was having a hand. Human psychology is hard to read.

I remember a case in one of the Dets. Prior to being identified as a target, his wife had been tragically hit and killed by a plastic bullet fired by an Army patrol during rioting. She had been making her way home after visiting local shops and had been caught up in the disturbance. This was a tragic accident but one capable of evoking the drama, emotion and pathos to either unite or tear families and communities apart. This family lost a wife and mother, a daughter and an aunt, not to sickness or illness, somehow comprehensible as the will of God, but to the act of man. And not just man. In the eyes of these residents, to the oppressive presence of an army of occupation. Had they not responded to the unrest on this street on this day, their love would have been out shopping the following day. But perversely, the husband, instead of holding the Army responsible and joining the IRA to seek revenge, blamed PIRA for inciting the riot as the catalyst for the patrol's very presence on his street that awful day. He was subsequently approached and recruited.

An eyes and ears agent in Londonderry had been beaten up by IRSP thugs, the political wing of the INLA – he was successfully recruited. An older couple in Belfast were recruited for their eyes and ears access exploiting their fear for their grandchildren's future in the gangland of the west of the city.

Exploiting a sexual theme, the FRU recruited a young woman, using one of our more handsome handlers to reinforce the rapport building, because we knew of her promiscuous reputation – not our analysis and comment, but reporting from another agent. Our motivation was to steer her and dangle her as a potential girlfriend for active ASU members. It has to be stated that this was a whole area and arena that required the utmost care, control and professional discipline to ensure that operational focus was maintained.

Whatever primary factors motivated agents, handlers would always attempt to re-root the relationship so that bonds of friendship and team identity were fostered and developed as rapidly as feasible. Friendship could be genuine or it could be faked by the handlers, but in most cases it played a disproportionately positive and important role. In many cases our agents were people we could like and look forward to being in their company – good handlers are essentially 'people' people. But not always. Effective handling always had to incorporate some facet of acting and playing a role or part. A common and important aspect of agent relationships was the handler providing guiding, almost priest-like support. It was commonplace for handlers to support their assets, where required, sharing advice with them on the issues and pressures of family life, offering guidance on work-related issues, for those who had regular jobs, mediating on relationship issues, providing financial advice, etc., etc. Female handlers, generally possessing greater emotional acumen, although not especially well represented in the ranks of the FRU, were particularly skilled in these aspects of source handling. And there could always be a sexual undercurrent to the relationship.* This tool to aid recruitment, or as a feature of casework, had to be specifically cleared at HQ level with either the CO or Ops Offr. Even then, the tightest rein was kept on casework. If a sexual motive existed it was switched off as soon as feasibly possible. Agents becoming emotionally attached to handlers and handlers developing feelings for their assets, and resultant complications, were all potentially nightmare scenarios and needed to be nipped very promptly in the bud when identified as issues, real or potential. Sex clouds emotions and clouds objectivity. If nothing else, agent handlers must retain an icy detachment at all times. At the start of my career, I ran a case where I had to work hard to prevent sex clouding the relationship while not offending the agent – I'm happy to say that I was successful. As the OC, later, I had to manage a few such operations in addition to the one briefly detailed several paragraphs above. They were always troublesome. During my time working for TC, I saw one handler on the next plane home after losing his head.

To paint in a bit of context, the handler was handling a good-looking female agent. She had been at school with a number of peripheral PIRA players and still saw them periodically socially. Our motive for recruiting her and subsequently keeping her on the books was to exploit the second-hand indirect access to these PIRA members. The added rationale was to position her with the intent of her becoming the girlfriend of one of them. With that her access would undoubtedly increase, even should the boyfriend be tight-lipped and more security conscious. I don't know how long the handler had been handling her, metaphorically or professionally, but clearly the relationship had mutated into something unhealthy and potentially dangerous. It was compromised and therefore so were both handler and agent. Meet locations were alternated. This was before our tactics had evolved to the point where some locations were only considered for short-duration emergency meets.

* The FRU treated male and female handlers as complete equals. I witnessed absolutely no institutional discrimination of any sort in the unit – I think the foundation of this attitude was born of the fact that the Int Corps was the first cap badge in the British Army to employ, and deploy, men and women on an equal footing. I know that this was not the case with other specialist units.

At this juncture, our main debriefing location was co-located with the office in the Mill. This, clearly, was not conducive to the type of meets that handler and source had obviously begun to prefer. So progressively, more debriefs were conducted in the area in and around a well-known forest park to our north.

On the fateful day, the cover team had obviously pulled off, no doubt on the tacit understanding that its presence was not appreciated, leaving the source and handler exposed, alone, unprotected and potentially vulnerable. When there had been no confirmation that the drop-off had been successfully effected, and the operation's cut-off had passed with no contact from, or to, the team, the ops desk initiated the emergency compromise plan. The handler's vehicle details and personal photo montage were raced round to the battalion QRF/ARF so they could begin an aerial helicopter search for the car. Our own handlers scrambled to search known points briefed on in the operational orders. It was a period of supreme tension. We all entertained our version of images of the worst-case scenario – a handler and agent shot dead by ambushing gunmen, or worst worst-case situation, kidnapped and en route to a safe house in the Republic.

The cool, rational, professional side of one's brain balances the source's background and risk status, the meet location, etc., to conduct a risk analysis, and concludes that all should be well. A less rational but no less informed appreciation starts to tick off all the little things that could go wrong, all the chance occurrences that could combine to conspire to produce disaster – an accident is, after all, a chain of little things going wrong that in the combination of their totality result in unanticipated and potentially catastrophic failure. Just a chance sighting of the source and handler could precipitate disaster.

It did not take long, predictably, to quickly drive up to the forest park and find our team safe and sound. The unit suffered some limited embarrassment, even though the truth was massaged and repackaged into a credible and more innocuous box, but a talented, charismatic and experienced operator, who should have known better, was lost to the unit. I don't believe his career ever recovered from this major error of professional judgement. The plus side of these types of rogue activity was that it focussed the mind of other operators in the Dets who might be tempted to engage in similar fraught behaviour – I prefer to believe that our colleague represented the lone bad apple. He was missed by the whole Det.

If sex were to insidiously take over the motivation for meeting, the whole handling and intelligence dynamic would be corrupted. To reclaim a professional even keel then requires a heavy hand – it was applied in this instance without compromise. If this remedial action is lacking, the case progressively, and quite likely rapidly, spirals out of control. Looking laterally, no secrets remained secret for long in the tight confines of the Dets. Knowledge of this type of indiscretion might take longer to reach the ears of the bosses, but fellow handlers would very quickly guess the reality. It would become a pervasive sore on the rump of team integrity and morale. When control is gone, the vacuum is filled by risk and danger. Meets become organised not for the primary purpose of engaging in intelligence collection but for baser reasons. Meet locations and meet tradecraft become tailored and adjusted to aid the convenience of lovers, not clandestine warriors engaged in the existential fight against terror. Judgement clouds, decision-making lacks focus and clarity. The aim narrows into a single point of light that might exclude all other considerations. This will not be a normal consenting adult relationship. The circumstances, the cover, the whole dynamic governing the covert relationship will corrupt and likely intensify the madness. It can only end badly. It is to be hoped that the worst-case scenario is limited to a plane home for the handler, and a new, and very carefully and specifically briefed, handler for the agent. This was the outcome of our instance of indiscretion.

On another occasion during my tenure as the boss in Bessbrook, I had to fire a warning shot across the bows of a handler who I had begun to suspect was losing objectivity in another case, and who definitely knew better. He began giving off signals that suggested less than professional conduct, adversely arousing my instincts. I was able to have a timely word and nip this in the bud, but my instinct was confirmed by the reaction I received. The resentment was short-lived – the operator in question was too smart not to realise the danger and too aware that there were other more important and pressing priorities. And female company was readily abundant a mere thirty minutes north without jeopardising his career and ultimately his life.

The wider point is that there is no single point of motivation. There will be more important and less important motives but ultimately recruitments are based, and cases endure, on a blended cocktail. And like a marriage, handlers must work to maintain motivation, identify new drivers, but above all, labour to preserve the spark and 'feed the love'.

9

MORE LESSONS

All the good, diligent work of the handling team identifying targets with promising access, and the toil to postulate on points of motivation, is futile and for nought if the target cannot be isolated, physically approached and a dialogue entered into – agents were not recruited by telepathy, and as far as I know are still not, even in this new age. The third pillar of any recruitment plan requires a point, or points, of contact to be established upon which handler and target can converge in seeming random innocence. Points of contact will only fall out of a thorough understanding of the target's lifestyle, routine, hobbies, interests and obligations. The most secure and effective points of contact will result from the convergence of this pattern of study and the imagination of a good creative handler.

Building an exploitable pattern of life may be an extremely time-intensive exercise. It may require reaching outside of the Det to other agencies to identify information they hold, in order to bolster whatever internal agent reporting the handler can access. Approaching the green army to source patrolling reports, particularly in the rural areas, was always particularly fruitful. Certainly in S Det, we maintained excellent relations with every battalion and their subordinate companies, and their intelligence cells, during their short tours of duty – we worked hard to be able to tap into their information. This was especially the case in situations where targets' homes, workplaces or other venues of relevance were covered by defensive CCTV cameras mounted on bases and operated by the resident battalion, or were within the considerable arcs of view of the OP MAGISTRATE towers. Contact with other units or organisations always had to be tempered by security concerns – we wanted to restrict to the bare minimum the circle of knowledge of whom we were targeting. Today's targets are tomorrow's, or more likely the day after's, agents.

Country handlers certainly did not rely solely on green patrol approaches to targets, but opportunities for more creative early contacts were far more limited. Always an option, though, was bumping a target on dole day – most of our targets were drawing their 'brew' money even if they were in fact working, above or below the border.

I remember sitting on a low wall outside Newry DHSS office one day waiting for the target to appear and 'sign on'. As usual we had briefed back in the office in the Mill. My role was to approach the target for the first time and just get him talking. It was an opportunity job; we did not have much background on him, but knew from the reporting of another of our sources that he had potential. We assessed that if we could engineer a sit-down away from prying eyes, in a conducive environment, we might have a chance to build something. He certainly looked as though he had the connections and the capability to be steered into something useful.

It was a reasonable spring day, not so fine as to force me to dress down, so I was able to retain my duffle coat. It would keep me warm if I ended up sitting half the morning and provided perfect cover for my pistol and comms. I was dropped off by one of the lads just up from the dole office. As I walked down the road towards the building, I passed the cover car and its lone occupant pulled into position in a car park about 50 metres further up the road from my wall. A single handler inside, sitting waiting in the front passenger seat, is much less noteworthy than a lone figure sitting glued to the wheel. I ignored him, and he ignored me. As cover, he had a perfect field of view and would be able to watch me without hindrance. In addition, he was a useful additional pair of eyes looking out for the target.

I sat myself down on the wall I had pre-recced with my folded newspaper on my knee. Nothing outrageous, just a subtle prop somehow making me less potentially threatening and more like the wallflower I wanted to emulate. It was a busy part of town, shoppers and others with business in their heads passing left and right, but I could not sit there head rotating from side to side like an airport radar, so I had to adjust my 'point of aim' and attempt to lock on to our target in the middle distance rather than up close. This allowed me to slowly sweep my head and look more relaxed and natural. We were pretty sure he would be coming from the direction of the bus stop away to my left, so that made things easier still.

It's actually pretty hard for a lot of people to sit still doing nothing at the best of times, certainly for more than three or four minutes. In reality, it's a state of mind. But on a concrete wall your bum starts to get uncomfortable and the cold and damp begin to seep inexorably into your frame. Beyond that, we begin to progressively feel that we are sticking out, that passers-by are beginning to notice us and raise quizzical eyebrows. They are not. If we are relaxed, we appear to be relaxed – a relaxed person is a non-threatening person. Now, I knew that Newry certainly had its share of hoods and thugs, both PIRA and INLA – an increasingly rare breed, old Official IRA die-hards – but this town centre location, even though it was a stone's throw away from some of the hard estates, was much, much more cosmopolitan. Cosmopolitan meant more secure. Of course, PIRA had attacked RUC targets in the town, but these were carefully recced targets and the operations would be aborted at the first sign of danger to the gunmen or bombers. It was not generally PIRA's, or INLA's, way to hit opportunity targets. In the not too distant future, PIRA would attack a parked RUC armoured Cortina that they had noted was parked regularly, doors open, in the town centre. Two terrorists approached the car and lobbed hand grenades into the vehicle, killing all three policemen instantly. This was not going to happen to me, but as I sat there as an hour became an hour and a quarter, I began to feel less sanguine and began to look harder to see if I was being watched or if a passer-by passed by more than twice. The key in a situation such as this was to log the body language of those loitering in one's field of view – my field of view was potentially a gunman's field of fire.* What I had to do was separate the tense, taut and nervous from the casual and disinterested. They, the former, would be the ones posing any threat. Tradecraft demands that disinterested direct eye contact is avoided unless specifically necessary, but gaining a sense of a third party unduly focussing on me would definitely constitute an undesirable signal and demand an escalation in preparedness to respond, ultimately in a timely vacation of the scene. Always trust one's instincts. I believe that I have always been sensitive to the atmosphere around me, so have invariably felt able to relax until experiencing real discomfort.

The great concern, however, in this sort of situation was that someone, casually or not, would initiate a conversation, even if only to ask for the time or a light. An answering English, or even Scottish, accent would usually mean only one thing – Security Forces. And that meant unwanted attention. Time- or fire-seekers are easily dealt with. A flick of the wrist and a smile reveals the time, another quick flick operates a Zippo. A nod and the exchange is over, anonymity maintained. For anything more intrusive, I had a simple strategy ready and mentally rehearsed to hand. Possessing darker Celtic or quasi-Mediterranean features, I could be mistaken for a foreign visitor – take your pick for my reason for being there, but I easily, at least visually, passed for anything rather than an undercover soldier. If provoked into speech, I would assume a foreign-sounding accent and attempt to end any conversation as quickly but politely as possible.

★ Years later, no longer in the military, I was involved in a drugs raid in Lomé, the capital of Togo. A special squad from the Togolese police had arrested a group of Chinese in one of the city's more prosperous quarters. They were suspected of importing counterfeit medicines. We were out on the street, waiting for transport to arrive to take them away. Watching one of the four who had been arrested, his eyes were constantly flicking to a spot just up the street. I guessed he was involuntarily checking on one of the cars parked there – body language. I asked him for the car key and was handed it. Inside the vehicle I found incriminating documents and a weapon.

So, I felt OK in myself but more and more stressed that the target had not made an appearance. I was certain I had not missed him going in nor going out of the DHSS office, my cue to up and at him, but it was just possible that this had happened. But equally, the cover car had not spotted him and triggered me. I had been acknowledging the quarterly nothing-to-report SITREP sent over the net by the covering handler by double-clicking the pressle switch of my covert radio at the end of a thin cable running down the inside sleeve of my coat, secured at my wrist by my watch strap, indicating noiselessly that all was good with me too.

I checked my watch. My ninety minutes was up. In line with our operational plan, it was time to lift off. Another no-show. Deeply disappointing after all the planning and now my long wait on the wall. But we were all seasoned realists and understood the vagaries of the game. I had one long last searching look in both directions and triggered my pressle four times. The duty op came back over the air into my earpiece instantly. "Is that you lifting off?" I double-clicked in response, confirming my intention, and stood, over-straightening my stiff legs, slackening off my bunched shoulder muscles, and hoping that life would soon return to my numb posterior. The net came to life again. "Roger that, lifting off now." The cover car acknowledged and I proceeded up the road to where he would pick me up and we would return to base.

The objective of these initial attempts to 'bump' targets, when they were successful, was to begin a twin-pronged process. The key objective was to start talking, to start attempting to build some sort of proto-relationship. In tradecraft parlance it was to start building 'rapport' – the cultivation phase of an operation. A sustained dialogue over time would serve ideally to establish, build and strengthen a bond between target and handler – we are humans, we respond to other humans, and we are always flattered when we are shown kindness and attention. As the bond developed, theory asserted that the motivating factors identified by the handler would be aired and could be exploited, and other complementary factors given room to flourish, not least the early seedlings of friendship. The secondary purpose was to assess just how viable the target was, set against the guiding criteria of access, motivation and capability – or were we wasting valuable time on a no-hoper?

Of course, the reality of covert operations, and the wider outcome of any plan in life, is that whatever approach we planned, it did not always work out. Life is so comprehensively governed by chance, freakish or predictable, by 'sod's law', or as we called it then, the 'paddy factor'. If it can go wrong, it will go wrong. The vagaries of chance just required us to spend even more time on targeting. But when all the cogs aligned, the targeting process would jump to Phase Two and the handler would begin to get a realistic feel about whether he was talking to a potential new agent. This cultivation phase could last weeks, months, even, in extremis, years. It could be a project to hand on to one's replacement when time just simply ran out. Alternatively, the pitch could be made in a one-time contact with little or no preamble. These ops, whatever the duration of the 'getting to know you' phase, were always challenging but also usually fun. When they went well, the feeling of accomplishment and well-being, and the electricity of anticipation, was near orgasmic.

In protracted courtships, if the initial rapport building looked promising, a third key factor had to be considered if the targeting was to advance anywhere near to its final culmination – the recruitment 'pitch'. In situations where the early contacts were conducted in uniform, the target had to be brought to a place, mataphorically, were there was never any room for debate concerning the real identity of the handler – one army and that was an end to it. The underpinning psychological imperative was to subtly demonstrate that that immutable truth did, however, mask another. The target had to be brought to a place, metaphorically, where they began to see clearly that the handler was not ordinary Army but something reassuringly different, but at the same time benign and non-threatening. The handler had to plant the seed that when he invited the target to meet away from his home turf, this could be done effectively and securely with absolutely no risk to the target.

In the towns and cities of the Province, the targeting handler, in most circumstances, had to sustain some degree of cover story, masking his true identity as a soldier until the point when he chose to declare his true nature – certainly a crunch moment if by that stage in the operation the target still remained oblivious of the fact. The Israelis, for example, were expert at employing 'false flag' approaches to Arab targets, whereby they kept entirely hidden their real identities as Israeli intelligence operatives – we did not maintain a cover for any longer than was necessary.

Illustrating the inventiveness that consistently drove targeting operations, I have outlined three diverse, but typical, examples creating that first crucial point of contact. Two relate to the city, the third to the sticks.

This particular target lived with his family in the tightly packed sprawl of a Republican housing estate. Not an easy or safe place for a covert operator to loiter. Not an easy place in which to get alongside a target safely and purposefully. The targeting handler had done his best and a pattern of life study had been assembled, but it was pretty thin. The gaps suggested he was not going to be easily intercepted outside of his street, whereby a situation could be even superficially stage-managed to encourage that first conversation. A more radical and imaginative approach had to be proposed. One detail registered in his limited daily routine was that his Japanese hatchback was invariably parked overnight on the kerb directly in front of his garden gate. The seed of an idea was developed and a plan was put together.

Close to midnight, the handler would enter the area and await an all-clear call from a second car cruising past the target's house. On receipt of the radio message that the street was quiet and clear of possible onlookers, the handler would himself drive into the street and, in passing the parked hatchback, clip its front wing, causing enough damage to require professional repair.

All went exactly to plan. The handler stopped briefly, confirmed the extent of his handiwork, placed the brief, pre-prepared scribbled note of apology, his telephone number added at the bottom, under the front windscreen wiper, and exited the area in convoy with the cover car. The next morning an irritated target surveyed his broken car, unfolded the note, and later that day called the handler on the dedicated phone line installed in the Det offices, agreeing, in accordance with a rehearsed cover story, to meet the very humble and apologetic careless driver that evening in a safe bar in the city centre.

This approach demonstrated all the required imagination and lateral thinking to overcome the limited point-of-contact opportunities. As a ruse it was credible and realistic. The plan exploited the cover of darkness; the cover car guaranteed a real-time absence of witnesses; and a prior check of the Army patrol programme for the area revealed there would be no green army in the estate. The letter could be left under the wiper blade because the forecast was for a dry night, and the plan relied on the target's natural desire to have the offending driver's insurance cover the costs of repair. Accidents like this are commonplace and would arouse no suspicion of an elaborate FRU plan. The follow-up meeting took place. The handler maintained his cover and a follow-up social meeting was arranged. Initial success.

The next target was clearly a dog lover. Pattern-of-life revealed that twice daily, regularly as clockwork, he walked his female Alsatian from his house, along the river path, through some woodland and back home via a patch of scrubby wasteland. Set against the other details of routine, these looked like the most effective and secure slots in the target's day to begin his cultivation. It looked as though he always walked alone, and usually had the route exclusively to himself. The assessment was made that, as an added bonus, he was likely to be at his most relaxed during these walks and consequently more receptive to any advances made by the handler.

The handler negotiated access to a dog, I guess from a personal friend, probably delighted to be spared the ordeal of daily walks themselves, at least for a time, and began walking it, coincidentally at exactly the same time as his target, but in a counter-wise direction. For the first week he passed the Alsatian and its master once daily without any form of acknowledgement. The second week, the two exchanged nods. You've probably guessed it – the third week they began halting briefly to exchange initially dog-related banter and the exchanges began to become longer and more meaningful.

This particular operation perfectly exemplifies the exploitation of a target's routine. As an illustration of engineering a point of contact, it is flawless. It provides a perfect cover story, substantive and visual, for the handler to be where he was, and exploits not only the target's routine, but, initially at least, as a dog lover, a personal motivation and a pretext for engaging him in conversation.

The third illustration is set against a rural backdrop. The target was a poacher over the border in the south of Ireland. It was reported to the Det that the poacher was not only a game eater, but also a game salesman, discreetly selling on the bulk of his cull to local people.

The handler duly contacted the hunter and began meeting him regularly on the pretext of buying game. Despite the apparent casualness of this arrangement, it was planned, briefed and executed as a full-blown covert operation. The handler arrived at the prearranged meeting point – not ideal as we tried to avoid meets at fixed pre-briefed locations, but unavoidable due to the nature of the contact. He would be covered all the way through the operation by his cover team, extra vigilant and very conscious of the enhanced threat level in the circumstances.

The relationship prospered and the frequency of contact increased. In this instance, however, the team became a little distracted and the mechanics of purchasing illicit rabbits and the odd pheasant initially blunted the pointed end of the stick. With a little sharpening from HQ, however, the operation did regain its focus and the business of intelligence collection resumed its priority status.

What role does capability, the final fourth pillar, play in the targeting mix? Capability is critical. It is the final determinant as to whether a target can handle the practicalities of functioning and surviving as an agent. A target may have wonderful access. They might be motivated, and despite the risks and dangers, unequivocally commit themselves to working for the Crown, but with an absence of capability they are worthless – they will be incapable of delivering the goods. This lack of capability might manifest itself in abject terror of being compromised that no amount of reassurance from the handler can overcome. The source might be effectively paralysed, and totally incapable of performing the necessary physical tasks and remaining discreet without betraying their fear. A heavy drinker might be so indiscreet that in a drunken moment they compromise themselves. A potential agent may not have the necessary common sense or mental facility to process information and pass it on to his handler with coherence and accuracy. A likely agent may be able to mix in their own immediate environment, but not, as the result of injury, illness or means of transportation, possess the mobility to meet covertly, away from their homes, as dictated by the requirements of sound, secure tradecraft.

But at some point, if all the variables, unknowns and plain fates came together, the assessment would be made, usually in conjunction with a nod and with some guidance from HQ, to move to the third and final phase of the targeting process. This is the recruitment phase, during which the recruitment 'pitch' is made. At the outset it has to be noted that most targeting operations do not thrive and reach this final climax. Those that do are more often than not unsuccessful. The target refuses to work, either in a state of complete shock and surprise having had no inkling of the handler's real identity or intention, or with a complete understanding of the situation. Failed attempts are frustrating because they represent the culmination of a tremendous expenditure of time and resources, but as the saying goes, every cloud has a silver lining. When a recruitment attempt was declared by the target and was published in the media, particularly in the IRA's own propaganda sheet, *An Phoblacht*, a shiver of dread and doubt would run down the collective spine of the terrorist organisations. If this attempt was unsuccessful and blown, they would speculate, how many remained undeclared and were successful? Beautiful. We were able to throw back the fears and dread of the informer, stoked up by the lessons of Irish history, right back into the laps of the latest generation of Republicans.

The final phase of the recruitment process was always heavily stage-managed and would constitute a significant event in the unit diary. In most recruitment operations the finale would usually follow an already existing pattern of contacts and meetings. Sometimes the confidence to 'pitch' the target came relatively close on the heels of the initial contact. At the other extreme, it could be at the end of a protracted sequence lasting months and months.

It was a situation where the man on point, the handler, would be able to provide the best assessment of when the target was 'ready'. It was not unusual for most members in the Det to have a role to play and even, on occasion, we would commandeer wives and members from other Dets to play supporting roles. Clearly there was absolutely no way that wives were used in any role that was dangerous, or that required training. This was always a situation where handlers with local accents were consistently in demand and worth their weight in poteen – one thing that serving in the Province reinforced to me was never, ever to try and put on an Irish accent.*

A key point at this stage: as an agency we did not condone blackmail as a recruitment tactic. This is not to say that there would not be occasions when pressure was implied or applied, but our philosophy was based on pure, practical assessment. If you unduly pressure a target, he or she may agree to work for you, but this commitment will be founded, not on good faith, but on duress. Could such an agent be trusted? We would always respond with an unreserved negative. An agent being blackmailed to work will likely fabricate his or her intelligence to reduce the pressure, or ultimately, try to set up the handler. To run an effective case, the agent must be positively, not negatively, motivated. The RUC operated by another creed, and certainly used their ability to prosecute a target if they had a case, and the target initially refused to work. This is not to say, of course, that all SB sources were being

* In his very candid and comprehensive exposé of 14 Coy tactics and capabilities, *The Operators*, James Rennie describes 'language' training whereby potential operators received coaching on the course to enable them to put on local accents. Review the instances in film and TV where professional actors have attempted to do the same, and failed, even with the benefit of retakes and far more intensive training – then assume that an operator would have to slip instantly into giving a credible performance, in one take, and against what would be potentially a very stressful backdrop. I am far from convinced that they would get away with it. On a separate note but allied theme, I suggested to the Top that operators, particularly in the border areas, received some basic Gaelic language training. With over 40 per cent of southern Irish citizens, and an even higher ratio of hard-line Republicans, speaking the language, how much would this do to not only cause instant surprise but potentially break down barriers and enhance rapport with a target?

blackmailed – the majority were run exploiting the same matrix of motivating factors as we based our cases on.

If an operation achieved the ultimate success and the target agreed to work, it was an occasion for celebration, but absolutely not a time for laurels to be rested upon. An additional asset increased the collective workload on the whole Det but this was a burden that no one resented. The really hard work was just beginning, however. The new agent, with their new source number, had to be rapidly schooled in their new art, assimilating the tools of the trade, starting with the lessons of faultless security, security and more security training. They had to understand enough, right from this initial meeting, to keep them safe until the second. Then it was a process of drumming into them the need to be perpetually cautious about how others, including close family, interpreted their every word and act, and how they collected their intelligence without drawing any undue attention from those same third parties. We always instructed agents to keep their new roles from even the closest of family members and not to share even with wives. Sometimes, of course, an agent would make the decision to tell their spouse or would somehow betray themselves. We did run a few husband and wife teams, either resulting from a targeted joint recruitment or in pragmatic recognition of this, sometimes inevitable and unavoidable, security breach.

Training drilled down into how to unobtrusively follow the elements of tradecraft required to meet covertly, the telephone drills to maintain irregular contact if required, the continuous requirement to create and rehearse cover stories, sometimes multi-layered, etc., etc. During the course of their career as an agent this training would never cease and would be continually refined, updated and modified as the circumstances pertaining to the case developed. This need for good security was a constant source of stress and pressure for the agent, but at the same time was a confidence-boosting measure because it demonstrated our care, concern and commitment to them and persuaded and reassured them that there were logical, tried and tested ways to keep safe.

10

TACTICS, TRADECRAFT AND TRICKS

I am now moving from the fraught and uncertain task of the recruiter to the certainties that agent-handling operational fieldcraft involved. Our fieldcraft had evolved over time. While the guiding principles remained immutable, tactics underwent continual subtle changes, largely in response to the adaptation of changing technology but also in response to the continual assessment and reassessment of the threat. By the early to mid-1980s it is probably true to say that it had reached a pre-microchip hiatus, a gold-plated one, that was to last until the comprehensive adoption of mobile phones and home computers. I have nothing to say on agent operations post this technological revolution.

Tradecraft codifies tactics, processes and procedures. Its primary function is to allow handler and agent to meet in conditions of maximum security. In a permissive environment, effective tradecraft prevents a 'soft' compromise to a counter-intelligence agency. A worst-case scenario would be arrest of the agent and subsequent conviction in a court of law. Against a non-permissive backdrop like Northern Ireland, the 'hard' compromise would likely mean an ambush and death for both handler and agent, or the nightmare contingency of capture by terrorist personnel and a slower death. There is one poignant and simple point to make concerning our tradecraft. During the operational life of the FRU, and its reincarnation as JSG, the unit did not suffer a single operational compromise that threatened the physical safety of either an agent or a handler. This is a bold claim but one that cannot be refuted. We did have very few compromises, but they were not the result of failures of tradecraft out on the ground. No one died as a direct consequence. I think we could, and should, be very proud of this ultimate affirmation and testament to the way we conducted our business in the testing environments we operated in.

FRU tradecraft was not complicated but it was relatively sophisticated when weighed against the modus operandi of other intelligence agencies, especially those working in the Province. The RUC SB were certainly a generational leap behind the FRU in terms of employing secure meet procedures the day my Ashford course kicked-off. They would not catch up for a number of years, well into the late 1980s, with the realisation that the continuing loss of agents had to force change.

The driving principle was to meet agents, wherever feasible, in secure, controlled locations where the meet could be stage managed and both handling team and agent could relax. At the point of being picked up by the handling team, and dropped off at meet's end, the imperative was that the agent would be well outside his or her normal 'habitat'. Only in a situation of extreme emergency, where time was severely limited, would an agent be met close to home – in this situation it might even actually require the handlers to go to the source's home. If this option was unavoidable, security considerations would be even more rigorously woven into the handlers' planning.

The aspect of security training and planning that exercised us disproportionally was the constant rehearsing and evolving of cover stories. Every action taken by the source would be covered by a credible cover story that reflected, as close to the truth as possible, the routines and realities, including the 'innocent' secrets that they might be living, of their 'real' lives. Cover stories were visual as well as verbal, so that in the event an agent was seen conducting 'business', either by a disinterested third party or, more sinisterly, a member of a terror grouping, they had a credible explanation to hand – critical and without doubt, in extremis, life preserving.

This was another area of endeavour that taxed the imagination of the handlers but always produced the best finished product when the ideas and input of the agents themselves were respected – who, after all, knew their lives better? Pause for a moment and look into the mirror. We all use cover stories to conceal things that we do not wish others to know about us, whether they be partners, colleagues or bosses. Consider how we put those stories together and which ones work best and which ones we feel most comfortable trotting out. Now, imagine that the purpose of your cover story is not merely to ease you out of a potentially embarrassing or difficult situation, but might be required to save you from torture and death. An interesting concept.

The next meetings between agent and handler were usually arranged during the routine face-to-face meets, all details being mutually confirmed before drop-off. A productive agent would be met weekly or even several times a week if the pace and volume of their reporting demanded it. Low-level eyes-and-ears sources may not have been met more regularly than monthly. In the event that agent, or handler, required an impromptu or emergency meeting, a pre-arranged visual signal could be invoked. In XMG, the county town of Bandit Country, over a period, a coloured patch was inserted by the handler in the armoured window of Borucki Sanger overlooking the main square. For another of our agents in my time, we trialled something similar. But more conventionally, the telephone would be used and simple coding would be passed in whichever direction was appropriate. Every detachment had at least one dedicated 'source line' that was permanently cleared only for agent use. Whenever they rang in, the Det duty operator would always experience a brief involuntary rush of adrenalin. Whenever an agent used the telephone to call his handler, especially when that call was made from a public call box, it was SOP for him or her to make a second call directly afterwards to a friend, relation or colleague. In the event that they were seen making the call, by any third party, this second call would provide their alibi – back to cover stories. On one occasion, one of our less intellectually endowed sources phoned in to the Det reversing the charges. We were forced to locate the exchange and conduct damage limitation. We assessed there was no threat to him but that the source line had henceforth to be considered compromised. It had to be changed and the tiresome process of passing the new number to all agents enacted.

No matter how routine, every covert meet was a stand-alone covert operation. There was no corner cutting, no just 'cuffing' it. Every meeting was planned to maximise security protection for all players against the worst-case scenario of a deliberate terrorist ambush. Under no circumstances would a handler meet an agent without at least one other operator being on the ground in close proximity to him at the point of picking up, or dropping off, the agent – the moment of greatest risk. This was the 'cover team'. In low-risk scenarios, this second operator would be the co-handler.

All cases were run on the basis of a lead handler 'commanding' the operation and providing first-line direction to the agent during the meet. The co-handler's role was to directly support the prime handler, most usefully during the debrief – two heads, or rather two pairs of ears, are always better than one. He could fill in gaps the handler might have missed or provide context overlooked by the handler, and chip in with pointed questions, if again they were missed by the main debriefer. The co-handler fulfilled the role of an understudy, and usually, but not always, dependent on interpersonal dynamics and, frankly, manning contingencies, took over the case on the posting out of the unit of the more senior operator. Beyond this, the co-handler's presence most importantly provided additional security and protection for the handler. And he made the tea! Shifting the operational context for a minute, Israeli military intelligence lost a number of their handlers because they conducted their debriefs without the second pair of protective and supportive hands of a co-handler. In one such incident, when sitting safely alongside his handler, the agent produced a weapon and murdered him.

In preparation for the meet, the handler would prepare and deliver formal orders, in exactly the same way as an infantry platoon commander or multiple commander would prepare his patrol, using the identical orders format and phases, briefing all participants in the operation including the duty NCO, who would monitor the radio net and coordinate actions in the event of a problem. His orders would include all the various contingencies and 'actions on' – admittedly, for routine low-risk operations these paragraphs would be fairly standard in content. When preparing to deploy on recruitment operations these orders groups could be high tension, complex and of long duration. There would always be time for questions or follow-on discussion if it was appropriate. I remember regularly sitting in on orders groups for recruitment operations that lasted an hour and a half.

As already stated, in most scenarios the agent would be instructed to travel away from their home area, where they would be more readily recognised and known. Agents working for S Det who lived in the border country would be instructed to travel north to the larger, more cosmopolitan town of Newry, or further afield to Banbridge or Hillsborough or even Belfast, time permitting. Their cover story, and the closeness of it to features of their real day-to-day lives, would determine where we could risk them being spotted.

Pick-ups were effected either on foot or more routinely by vehicle. Pick-up mechanics were predicated on the requirement to confirm that the agent was not under any form of surveillance. We progressively put more and more effort into anti- and counter-surveillance measures to bolster our security drills. Numerous different methods were used to get the agent safely into the handler's car, some simple, some more complex – but all would take into account the area, the level of risk, and the capabilities and circumstances of the individual agent. All the methods would include an element of counter-surveillance, and chime with the agent's personal cover story. Everything had to be consistent with, and backed up by, the cover story, the continuing need for that credible business-related, romance-related, crime-related, no limit to the imagination-related, cover story. It was doctrine that agents were never picked up at a fixed point. This significantly reduced the possibility that terrorists could use a turned or compromised agent to lead them to the handler.

To conduct an optimum debrief, agents were taken to secret dedicated safe houses. Each Det ran several, one of which was always inside a barracks location for maximum security. The remainder were ordinary houses that were occupied by some of the single, or unaccompanied, operators. These houses were predominantly located in the community, that is to say not in any barracks. The houses were located in safe areas predominantly of lower population density to negate the issue of prying eyes and twitching curtains. When I returned to S Det at the end of the course, I moved into a safe house in the leafy outskirts of one of the safe small towns in central mid-Down. I shared the house – cooking, cleaning, and everything else – with the handler working the unit's most important case, Mick L. We were not close and did not become close. Looking back, I realise that was a great shame and a wasted opportunity, on my part, to learn from this seasoned operator and mine the goldmine of his experience and the case he was working. Rather than young 'flatmates' caught up in life's bright new adventure together, our relationship was more akin to the gruff acknowledgement of the fellow passenger one sits daily opposite on the 0821 to Charing Cross. He was a fair bit older than me, with hair a little too coiffed for my taste and hipster slacks a little too low on the waist. We basically lived our separate lives, professionally and socially, but that worked perfectly for each of us – in reality, neither of us spent much of the week there anyway.

One such brief social interaction did come late one afternoon. I had returned to the house to pick up something trivial, and as I entered through the front door I was greeted by a cloud of dense grey swirling smoke. I made my way smartly to the small functional kitchen and there was the seat of the problem, as I had expected. Acrid smoke was billowing forth from the grill of the old electric cooker – it had clearly been left on. As yet there were no flames. I pulled the plug from the wall and went to check the rest of the bungalow. Poking my head into the small smoke-filled sitting room, there was Mick sprawled out on the couch, fast asleep. I shook him roughly awake. He was dazed and disorientated but quickly took in the scenario. We threw open all the windows throughout the place and it did not take too long for the atmosphere to clear as the cold, fresh winter air purged the smoke. Clearly it had not been toxic, there had been no fire, but maybe the grill would at some point have ignited – then the story would have unfolded in a far more dangerous and potentially life-threatening way. The incident changed nothing, and in very few minutes we again separated on our separate paths for the evening.

I heard some time later that he had been involved in organising a 'disco' in the sergeants' mess and had provided the music, transferred to cassette tape. At some point in the evening the tunes abruptly stopped, and instead of the Bee Gees booming out of the speakers, the voice of his agent dramatically addressed the frozen dancers, the thick Irish accent replacing 'Saturday Night Fever'. Somehow it would appear that Mick had mixed his tapes up and had inadvertently supplied an old debrief tape. Excellent lyrics but not an easy tune to dance to.

Within the secure confines of the safe house, especially those within 'the wire', handling team and agent could relax, eat, drink, conduct the gritty business of the day and work to strengthen and solidify professional and personal bonds. This was critical. In days of yesteryear, debriefs were largely conducted beyond the secure environment of the safe houses, inside handlers' vehicles. This tactic offered none of the security or comfort of dedicated premises. The RUC SB continued using this approach long after the FRU curtailed this insecure and cramped approach.

At meet's end, intelligence having been passed to the handlers and tasking passed to the agent, the next meet arranged and, if appropriate, retainer paid, the convoluted but secure process of reuniting the source usually with his car, and his or her normal life, would be carried out. Again, various different tactics were employed to avoid pattern setting, to detect and avoid any enemy activity, and to carry out the whole thing as safely as possible. Both halves of the team would then 'bomb-burst'; the handlers back to base, and the agent back home, to work or wherever. Just another ordinary routine day continuing to unfold, rather than the marking of the end of a potentially life-threatening event in both parties' doppelganger lives.

As every phase of the operation was concluded, the duty operator back in the unit ops room would be kept appraised of operational progress, and informed of the team's geographic location to and from pick-up to secure location, to drop-off. This was critical, because in the event of an incident, pre-GPS locating days, they would be responsible for tasking the response of the Quick Reaction Force, the QRF.

With the arrival of the new CO, we adopted the colour-coded numerical spots used by the surveillance teams of 14 Coy to bring brevity and clarity in identifying key road junctions and topographical features. Hamish had served with 14 Coy in the 1970s. While I thought it was a good idea for the city, I was not a fan for country areas, where quite simply the paucity of features did not justify change. He was the boss, so we all sat down to 'spot' our map books and learn the bloody things.

Those were the lessons we learnt in the classroom and practised on the other side of Templer's main gate.

11

MORE TRAINING, MORE TESTING

One of the key practical exercises that tested us in the earliest days of the course, and is, I would suspect, potentially replicated in any credible contact handling training anywhere, is the requirement to approach a complete stranger and learn their life story without compromising one's true identity and intent. So simple sounding a task, it is in reality one of the toughest tests for the normally reticent and essentially private creatures that we human beings are. But again, it is an ordeal that we all at some time in our private lives grasp when we move to break the ice with that person of special interest.

Because we are Brits, it is natural that this exercise was staged not in a supermarket, library or on the touchline of a sporting event, but in the pub. On the evening in question we were briefed on the rules for the engagement before we were detailed off to the numerous pubs in the Ashford town centre, one would-be handler per bar. Once inside, we had to select our targets, strictly discounting members of the bar staff and members of the opposite sex – what had seemed tricky now became exponentially more daunting. We were given a number of specific questions to answer, to supplement the general overview of the target's life story, and instructed to arrange a follow-up meeting.

My target was a typical rough Ashford local that had seen better days, and, I think, has long since closed down, probably with the introduction of the strict public ban on smoking. I was certainly apprehensive – we all saw this exercise as a make or break ordeal. Coming away empty-handed would be an unequivocal indicator that, as agent handlers, we would make good tank drivers. As my pub was just half a mile from the main gate, I planned to walk; and anyway, I would, of course, be drinking. I had already settled on my strategic approach but there was no guarantee on a mid-week evening that the place would even be hosting any drinkers.

On opening the peeling front door and entering the single bar it was as quiet as a downtown Damascus pork butcher on a Friday evening. There is, or was, no smell like a down-at-heel urban English pub. Stale tobacco, stale beer, stale lives. Somehow the décor, the furniture, the bar, could only be British. I surveyed the three maudlin drinkers, and there at the bar, on his stool, was my target straight from central casting. Target lock-on! Early-to-mid 60s, male, inwardly surveying a future as uninspiring as his past, and as flat as the solitary pint he was nursing. Unless he was a deaf mute, I knew that this was the perfect scenario and that everything was going to be alright. Buoyed by my reinvigorated confidence, I perched on the neighbouring stool and ordered a very un-officer-like lager.

Within an hour I had everything I needed, with one trip to the gents to top up the keg and make some hurriedly scribbled notes. The big lesson of life that I have witnessed first-hand time and time again is that no challenge is ever larger or more burdensome than its anticipation. And that if you take the plunge and crack the ice, treat people with respect and show interest in them as fellow human beings, there are not many insurmountable hurdles in life.

I returned to the Manor and carefully and comprehensively wrote up my report, concentrating on detail and staff duties, the military way to communicate succinctly and clearly on paper – bettered, in my experience, by no other corporation or organisation – to produce a polished document. As it transpired, I had got off to the best start possible, collecting and presenting the best and fullest picture of the exercise. Another lesson I learned early in my professional life: if things start well, they normally end well. And, of course, invariably vice versa.

Just to demonstrate how well others performed, I heard that on later courses one student had done so well he had actually been offered a job; probably, knowing Ashford, one that involved sailing close to the wind with a fair to even chance of jail time. On another, the flair of the would-be handler's opening gambit had seen him poised at the start of a homosexual relationship that no doubt would have changed the course of his life. It's possible he had mischievously been tasked to a gay bar, or perhaps more likely some other dynamic had been at play. Whatever, I am pretty sure his determination to continue his quest to become a handler won through and he navigated his way through this potential crossroads unscathed.

The practical debriefing exercises began unfolding just as positively. I found that I liked to listen, had a good memory for detail, and could quickly process the 'storylines'. When it became my turn to speak and drill down into the source's information, I had already identified the 'thread' and assembled the questions that were required to close the gaps, elicit that extra ounce of information, and present a coherent and comprehensive intelligence picture. My time in the Province, though limited, had, by this stage in my career, given me sufficient feel for how the terrorist groupings planned and executed operations – this helped me enormously because the course scenarios were logically modelled on current NI MOs.

Early recruitment exercises were similarly fairly straightforward and the cues invariably clearly identifiable. By effectively pushing and leading the role-playing targets – a mix of staff employed throughout the barracks, some family members, and returning handlers on active duty in the unit – their potential motivations soon became apparent and transparent enough for the moment of truth when one was required to 'close the deal' and go 'in for the kill' – all apt euphemisms. One exercise I remember involved a female target. As soon as my questioning had revealed that her husband had been murdered by terrorist gunmen, it was job done. Like an angler landing a perch, I was able to reel her in and secure her commitment to work while she watched me from the keepnet.

We practised conducting recces for pick-ups and drop-offs, and then the drills to execute real-life procedures, as part of our exercises. We spent a lot of time in the suburbs of South Ashford because of the physical and psychological similarity to parts of West Belfast. I remember on one occasion providing cover for a pick-up and finding myself in a rather exposed position. There was a nearby post box, so I ripped a page out of the back of a notebook I had with me in my meet bag, what the Americans call a 'bug-out' bag, jumped out of the car, and dropped it into the box. A good visual cover story – a reason for being there to assuage the curiosity of the casual or more motivated onlooker. The DS with me (we were usually accompanied on all serials by assessing members of the training team) seemed delighted by my simple initiative.

I found the extensive range work tremendous fun and experienced absolutely no problems, especially during the anti-ambush drills we rehearsed on foot and in our cars. We learnt that our vehicle was probably our best weapon and provided us with the best protection in the event of an ambush. We practised the manoeuvres that would get us out of trouble – fast reverses, J and hand-brake turns, and the theory, but sadly only the theory, of where to hit a blocking vehicle to burst past and through.

If encountering situations that constituted threats while on foot, we learnt that it was equally critical to act decisively, with speed, and to use violence with proportionality, but above all with intent. The haunting images from the ambush of the two corporals who ran unintentionally into the funeral cortège in Belfast in 1988 irrefutably demonstrate two clear lessons. Firstly, anyone operating in plain clothes must receive adequate training so that they are able to defend themselves effectively. The news footage revealed unambiguously that if the pair had received any schooling, it had been insufficient. The second lesson was that this training must be assimilated and practised to the point that its application becomes instinctive. Clearly they had not assimilated any lessons nor had they practised them. Their reaction to the crowd exemplified everything that one should not do. They did everything wrong and paid with their lives. It was a tragic, freakish, and needless loss of life from every perspective.

My physical fitness and familiarity with weapons handling eased my passage through this phase of the training. In the gym, even though I am not particularly light and agile on my toes, my boxing experience proved a handy aid in handling the unarmed combat training. Not too far in the future, SIW would ensure that all firearms and close combat training was conducted by expert and highly experienced, seasoned specialist NCOs from a well-known, high-profile regiment within the British Army. I clearly remember four of them, all first-class soldiers and professionals. One subsequently put his experiences down on paper and significantly referred to his time at SIW as the highlight of his career.*

We trained to tick off one final, but potentially crucial, box of the syllabus – first aid. I have always believed that even the most elementary awareness of the subject should be a mandatory life skill for everyone. Even a little knowledge can potentially save a life. For us the requirement was a little more serious and focussed. We had to be capable of dealing with some specific and role-related threats to life. These centred on the blunt force trauma consistent with RTAs, and the loss of blood and resultant clinical shock associated with gunshot wounds. I have always enjoyed and been interested in medical-related matters, so this was enjoyable training, unreservedly relevant, and compared to the intensity of the training that SAS medics undergo, frankly much too cursory. Fortunately, I have never had to deal with any serious injury sustained by a unit member, or to myself.

I did, however, a few years later – just after the Wall had come down and I had stayed on and was serving with the unit that had evolved out of BRIXMIS, the British Military Mission – attend to the victim of a head-on car crash in the middle of the former East Germany. A small Western car, I think a VW Golf or Jetta, had crossed the barrier-less motorway central reservation and had ploughed headlong into the front of a GAZ lorry coming from the opposite direction. The car was registered in Hamburg in West Germany with its distinctive HH number plate prefix. The driver must presumably have been a visiting businessman.

Cars and trucks continued to pass the wreckage. This was East Germany – no one wanted to get involved if they could avoid it. I did not need to share their understandable reticence. Potentially, I

---

* See Mike Curtis's *Close Quarter Battle*.

could help. I pulled onto the hard shoulder. Controlling the urge to rush to the scene, I waited for a break in the traffic before crossing the carriageways. The scene was a bit of a mess. The truck driver was unscathed but looked to be in a state of shock. His flat-fronted Russian-made truck was largely undamaged – the front had been designed to be flat. Not so the capitalist-made machine. The front of the VW was crumpled, twisted metal. Its engine was off, I guess as a result of the impact. Broken glass was everywhere.

There was a single occupant inside. He looked about 30, short mid-brown hair, his round face pallid and bloodless-looking. I could see teeth on the dash and clinging to the front of his jacket. He was wedged in place, still seat-belted but at an angle across the front passenger seat. There was a cassette tape protruding from the player mounted in the dashboard. Somehow I knew instinctively that he had been focussed on changing the tape, probably removing it in order to change sides, had lost control and veered into the path of the unsuspecting GAZ.

The door was jammed shut, so I leaned in through the shattered front passenger window and, inserting my fingers into his mouth, cleared the driver's airway of tongue and bloody mess – these were pre-AIDS days when only squeamishness prevented one from coming casually into contact with another's blood or bodily fluids. I checked for any external bleeding as best I could. I felt pretty powerless but fundamentally unfeelingly detached as I watched his laboured breathing – this was not any lack of humanity on my part but a coping mechanism. I find that I am able to switch on and off when confronted by extreme situations. Undoubtedly his severe head injuries were compounded by internal injuries, which probably included chest and resultant lung damage caused by the seat belt. I wondered who he was, what his story was, how his day had started and what his concerns or worries or expectations for the unfolding day had been. I wondered whom he was missing and who was missing him back home on the other side of the Iron Curtain in Hamburg. I wondered if anyone had had any premonition as to how the day would end, his final day, cut short in a pointless accident on a nondescript stretch of motorway in the middle of nowhere, in a land that no longer even exists. Whatever injuries he had sustained proved so severe that he died within minutes, peacefully and almost imperceptibly, still wedged inside his car before the East German ambulance arrived.

By the mid-point of the course we were all pretty tired. On the range at Lydd, a gale blowing off the English Channel, I had trudged all the way up the range, what seemed like miles, *crunch, crunch, crunching* on the gravel of the shooting lanes, up to the firing point, getting there to find that I had left my ammunition way back at my start point. But when things are going well you are forgiven these lapses, and it's laughs rather than harsh, derisive words that greet you.

The final exercise came and we put into effect all the lessons, all the drills, all the tradecraft, all the procedures and the tricks that we had worked so hard to practise and perfect. Everything went well over the three days and FRO Ashford performed well, gathering valuable intelligence, and recruiting some good guys to get the bad guys. As an interesting and relevant novelty, the issue of the failed meeting was introduced to add even more realism. The 'fail to meet' scenario is a prevalent reality of agent operations, particularly in the targeting context, when, for whatever reasons, after all the preparation, the source or target does not appear. The team goes through its missed meet drills and ultimately aborts the operation, returning 'empty-handed' to base. There are few bigger let-downs – good to face this reality in training. The price to pay is that a new meet now has to be crowbarred into the busy operational diary – a great test of flexibility and time management.

I sat down for my final interview with Pete Giddy and stood up again having passed the course. I probably have a course report somewhere but have not found it. I certainly did not put in a perfect, flawless performance, and weaknesses and areas for improvement were identified. But I had done enough, and performed well enough across the board, to persuade the team that I had the tradecraft, interpersonnel and defensive skills to become an agent handler. Ultimately, I had a face that the team assessed would fit in the unit across the Irish Sea. As a 23-year-old Regular officer, I would be returning to the FRU as a fully-fledged operator. I was ecstatic – absolutely no sense of the anticlimax I had experienced just two short years before, at the end of my university career, after my final exam, when I had gone to bed – to sleep – at 1830 hours.

I don't think I fully appreciated it as I returned to my room to pack, but this was the most important and far-reaching single event in my life so far. Passing the course changed my life forever. From this moment on, I did not look back once in life, for a single moment, and never once regretted the path that I had chosen, and that had in equal measure been chosen for me, and that I had the good fortune to have followed.

12

BANDIT COUNTRY

I arrived back in Bessbrook to ready myself, as autumn intensified, for the joys of a long, damp south Armagh winter in a rural agent-handling detachment.

The welcome I received was warm and familiar – I felt I had not actually been away. But if I had left to attend the course at 5ft 10in tall, I felt I had returned at least a full foot taller. There is no feeling akin to belonging to a small, tight, focussed team. TC seemed particularly happy to see me back and ready for work. In so small a team, one extra pair of hands is an exponential increase in capability. He briefed me that I would be handling assets in Newry, co-handling our sources in the Forkhill area to the east of our TAOR, and supporting targeting ops around Crossmaglen. Could any job spec surpass this?

I found myself in an extremely unusual position. I was the only officer in the Det but had no command responsibilities. TC was the boss and I worked for him despite my commissioned status and his as a senior non-commissioned Warrant Officer. This may have been of concern to others but to me it mattered not one iota. I was here to learn, and who better to learn from than a handling legend like TC, and frankly the rest of the lads. My eye was beginning to look to the future, and although not yet focussed on running an FRU Det, I was aware that I now had a unique opportunity to learn not only this trade from the inside out, but working shoulder to shoulder with the operators as an equal, I would be able to see first-hand any tricks, real-world retakes, or indeed sleights of hand, that SIW did not pass on. At this juncture I did not know how long this would be my reality, but I guessed that soon there would be discussions as to next steps and that these could very likely, and unfortunately, see pressure to return to the more regular and normal employment of a young officer. I chose not to brood on this, but rather to grab as much as I could from this unique opportunity and maintain as tight a grip as I could for as long as I could.

I applied myself and settled deliberately and quickly into my daily routine, just in case I would awake from my slumbers and find that it was all just a dream. I had my photographs taken from all profiles, mugshot style, for the folder kept on the ops desk. This included pictures and descriptions of all the Det members who could be deployed on the ground. In the event of an incident, the relevant sheets would be passed to the aerial quick reaction force who would likely be the first to arrive at any incident scene. The photos would allow them to identify us and significantly lower the risk of any 'blue on blue' shootout – armed covert soldiers do not mix well in the same grid square with armed regular soldiers – or police – in any circumstance, and we certainly did not use the baseball caps and armbands that Holywood FRU members would have. There was an operation name covering this contingency but for the life of me I cannot remember it. On returning to the Det as the OC, we updated this approach using video, which crucially captured far more lifelike and usable images. And, of course, I finished putting together my map books and terrorist recognition photo montages. The Bessbrook office covered an enormous area so we worked with 1:50,000 mapping, saving the large-scale coverage solely for significant towns like Newry, Crossmaglen and Forkhill.

I also rapidly got to grips reading through our source files and our paperwork dealing with ongoing targeting operations, and assessing the standard and breadth of the office's reporting. In the same way that effective security procedures underpin effective agent operations, effective paperwork and efficient administrative support underpin the dissemination of human source intelligence.

Top: Bessbrook burns. A few short minutes after the Mill was hit by a barrage of PIRA Mk 10 mortar bombs in April 1987. It was a miracle that there were no casualties.

Bottom: Another view of the damage, adjacent to the base's main entrance.

Ready to deploy on an agent meeting. The author and his deliberately unprepossessing covert ops car.

Bleak mid-winter patrolling on the Square in Crossmaglen. Behind the author, utilising the uniform of on of the Guards Battalions to discreetly 'bump' a potential recruitment target, an early iteration of Borucki Sangar can be seen.

bove: The Victorian rooftops of Bessbrook Mill, the Army's headquarters from which the war in South rmagh was run, and the offices and covert debriefing centre of South Det FRU.

elow left: Coming in to land at the Bessbrook Mill helipad in a Gazelle helicopter. The Mill was Europe's ısiest heliport.

elow right: A part of the helipad just visible behind its protective 'wriggly tin' perimeter.

Above left: The author right on the border with the Republic at 'Slab' Murphy's farm. Straddling the frontier, the farm was ideally placed both for smuggling and terror- related operations.

Above right: Down near the border in the early stages of a targeting operation, utilising a uniformed approach to begin the process of establishing a pattern of life for the target.

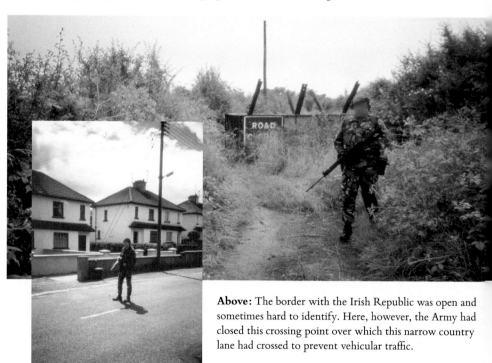

Above: The border with the Irish Republic was open and sometimes hard to identify. Here, however, the Army had closed this crossing point over which this narrow country lane had crossed to prevent vehicular traffic.

Left: The author on patrol in Crossmaglen mounting a VCP, this time wearing a Paras beret, the ARB at the time.

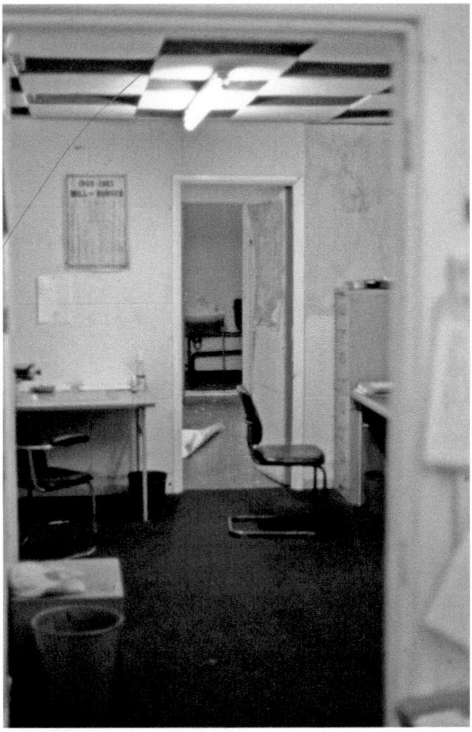

bove left: An aerial view of the town of Newry. The biggest town in this corner of the Province, it rovided ample cover for S Det FRU to mount the majority of its covert agent pick ups and drop offs.

bove right: Spartan and utilitarian, the FRU office space in Bessbrook Mill. The MOD was persuaded to p into its pocket and re-furbish it to a more professional level.

ossmaglen Square with its distinctive, and rather sinister, Republican Memorial, which was unveiled in 79 and dedicated to the Provisional IRA.

Left: One of the Army's Op MAGISTRATE towers set back from the South Armagh border, creating an extensive and formidable observation screen. S Det utilised the de visu intelligence the OPs provided to inform its targeting operations. At the same time the towers provided PIRA with a never-ending targeting option that they fully exploited.

Right: A senior PIRA terror commander working at his day job. The blood on his hands was certainly not just that of his sheep.

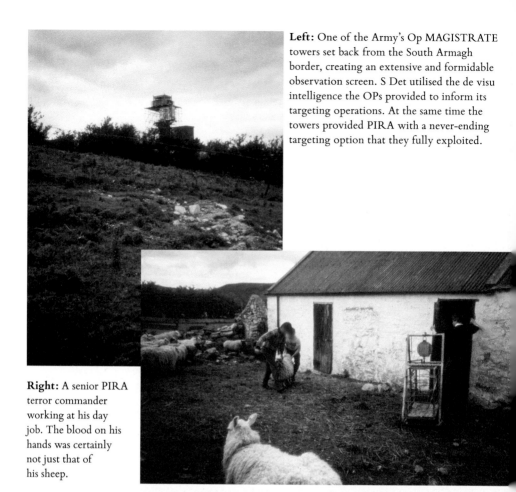

The HK 53 was a perfect weapon for covert rural operations. Easily concealed, with the telescopic stock extended it could become an effective assault rifle.

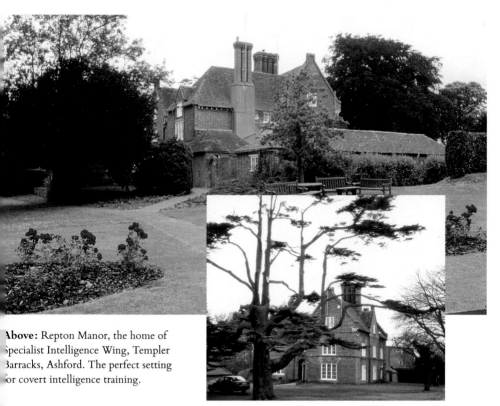

Above: Repton Manor, the home of Specialist Intelligence Wing, Templer Barracks, Ashford. The perfect setting for covert intelligence training.

Right: The main entrance to the Manor, as SIW was known to us, just visible. Now that Templer Barracks has relocated to Bedfordshire, the old Elizabethan house looks very forlorn.

Below: The first phase of the handling course's Resistance to Interrogation exercise, a chillingly realistic 'snatch' operation on a narrow lane in the Kent countryside. Students were kidnapped at gunpoint by masked terrorists and whisked away 'south of the border'.

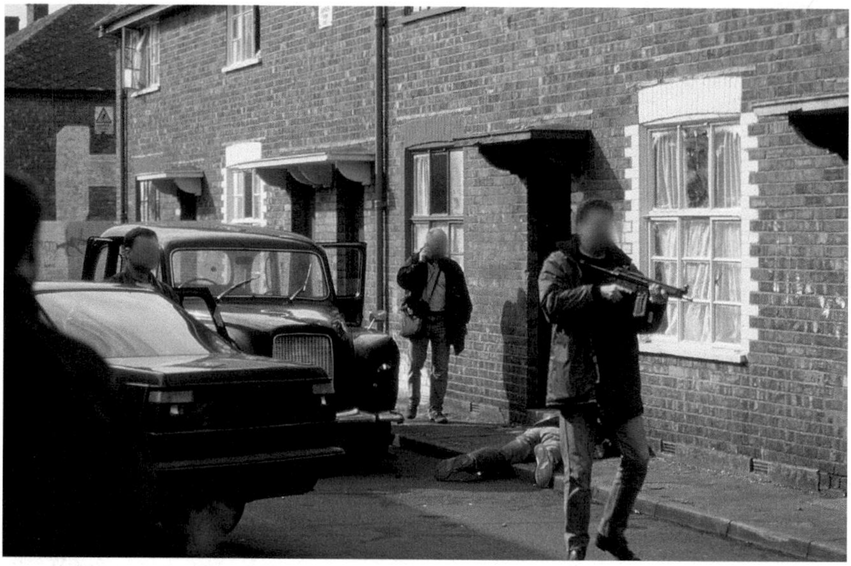

Close Quarter Battle training in Rype Village on the Kent coast, replicating all the situations an operator might face in the Province if things went wrong.

Above: More scenario training: a covert operator is caught in an illegal PIRA Vehicle Check Point and surprises the gunman.

Right: The author going for the line. Hamish's FRU rugby team – complete with white Fijian Rugby Union shirts!

This is how the process worked. We've already seen how an operation is prepared, and how it shakes out on the ground and how the meet is conducted. On returning to base, the handling team de-kits, returning support weapons and all other equipment to the office lock-up. Having checked in with the ops desk, the handler and co-handler would alert the FSC, in conventional Army-speak the Operations Warrant Officer, or Ops WO. This was TC. He would be briefed on any significant intelligence. TC would assess whether HQ FRU – at this stage in the unit's evolution the Ops Offr, then Bill W, now tragically deceased – needed a quick and dirty update. Based on this conversation, we would decide whether any external agency, such as TCG or Special Branch, needed the information quickly for defensive or offensive exploitation.

The handlers would then begin to write the Contact Form, or CF as it was always referred to, as we have already covered fatefully in the flawed case of 1001. A handler running a number of busy cases would himself be a very busy bee. The CF was the 'story' of the meet. It would be completed in full and key sections relating to the source updated religiously as the case developed or circumstances changed. The rationale was that, by reading the CFs in the case file, a new handler could step in and run the agent effectively and securely with minimal operational step change.

Each CF, FRU-wide, was written in several parts. As I have already described, it contained a brief operational overview including source number. The agent names were never recorded at any time or in any place within any paperwork. Handler and co-handler cover names and real identities were logged. We used false names in all our one-to-one contact with our sources – they did not know our true identities. The FRU did not, however, adopt false identities backed up with fake military ID cards, but we did routinely use NI driving licence covers to mask our military IDs when we were stopped in VCPs and asked to show identification. Also included were date, times and locations of pick-ups and drop-offs, debrief location, and vehicles used.

Further, they included the meat of the storytelling, providing an in-depth flavour for the debrief itself with salient details about stage management, mood, interplay of characters, etc., then drilled down into the key factors underpinning security, access, motivation, work issues, welfare and family matters, and all other relevant circumstances and matters relating to performance. Another case critical paragraph, Case Development, relayed the handler's assessment regarding how and in what direction the case could grow and increase in value. It was important that the key paragraphs were critically assessed and reassessed because these impinged directly on the continued running of the case. Where there was no change from the last meeting it was acceptable to annotate the paragraph 'No Change', but this response had to be carefully weighed against laziness.

The Det hierarchy played a critical role in quality controlling all paperwork and ensuring that it consistently reflected the highest standards. When I returned as OC, I always had half a mind focussed on the fact that future generations would critically review our work, and I wanted our legacy to be one for which we could always be proud and continue to boast our professional prowess, as well as producing top quality reports as an indication of our own commitment. Under Hamish Norrie's direction, CFs were modified to make them less time-consuming and arduous to complete and to reflect our increased use of counter-surveillance tactics to ensure that our agents were not being followed by hostile third parties, potential or real.

Critically and obviously, CFs included the information gleaned from the source during the meeting. This had to be recorded with scrupulous accuracy and attention to nuance and fine detail. Value was added by the handler adding 'Comment'. This had to be clearly delineated from the information delivered up by the source, but if handled well could provide valuable assessment based on the knowledge and experience of the handler. This was always an issue and some handlers never succeeded in understanding the nuances, let alone mastering the practical application. It was consistently a matter that required attention, right from the earliest lessons on the course at SIW. During the internal review process, the FSC and/or OC might also add Comment from their perspective.

Once written, the FSC or OC reviewed the CF for accuracy, clarity of detail, and style. As OC S Det I always checked and corrected every CF before 'publication' – in the case of a couple of handlers, I had to basically rewrite the whole document as their literary skills were a tad less than perfect. My view has always been that if a document contains mistakes, its credibility will always suffer in the eye of the reader, and by extension this impacts on the view taken of the Det as a whole. This was always time-consuming, especially as one of these cases in question was our most productive, but I never once resented this – the handlers had worked hard to produce the intelligence and always given of their best, so what was a little wordsmithing.

With regard to the intelligence gained, a decision was made – in the case of higher-grade intelligence usually after consultation, by secure telephone, with the Top, the Ops Offr, or later the Ops WO – about what exactly we would disseminate to the wider 'community'. The vehicle for passing on the intelligence was the MISR, the Military Intelligence Source Report. This was annotated at different levels depending on the sensitivity of the intelligence. Each MISR was graded according to the universal matrix that reflected the reliability of the source – A to E in descending order of merit – and the accuracy of the item of intelligence – 1 to 6 from fact to fabrication. Intelligence from a good agent would usually be disseminated with a B2 rating. F6 would often denote the reporting of a new asset – basically not yet verifiable. E5 MISRs would be found in the gents.

Intelligence of a targeting nature that impacted on lives was never sat on regardless of source sensitivity. In these instances exploitation became a real art form, and could end up being a collaborative joint effort with SB and TCG, depending on a case by case basis. We really earned our money and displayed our professionalism in these instances.

The key point is that in these pre-IT days, Dark Age rules and procedures reigned supreme. Everything was initially handwritten in a classified draft. Once the internal reviewing process had been completed, the CF or MISR was typed up manually by the Det clerk(s) and type-checked, probably by the FSC. The dissemination phase would then occur. In the case of CFs, only three copies existed – the first remained in the Det, the second was put on file in HQ FRU sitting within the HQNI compound, and the third was held by the ASP, the Security Service officer and his small staff, then co-located with HQ FRU. This was a clunky, slow, and laborious process but usually worked effectively and efficiently if everyone in the chain performed their roles and completed their work diligently, in a timely manner, and with security always at the forefront of every process – the 1001 case apart.

When sources were contacted, or contacted their handlers, by phone, a truncated Telephone Contact Form was initiated.

Similar paperwork governed and recorded contact with targets and CASCONs.

Each and every case file contained what was called a '12-Pager'. This served as an overview of the case and recorded all salient details, except agent identities, especially detailing the key factors of access, motivation, security and case development, in one document. They were updated every six months to retain relevancy. Picking up and reading a 12-Pager of each case provided the reader with a sufficiently detailed overview that they could have conducted a meet and not been too lost.

Before I knew it, I was fully integrated into the operational rhythm of the Det. I was patrolling regularly across the TAOR, not just around Crossmaglen, although I got to know the square miles around this ugly small town, arguably, better than anywhere else on the planet. Over my time with the FRU I have lost count of how many different cap badges I have worn, from Guards regiments to the Paras. I was getting to know a number of cases as the co-handler, and running a couple of my cases as the prime handler in Newry. Sadly, our most promising source in the town had gone out of contact with the office after some issues developed before I arrived. During my time on this tour I did not meet with him.

My main asset I met fortnightly, picking him up on different alternating routes in Newry and usually using our office secure meet location for the meets. We had operated three separate safe houses, one beyond the wire and two inside barracks, in Drumadd in Armagh city and in the Mill. We gave them church names and referred to them in all forums as St Patrick's, St Mary's and St Joseph's. When we later relocated our external safe house, we christened it St Malachy's. As an eyes-and-ears source he was able to report a constant volume of background information about the main players in the town, both PIRA and INLA, but I saw little chance of being able to develop the source's access to any significant degree. As a case to cut my teeth on, however, it was perfect – it is an interesting statement on the adaptability of homo sapiens that the extraordinary can very quickly become ordinary. To be brutally honest, at this time we, as a unit, were not yet producing much exploitable intelligence, but had developed better cases and access than our predecessors during the more buccaneering Brigade handling days when agent operations had a less unitary and pointed structure.

Daily life continued as we worked hard to identify new blood and push the sources that we were already running. I spent the largest proportion of my time out on patrol supporting the targeting effort. I enjoyed the freedom, the fresh air, the natural beauty of our surroundings, and the challenge of attempting to dent the institutional reticence of these tough, devout Nationalist country folk to even acknowledge our presence as we met in the farmyard, in the village square, or on the roads and lanes.

The vast majority of patrols were inserted by helicopter to counter the deadly threat posed by PIRA roadside bombs. PIRA's bomb-making sophistry was unmatched anywhere in the world by any terrorist organisation. Their electronic expertise posed a continual existential challenge to government scientists at the various scientific research establishments. It was a constant game of catch-up. PIRA would develop a new technique which we would then negate, in the case of electronically detonated devices by the deployment of sophisticated Electronic Countermeasures, or ECM, hardware – innovation inspiring counter-innovation, requiring fresh innovation, and onwards. Up until his arrest, PIRA's leading electronics expert was a Crossmaglen man. He had studied the subject at university to degree level and, although it was not possible to gain a BSc in applied bomb making, he had obviously gained sufficient theoretical knowledge to assume his technical mantle and contribute to the deaths of as many security force members as he had. To defeat our countermeasure, PIRA would then develop, test and deploy an enhancement in a colossally expensive vicious spiral.

We would either fly straight out to a drop-off point or into one of the forward bases, usually XMG or Forkhill, and patrol out from there. At patrol's end the helicopter – then the Wessex, later to be replaced by the much faster, larger Puma and smaller but nippy Lynx – would swoop in and take us home. Most crews were RAF. They were good, but with the first hint of bad weather, a day of good weather during a south Armagh winter was a flag day, they would refuse to fly. That meant more cold and wet, either waiting for the weather to lift or for a van pick-up to be coordinated – never a favourite tactic of mine. I remember at the end of one patrol on a particularly cold, wet, windy day when the RAF were flying, or rather not flying, we were told over the net that our pick-up had been indefinitely delayed. Hunkering down to wait, I have never been colder in my life – except perhaps during the winter of 1995 in the Bosnian mountains. When finally we got the good news that our lift home was up and running again, we had to break the patrol in two. I was on the second lift. Those forty minutes awaiting the round trip were some of the longest minutes of my life. Some flights, however, were crewed by the Royal Navy. These guys were fantastic and rarely left us in the lurch. I think their experience of conditions at sea moulded a completely different and more robust attitude to flying. Perhaps they were also motivated by a different ethos of commitment and team spirit. As a point of interest, the helipad in Bessbrook served, at this time, as the busiest heliport in Europe. The sound of whirring rotors was almost a twenty-four-hour feature of life for all us residents.

Bandit Country was not named casually or without cause. Patrolling was inherently dangerous. Every time a multiple exited one of the south Armagh bases, they confronted the prospect of premature and violent death. PIRA knew every field, every blackthorn hedgeline, every copse, and more relevantly every dead spot and dead ground-covered approach. Collectively we faced the dual threat of sniping attacks or patrolling over or next to a concealed Improvised Explosive Device, expertly constructed and positioned to be detonated remotely by command wire or electronic pulse.

Even a small quantity of Czech-made, Libyan-supplied Semtex would shred a human body, the shock wave causing life-changing injury to anyone caught within its explosive arc. Once south Armagh took possession of a number of .50 calibre Barrett M82 and M90 sniper rifles, the normal unease the troops experienced towards the prospect of a sniper attack escalated to levels of real existential fear as the enormous kinetic energy of the rounds punctured body armour with the ease that air rifle pellets penetrate Coke cans.

Two years previously some members of the office had accompanied the Army Intelligence liaison officer co-located with the local SB office in Newry out on patrol in the Jonesboro area, to the east of the patch. They were caught by the blast when a concealed IED exploded. Miraculously for them, it only partially detonated and the worst injury sustained was some temporary deafness. It was not something any of us in the office dwelt upon, but the collective, repetitive stress exacted its insidious toll and every casualty and every fatality certainly provoked at least a brief moment of introspection, and another incremental transfer of sand from the bucket that represented the finite limit of our stress reserves.

By the time I returned to the Mill, PIRA had conceded to our temporary victory in the IED/ECM localised arms race, and had abandoned landmines in favour of mounting attacks utilising home-made mortars, as we were to personally experience when the Mill was attacked.

We had come down to the Mill early for a dawn flight into XMG. We were going to spend the day in the cuds around the town and fly back early evening. We watched the Wessex pull away from the SF base helipad and wandered into the Cross cookhouse to have a quick greasy breakfast before heading off with a patrol from the local ARB company. We were, of course, in full combat gear, conforming in every way to the other patrol members, except perhaps Phil's and my hair was a little longer at the back, but with none of the waves and curls of the E Det perms. While we waited to brief the patrol, our carbohydrate load beginning to digest, I began to feel slightly queasy. I assumed I had eaten too much too quickly, but felt that I would not regret my infusion of energy in four hours' time when we started to get cold and tired.

As the morning wore on and we worked our way over our pre-planned patrol trace, I began to feel more and more unwell and began to experience more and more pain. By early afternoon, frankly, I was struggling, but what to do? There was no way that I was going to sit down and refuse to continue – "FRU nobbers can't take the pace and start crying!" I could hear the comments already as they raced around the battalion with brush-fire velocity. We would lose all credibility.

Eventually, thankfully, the end came and we made our pick-up point and awaited extraction back to Cross, and then onwards to Bessbrook. Back at the Mill, I got changed and downed some pain-killers before driving back north in convoy with Phil, for security.

When I got home, I knew that something was really not quite right, so I rang the medical centre at Thiepval and spoke to the duty doc. He listened to my symptoms and asked me if I could stand driving another half hour. He told me to go straight to the military hospital at Musgrave Park, dump my car there, and check myself in.

I was examined, and within thirty minutes was in surgery with, apparently, an appendix on the verge of rupturing. I am so glad that that day's patrol had not been an overnighter or I really would have had to sit down and cry. I had a great ten-day holiday on the ward afterwards. It taught me a lesson, though – always listen to what your body is trying to tell you.

I started to patrol more in the red-brick hardcore estates on the outskirts of Newry and a couple of the hard-line neighbouring villages. The town was claimed by the RUC as their territory, but for whatever reason their parochial attitude relaxed and the Army began mounting green patrols, getting to know the western estates – but never venturing into the town's centre. I have already stated my preference for urban patrolling because of the much higher density of population, and the reality that townsfolk are more open and will readily chat with less reticence than their country cousins. Even some heavily traced PIRA and INLA members in the estates would talk, although others remained fiercely hostile. Obviously there is a quantum gap between having a laugh and exchanging some playful banter, and expecting a winning smile to draw a hardened terrorist into working for you. But by building a level of rapport and displaying that you are subtly different from the average young patrol member, it could plant the seed, or continue the nurturing of a seed already beginning to sprout, for something fundamentally more significant, exploiting motivations that at that point in time remain well hidden. This 'differentness' might also be spotted by an onlooker and provoke them to seek you out. I was able to pass the time of day with some of the key pivotal players who we knew were active and dedicated terrorists, and some of the peripheral younger up-and-comers like Fergus Conlon and Eoin Morley. Conlon was easy company and had a sense of humour, but I sensed that his potential was limited. I really liked Morley, and think that we could have advanced the relationship. In situations like this, particularly where we had almost zero opportunity to stage-manage these nascent contacts, any prospect of success was founded on the ability to be able to project beyond the immediacy of uniform, gun and the precedent of fifteen years of pattern. Handlers had to be able to transcend the expectation of the normal. It was fundamentally about projection of character and communicating, spontaneously, on a different level. If this initial spark was lacking, that was that. There was no further contact.

Some handlers struggled to do this effectively within the context and constraints of patrolling, and I certainly was not able to 'click' with everyone I tried to talk to. This was a trait that the Ashford course would reveal, but not something it could teach. I am not even convinced that practice can develop the capability. As our private lives reveal, there are those with whom it just seems impossible to connect – back to the point, we are, after all, animals. But Morley was very easy to talk to and showed no reticence talking openly, confidently, intelligently and with humour. I think he enjoyed this close proximity to the forbidden fruit of contact with the Brits. Maybe it gave him some sort of buzz. Maybe he was able to big himself up, boasting about his contact with the enemy, how he had controlled that contact, and even maybe exaggerated about developing his own potential source. We had a couple of forthright exchanges about Republicanism and the future of the Province. It was a pity that I moved on before I could move things on with him.

I was saddened to hear that both he and Conlon were later shot dead by their own, in the case of Conlon as a supected police informer.

I was able, however, to bump one young lad on one of the Republican estates in Newry during one of these patrols when everything seemed to click even more solidly. On researching his background, he had no subversive trace but appeared to be popular and just the sort of new blood with which INLA or PIRA were, like us, seeking to feed their campaigns. We quickly developed a good rapport and, returning on patrol, I had already assessed that he had potential for steering into a position of potential access, if only initially low-level eyes and ears. I said it would be fun to meet up, me out of uniform, and away from the restrictions of the town, to have a laugh and a drink. Somewhat to my surprise, he agreed and I gave him quick and simple instructions for a pick-up on the other side of the town for the following night.

I got to the Mill after the patrol and excitedly briefed TC on my first fresh, viable target. I think he was probably not overly excited about the lad's apparent potential, but he supported my request to meet and I sat down to plan the operation.

I wrote my orders and delivered them the following evening. I kept the plan as simple as it needed to be, and with enough time to get into position for a smooth, swift pick-up we left the base in two cars and headed down the hill past the Derrybeg and Carnegat estates, into Newry town centre. I was nervous and excited in equal measure. Projecting mind over matter, I willed my target to be walking his route. I did not want to have to return to base after a no show and have to admit failure, even though in reality in the ruthless and tough game of agent handling there was absolutely no shame, as the older hands knew personally, in a fail to meet.

Tommy W, who had accompanied me on the patrol, provided close cover, and lo and behold confirmed the target was there and complying with my hurried instructions. Good lad. I pulled in, leaned over, cracking the passenger door, and waited for him to jump in. I think the reality was that he was as pleased and surprised to see me as I was to be able to mentally tick off Phase One of the operation. We set off, Tommy now mobile in my rear-view mirror and no doubt confirming the pick-up, back up the road to the ops desk in the Mill. We headed north to one of the safe Loyalist towns in mid-Down for a drink and something to eat. Even in these 'safe' locations, we had to remain vigilant. The Province is a small place and one can never guarantee that someone totally unexpected will not pop up in the most unlikely place. Whatever the sectarian divide, it could always be crossed when reasons of commerce demanded cooperation and compromise. And we also had to be mindful of the suspicion and distrust of Loyalists towards unknown outsiders. In their eyes, why could we not be Republican extremists conducting recces for a sectarian attack?

At this early stage in an operation with an untraced target, a social meeting was acceptable, and indeed invariably absolutely necessary, to develop a new, budding relationship. Things went well. Tommy backed me up perfectly and his humour and likeable rogue personality contributed positively to the evening. The target was easy company and spoke freely about his life, the realities of living on a pretty tough estate, his mates, and touched on what he had witnessed personally and heard second-hand of the comings and goings of local hoods. He seemed to know everyone. Definitely looked worth following this up.

Following a routine and professional drop-off, we returned to base and de-kitted. Nothing to pass int-wise, so time to go home and start thinking about the Contact Form I would write the following day.

TC was pleased with my debrief and recognised that we should continue with the case. And we did. We had met another two of three times, by the end of which we had built a pretty solid relationship. He continued to answer both Tommy's and my seemingly harmless questions without reticence and clearly enjoyed the chance to engage with new people away from the confines of his own life. More importantly, I detected the glow from his own relish at doing something that was forbidden and completely beyond the bounds of acceptable behaviour. He was thrilled by secretly meeting two covert soldiers.

I decided that at the next meeting I would openly pitch him. There was no operational requirement to wait to build further rapport. It was time to confront and banish the lurking bogeyman of the pitch. No excuse not to. He had already expressed an interest in military matters, and perhaps, had he lived in another place at another time, he may have decided to become a soldier himself. I briefed TC on my approach: I would suggest that he became the third soldier in our little band, a covert soldier, of course, whereby he would keep his eyes and ears open for anything that would be of interest to a soldier. We would, of course, pay him a military salary in recognition of his service. Not an elaborate approach but focussed and realistic.

I was pretty confident the pitch would work – you can never be certain, though, that once the novelty has worn off, and hard reality kicks back in, this initial pledge survives. Another test for the handler and his skills. But we had a pretty good foundation to springboard from: we had a good relationship; he had fun with us; nothing he had experienced in our company appeared threatening; we were not asking anything of him that required him to change any overt aspect of his life; as an unemployed lad he would have some pocket money; and he was doing something that was actually exciting to spice up an otherwise totally mundane and pretty tedious existence.

I knew we could keep things simple and I wanted Tommy to be in on the pitch, as we worked together with a chemistry that was already tried and tested on the target. The only change I wanted to make was to push a bit further away to a place he had probably heard of but had never been. With no premonition as to how his life was about to change, our target was there bang on time on the pick-up route. Everything again went effortlessly according to plan as we drove the hour and a bit to Bangor, a safe town out on the coast east of Belfast where I had manipulated the broken garden gate to explain about the husband's ashes – maybe I could call it the Blackpool of Northern Ireland, but as I have never been to the Lancashire coast I won't.

We found a Chinese restaurant and sat down for, ostensibly, just another night out. The target was completely relaxed and easily slipped into the fun of another good night out with his new friends. He had never been to Bangor before. As we sat amidst the red paper lanterns, traditional music plinking away in the background, assailed by the aroma of soya sauce, boiled rice, and meat and vegetables sizzling in their woks, I could see that Tommy was a little constricted even though he had, ostensibly, a non-speaking part. I willed myself to remain calm on the outside, but inside I felt like I was out on a first date, fighting not to say the wrong thing and striving equally to say the right things. As we ate and laughed and chatted away all I could see were the massive words, pulsing in front of my mind's eye, that I was inwardly rehearsing. I could clearly see the wall that I knew very shortly I was going to have to assail. Not a nice feeling.

Then, suddenly, the mood was instantly lightened and the tension sliced in half like a chicken breast in sweet, rich plum sauce, when, without warning of any sort, if indeed there could have been any, a generously sized, if not to say huge, crust of desiccated nasal mucus dropped out of our boy's right nostril onto the tablecloth. As true professionals, not one of us reacted. But at that moment my nerves instantly unknotted and I knew everything was going to be OK. I was still the taut, poised hunter, but as I waited for the right moment to pounce, I found that now I was actively enjoying myself and weighing the conversation for the right moment to strike. It was now actually fun. When I gauged that that moment had arrived and I started my 'sales pitch', the words just flowed like water through the stone arches of the mandarin Anji bridge. I was word perfect. Even I felt the rhythm – smooth, faultless, convincing – and with it my confidence grew and grew, and the credibility of my pitch appeared incontestable – again, reality is never as bad as its expectation. Without a blink of an eye, or a crossed word, our target became, seamlessly, our agent.

Nothing and everything changed at that moment. I had made my first agent recruitment, and on our next meeting we would sit down as handler and source, although to a disinterested observer this meeting would be no different from any of those we had already staged, except that it would take place in the security and privacy of a safe house. The only exception would be that a small handful of notes would now pass hand to hand before the drop-off took place. I felt so buoyed up that I could not wait for my next opportunity with my next target. Hubris, of course.

I was naturally delighted and received congratulations from the Top and from the rest of the team, but in reality nothing did change day to day. I continued to meet my agent until I left the Det, picking up useful but not campaign-winning bits and pieces. There were no issues and the case ran smoothly. In fact, from start to finish I had this strange sensation that everything had the feel of an Ashford exercise about it – minus the awful basement cells.

As a Det we spent a fair amount of time out on the patch in plain clothes in our non-standard cars. We would conduct recces for ops, confirm intelligence passed to us from our own assets and from other agency reporting, and generally just keep our knowledge of the patch up to date to reinforce our credibility and aid meeting our agents. This was dangerous and potentially deadly if patterns were set over a protracted period. We sought to scrupulously avoid this and managed the risk effectively, and above all professionally. If we considered that we, or our cars, were compromised to any significant degree, we would at the very least change the number plate through HQNI; in extremis, we would move the car, or van, out of the Det, probably rotating it through another FRU Det. Before Hamish established our own vehicle detachment, our fleet was managed by the 12 Coy transport office. They handled the transfer and all the logistics and maintained a track on the history of each vehicle.

With regard to ourselves, the issue of a compromise was not a welcome development but it caused us no undue concern – neither TC nor I were perturbed at the prospect that PIRA and INLA had our real names after our extraction operation. PIRA almost certainly assumed that the names they had discovered were not real anyway. I think in these contemporary days of digital photography and mobile phones, handlers would be more concerned about the risk of being captured on film, but for us this potential danger did not even feature on the group radar. If we felt we were 'warm', a change of appearance was not taxing – get a haircut, or grow our hair longer, shave or cultivate facial hair, change a favourite jacket – a little less flexibility for female handlers, but we had none in Bessbrook. The issue did not even garner a mention on the course. As a point of clarification, in the

FRU we did not use disguises. Back at SIW, Surveillance Branch liaised with other agencies and had access to their specialists. The disguises they used, sparingly, in support of surveillance training exercises were extremely effective, but for them the issue of exposure to their target was more 'critical'.

A key member of PIRA in the border area, an ex-Chief of Staff of PIRA's Northern Command, and an active big businessman and smuggler, was Thomas 'Slab' Murphy. He has been named more times in the media and his role highlighted in more documentaries than the amount of times Gerry Adams has denied IRA membership and complicity in the cases of the 'Disappeared'. Slab was a real archetypal godfather figure. The farm complex that was his home was literally right down on the border to the east of Crossmaglen. It straddled the international frontier, some buildings in the north, the rest in the south. His yard was ideally placed as a funnel through which goods moved north and south and south and north, taking advantage of the various EU cross-border subsidies. It was also a perfect point through which to move PIRA munitions. He farmed it with the help of his two brothers, Patrick and Frank (the former a useful boxer in his day), supported by a retinue of henchmen, some of them employed specifically as bodyguards. We received intelligence over the years updating us on the identities of some of them. All three Murphys were hard men. There can be no debate that Slab's leadership was responsible for innumerable deaths and an unquantifiable scale of destruction. Slab's PIRA status ensured his presence at the top of the Army's arrest-on-sight list.

Bob M and myself were conducting a recce, two-up in a single car, down through the narrow country lanes that bisected the tiny heavily hedged fields of the patch, the southern extent swinging past Slab's place as we brushed the border. The journey to this point had been unremarkable and routine. As we approached the border and the Murphy farm, we could clearly see three men working at the roadside, uncompromisingly toiling on this British verge. A sighting like this will inevitably quicken the pulse and focus a mind already in command of a fairly taut nervous system. One of the by-products of adrenalin is the sharpening of one's eyesight. It was clear that the trio were not overtly armed, not that this conclusion could rule out the potentiality of concealed pistols. It was also clear that this was genuine, innocent rural husbandry. As we drew closer, the surprise we did receive was that there, in the North, were the three Murphy boys, 'Slab' flanked by both siblings. It was one of those surreal moments. We looked at them looking at us, looking at them. Our status as outsiders would have been immediately apparent even though our car had County Armagh plates, with their alphabetical IB prefix – so much better if we had had the resource to fit southern Irish red plates to our vehicles. As the driver, I gave the raised first finger acknowledgement of countryfolk, but I am confident that they rightly assumed we were undercover soldiers.

As we swung slowly past on the southern apex of the gentle bend in this narrow country lane, Bob attempted to call in the sighting to the ops desk for potential exploitation. Predictably we were in a dead spot, most demonstrably in PIRA's world, and totally cut off from our own. We were probably safe because PIRA rarely reacted on an operational whim. Attacks, especially down here, were always meticulously planned and executed. Any operational concern regarding their security would lead to an operation being aborted and mounted another day. Without a clear understanding of who we were and the exact nature of the operational environment extant at that precise moment, 'Slab' would not have risked an ad hoc reaction. For our part, we were pretty excited. We had come face to face with infamy, with PIRA's top terrorist, but maintained an equally non-reactive posture – what could we do? So nothing happened, we went our way and, as far as we knew, the Murphys continued working until lunchtime. It must have been a similar situation for Eliot Ness when he first cast eyes on his nemesis, Al Capone. That story ended with Capone in prison. Slab remains a free man. Regardless, we all lived to fight another day. In all my time in PIRA's back yard, I never again saw any of the Murphy clan.*

The office maintained the precedent of employing a Royal Marines handler, filling one of the so-called resident unit handler posts. The Naval presence in the Province, commanded by the

* Patrick Murphy died in his bed in December 2019.

Senior Naval Officer Northern Ireland, abbreviated to SNONI, was specifically responsible for patrolling Carlingford Lough and the broader coastline; the mission, to deter PIRA, or any other terrorist group, from attempting to land arms into the north by sea. To this end, HMS *Kingfisher*, a small minesweeper, flew the Red Ensign, with its small contingent of RM Commandos cramped on board to mount any necessary boardings of suspect vessels. Jock McN was the Det's Marine at this time, a tough Scotsman, and he organised for me to spend a day on board to see how the senior service operated.

It was a fun and instructive day as my first experience of things naval. Kitted out in my rubber immersion suit, I was winched down onto the deck of the *Kingfisher* from the hovering Royal Navy Sea King helicopter in miserable wet and gusty winter weather. I found the small crew to be very professional and very welcoming as they continued their uneventful and lonely beat, patrolling up and down the coast. I thought it was somehow fitting that the ship's captain was himself an Ulsterman.

When it was time to leave, we raced to shore at breakneck speed in one of the ship's Rigid Raiders, like a scene from an RM recruitment video, hitting the beach north of Warrenpoint where one of the Det cars picked me up. Great personal and professional experience. I couldn't help but conclude, though, regardless of the ship's own professional crew and their commitment, that the mission had little chance of altering the zero impact they'd had on controlling the flow of munitions into the Province, set against the 6,000 or so kilometres of the Irish coastline.

I think all the special units shared the same philosophy when it came to work and play. Work was paramount and the alpha and omega of our collective existences, but when it had been successfully and diligently completed, it was time to play. This challenge was approached head-on with equal enthusiasm.

As a Det, then, we socialised pretty much together, except for the couple of guys who were married and accompanied. We stuck to safe Loyalist towns either side of the main road up to Belfast, but the best nights out were in and around the city. I began to have one or two drinks too many on nights out, influenced by my harder-drinking teammates. Not to the extent of it affecting my health, and certainly not my work or my personal security, but sometimes the wrong side of the safe driving limit. I recall one particular late night driving across the city, definitely a gin over the limit, with four RUC friends in the car absolutely carefree about the whole situation. Their attitude to alcohol was even more wayward than our own. The whole attitude to alcohol in military circles in those days was very different from today – in real terms, we belonged to a very different Army then than today's. The Whitehall Warriors working out of the MOD in London regularly downed pens at 1230 for a liquid lunch – no more today – and officers, SNCOs and men imbibed far greater quantities of booze than they do now. Paradoxically, the official attitude to drinking and driving in the 1980s was far stricter than it is now. As an officer, being caught at the wheel over the limit, one would reasonably expect to be cashiered and that would be that.

Late one night, I was driving home alone after being out with a couple of the guys and some RUC friends in south Belfast when I ran into a police checkpoint. I opened my window and produced my military ID, looking to any onlooker as though I was displaying my driving licence. The policeman was an older officer, probably a reservist. He looked at me and looked at my ID card. He must have concluded that I was not a member of a regular unit, then knowingly enquired whether I had been drinking. I admitted that I had had a couple as I watched myself boarding the plane at Aldergrove, no longer a member of the FRU and quite likely not much longer an Army officer. He leant in through the open car window and advised me to be careful how I went – spare, knowing words of wisdom. That was the last time in my life that I have driven with a blood alcohol level higher than the legal limit. Whoever he was, I thank him and remain eternally grateful for his worldly approach and for the wisdom he so markedly but unobtrusively passed on to me.

Closer to home, I went out a few times with an RUC girl from Newry. She was a lovely girl, intelligent and dedicated to doing her bit for the community. She was from an old County Down landed family; if I remember correctly, her father had spent some years as an Army officer way back. We had been out the night before. The following day, I was out on foot in Newry conducting a recce for a forthcoming job. She was on duty in uniform and driving an armoured Cortina along the street towards me. Being an observant police officer, she spotted me in my duffle coat and beeped the car horn and waved enthusiastically in my direction. I walked on obliviously, consciously seeking to shed six inches and drop my head even further into my hunched shoulders, feeling the eyes of forty Republican sympathisers burning into my back. That evening she called me shame-facedly and apologised profusely. We shared a good laugh about it.

I spent most of my free time up in Belfast, not quite teetotal but a chastened soul. I have always really loved the city, its warmth, variety, and paradoxically its sense of security. One evening, I had finished working and was in the east of the city on the arterial Newtownards Road. I had not eaten since lunchtime in the Mill, hours before, and felt that a late dinner on the run would be in order. In terms of fast food, burgers, kebabs and sushi were very much delights of the future. The Province was still a traditional land of fish and chips. These were still the days when pubs remained closed on Sundays, and in many areas every other billboard poster was an outpouring proclaiming the evils of the Devil's Vomit (all alcoholic beverages). I spotted a likely chippy and dropped in.

I am convinced fish-and-chip shops trigger some sort of prime-val pull in the British psyche. Certainly foreigners seem to think we survive eating nothing else. But there is the welcoming warmth that one feels, particularly on a cold, damp winter's evening, immediately one enters. The harsh bright lighting and aroma of super-heated fat instantaneously increases energy levels and dispels all notions of depression. I had the place to myself. I scanned the menu card pinned to the wall and surveyed the selection of pieces of fish, pies and saveloys that were warming in the warmer above the troughs of bubbling fat. I gave the lone proprietor my order and stepped back from the counter to wait while my chips were freshly fried.

Within a couple of minutes a second customer entered, a lad around 19 or 20. Instinctively, I gave him the once over. A bit shorter than me, so around 5ft 8in/5ft 9in – no problem. Short mid-brown hair. He was wearing a green parka and faded jeans – no problem. But the jacket was open and it was distinctly chilly out there – potential problem? He was wearing boots – they were German para style. There was something about his manner. There was an intensity and a tension literally pulsing from him – this did look and feel like a problem. He was fully charged and ready for something. I experienced the strangest sensation. He was staring fixedly at the owner, unmoving – this now was definitely a problem.

I took a discreet step back and made room to draw my pistol and shoot him dead if the worst happened. At that moment, he seemed to become aware of my presence. He turned on his heel and strode out without a backward glance, or a single spoken word. I moved forward. He was gone. The chippy breathed an audible sigh of relief. He told me he had been scared to death expecting the youth to pull a gun and either murder or rob him. I agreed that this had been my overwhelming feeling too. The suffocating tension had gone and the hot, fat-induced sense of peace and calm returned. It felt like the sudden exhalation of breath that greets the final whistle at a tense cup final.

I paid for my cod and left. It was a really bizarre experience – I felt 'something' coming off of him that I still cannot explain, and I think he almost certainly experienced the same sensation. Whatever his sensation or premonition, it might certainly have saved his life that evening. The power of non-verbal communication.

Two years later, when I had returned to S Det, I was up with E Det and we had just briefed to go into the west of the city on a recce. Chatting with two of the guys, we all three admitted to a strong premonition that something was going to happen while we were out on the ground. Operations, however, take no extra account of intangibles like this, readings of tea leaves or horoscopes or the word of Mystic Meg, and we set off. Halfway through our route, a contact report came over the air that there had been a shooting literally just off our route. It appeared to be an armed robbery, terror-related, as it turned out. There was, however, nothing we could do in terms of any timely reaction, but it seemed that this had been the focus of our collective sixth sense.

Only one other time in my career have I experienced this strange, powerful, foreboding sense of something dark lurking just beyond reach. It was a dark, moonless night, it had been raining and the air was chill with that cold, damp hand that reaches to one's bones and steals all warmth. I was out with Alistair D in uniform on a night-time job outside Crossmaglen. Suddenly, simultaneously, we both felt some invisible dark shadow pass between us and before our vision with a warning that evil was about to fall. The air chilled further, my shoulders tingled, and my grip on my rifle stock involuntarily tightened. It was quick, short-lived like the sense of space that suddenly emerges and just as instantaneously departs when someone very close behind you moves away.

Nothing happened in the event, but had we been marked out as victims before some inexplicable factor intervened to save us? It was an unnerving experience, all the more intense because it was shared and affected both of us – and Alistair was a very down-to-earth and cynical individual. I have always believed that we show supreme arrogance if we unquestioningly discount the myriad of unexplainable things that periodically and seemingly randomly cross our paths in life. There is something out there, probably positive and good, but equally beyond our comprehension – I have little doubt that we experienced *it* that night.

I had no premonition, sense of doom or upcoming incident as the Christmas of 1983 approached. I had popped up to the university in the Botanic Gardens area of Belfast to quickly see my girlfriend. As I was returning to my car, parked on a side street further down University Road, I heard the electrifying sound of gunshots. I instinctively counted two. Training – always count your rounds. They were low velocity, almost certainly pistol. This did not sound good. I broke into a cautious trot, scanning left and right as I made for the direction the shots had come from. I checked my open jacket and gave the hem a tug with my right hand to ensure I could reach my pistol, holstered on my right hip, unimpaired if I needed to.

By the time I had rounded the main university library building, I could see a male lying sprawled on the pavement. A brown leather briefcase, standing upright almost as if it had been carefully arranged as a supporting prop, sat beside him. No sign of weapons. It was clear to me that he was the victim. It was also obvious he had been shot dead, blood pooling from the wound to his head. I had no idea who it was at the time, but very quickly the news reported that Edgar Graham, the 29-year-old Unionist MP for Belfast South and a Queens University law lecturer, had been murdered. That sense of detachment and physical dislocation kicked in again. Time slowed. I took in the situation, mentally balanced the factors as they appeared to me, and acted. I did not dally. A UDR patrol was fast approaching. I could see two Land Rovers. I moved away resolutely but somehow still reluctantly, and returned to my car. There was nothing further I could do. I had not seen the gunmen nor had any clue as to the direction they had fled in, and there was no aid I could offer to a dead man. Being armed myself, it was better to be away from the scene than risk some sort of misunderstanding with highly adrenalised young soldiers. I felt increasing anger and frustration at my lack of empowerment, but above all a sense of realism. What was done was done.

The PIRA gunmen had, it transpired, escaped on foot towards the Nationalist Markets area off the Ormeau Road. I had been too late to do anything but had I parked a little closer to the university, or been briefer with my girlfriend, I might have been on hand, right place, right time. I was trained, the gunmen were not, and I would have had all the benefits of the element of surprise. Maybe this would not have saved Edgar Graham's life, but if I had been closer, I might have had a clear shot at his killers and, with their deaths, bought him some justice. The what-ifs of destiny as the butterfly's wings flutter.

As a soldier, I am probably not alone in sharing a passing admiration for PIRA's attacks on on-duty military, especially when they were prepared to engage us gun for gun in a firefight. But what were truly sickening were the murders of the Edgar Grahams, completely defenceless targets who were given absolutely no chance to defend themselves and were gunned down, or blown up, ruthlessly in cold blood. These were the acts of cowards, not soldiers – for them, from my standpoint, there is absolutely no room in the specious debate about terrorists and freedom fighters.

No one was ever charged with this murder.

Time advances and, however slowly, all future plans, no matter how far off they appear, eventually become the business of the day. My time to move on was nearly upon me. I had already been in discussion about my immediate future and my next posting with Colonel Tom. I had indicated my number one posting preference and personal desire to return to the FRU as a Det Commander. But against the current posting plot it looked a tricky fit, and I was not optimistic. I was out of sync in terms of tour lengths and upcoming vacancies. What he had promised me, however, was a place on the Long Surveillance course, and the chance, if things worked out, to be posted to the Corps' flagship unit in Germany – again out of the mainstream. The course was indeed long and trained operators to work against the unit's main target, the Soviet Military Mission, SOXMIS, that mirrored our BRIXMIS unit based in Berlin. The unit, referred to as 28, was based in Herford just up the road from the SOXMIS mission in Bunde, sitting close to the heart of the British Army of the Rhine.

As I had this discussion with the Colonel, Duncan had already arrived in South Det as the first OC of the newly independent detachment, effectively assuming command from TC. A Late Entry officer, commissioned from the ranks, he had settled in and started to inject new vigour into operations – he was a quiet Welshman from the north of the country who had served as a handler in the pre-FRU days in Londonderry and done time with 28, so was no novice. I'm not quite sure if he knew how to take my presence and was probably happy that I wasn't to be a presence for much longer.

The future did look bright, but regardless – with sadness – I said my farewells, inside and outside of the unit, packed up, and took leave of my fellow operators, having learnt more than I ever thought possible after so full and comprehensive a training course. I could wholeheartedly confirm the assertion that training really only started on reaching the unit. I felt I had experienced so much, seen so much and been a part of so much. If I had realised that I would be back in a little over a year there would have been more of a spring in my step and a less heavy weight pressing down on my heart as I boarded the ferry for Liverpool.

13

IN THE Q

Back at SIW, I very quickly learned my first lesson: surveillance operators are generally a different breed, and the philosophy binding them together and driving operations is very different from the craft of the Research world.

Covert operators, no matter the discipline they practise, are all required to blend into the background fabric of life. To describe them all as grey men is misrepresenting the case, and is invariably applied pejoratively by those who inhabit the world outside. However, whatever the nuance, Research operators and surveillance operators are different animals. An agent handler is not an agent handler if he or she lacks the personality to bond with, and motivate, others. The best handlers are brimming with charisma and are definitely larger than life characters, without overstepping the boundary into brashness and oafishness.

We used to joke that surveillance operators can thrive and prosper with little or no personal spark or charm – being a 'smaller than life' character implies no impairment to success. I do not want that to sound demeaning, it is just true. Of course, nothing is ever totally black or completely white, and there are surveillance boys and girls who are supremely balanced characters, certainly many whom I both like as friends and respect as professionals, and a small minority who have successfully bridged the gap and been just as successful on both sides of the house. Here I think of Simon H, Roger McF, Clive A, and one or two others. For a young officer, and young HUMINTer, it was interesting to witness this personality dichotomy at first hand.

I knew a couple of fellow course participants, including Harry T from E Det, and another ex-FRU guy, frankly an also ran. It was apparent to me that the majority had already successfully completed at least a Basic course, and another had served with 14 Company in the Province. This placed them considerably further along the learning curve and negated a lot of the early pressure that I experienced.

As we settled into the course, a further general truism became quickly apparent: the art of surveillance was far more driven by, and operational success was predicated to a much greater degree on, taming technology. We certainly learned to become pretty credible photographers, behind the lens and in the dark room. Surveillance cars were all fitted with covert cameras and video. Observation Post work, surveillance mounted from static covert positions, relied equally heavily on cameras with the addition of long lenses to enhance the ability to stand off from a target. Close Target Recce work relied on early generation night-viewing devices so we could see in the dark and remain covert without deploying additional light sources, and use infrared flash to take photography. We also learnt about, and exercised with, 'quick plant' beacons that enabled targets to be tracked remotely allowing the team in mobile follows to hang back from the target, minimising the risks of compromise. And contemporary surveillance was comprehensively neutered without effective and reliable secure communications. In real terms, now steam-driven antiques. I would truly love to see just how far surveillance technology supporting the twenty-first-century team has advanced.

The Surveillance course was split into two broad phases: in the first, we learned to mount both urban and rural static surveillance, establishing covert OPs. These were the skills that the Close Observation Platoons, and the rural operators of 14 Coy in NI, had deployed operationally. During the second phase, we learned to mount surveillance on mobile targets, both on foot and in vehicles. This included dealing with targets on public transport, and mastering the difficult transition when the target moves from foot to mobile and vice versa.

The teaching model mirrored the one I had seen on my NI Course with the Agent Handling Branch. I have to say that the instructors were just as professional and were, generally, a thoroughly good bunch. A couple of them had served with 14 Coy – no one lacked professional qualifications or credibility. The course was superb and I speculated that there was no better one anywhere in the world, East or West. All lessons started in the classroom, were practised outdoors, and then woven into increasingly tough, and long, practical exercises – no surprises, just like in the agent handling courses next door across the drive in the manor house.

In the context of the British military's employment of covert surveillance, the concept can be deployed following two distinct but not mutually exclusive methodologies. In the NI context, surveillance was fundamentally an operational tool. This is why it sat within Director Special Forces' orbit, although a past Director Intelligence Corps – DINT – had been offered command of 14 Coy by the MOD but had turned down the offer after assessing that he could not sustain the required manning level – a fateful decision. Teams within 14 Coy could be tasked to provide pure intelligence, as a pure intelligence-gathering tool – following a target to see what they did, where they went and whom they contacted – potentially identifying new persons of intelligence interest, and new targets to observe. But first and foremost their role was operational, to exploit intelligence provided by other source agencies and augment other operations in order to kill or capture terrorists.

Covert Passive Surveillance, as taught by SIW, and practised by units like 28, is, first and last, an intelligence-gathering tool. In contemporary Germany it provided intelligence, primarily, but not exclusively, reporting on the activities of SOXMIS and its intelligence-gathering missions.

The dichotomy in application resulted in a differing operational imperative. In the Province, if a 14 Coy team had a PIRA bomb under control it was imperative that the team maintained eyes on it at any cost, even if this ultimately resulted in the compromise of a team member – losing control of an explosive device almost certainly ensured that deaths would result, or at the very least that hundreds of thousands of pounds of damage to buildings and infrastructure occurred, when PIRA detonated the bomb. This was politically unacceptable. The operational driver for 28, on the other hand, was to remain covert and invisible to the target. Rather than risk compromise, the team would pull back and accept a loss against the rationale that employing effective lost contact drills would likely result in regaining control of the target later in the chase, even if the temporary loss was created by a competent 'enemy' operative to make time to conduct their covert task. As an aside, but critically offering an overarching comment, it is my view, based on my experience as a HUMINTer who has imposed surveillance and been the target of hostile surveillance, that a professional intelligence officer, employing effective anti-surveillance drills, will defeat even a highly skilled team every time he is required operationally to do so.

As budding OP experts we did indeed become very proficient photographers, a skill that was to be extremely relevant for my future posting to BRIXMS, five years hence. I was amazed to learn how it was possible to take a picture in the middle of the darkest night, as though the object was lit by the noonday sun, using long-duration exposures. Occupying an urban op was easy, straightforward and comfortable. We frequently mounted observation from within small, cheap hotel rooms – dry, warm and well plumbed. On one occasion, we occupied a disused room in a local TA centre. Thankfully, as the course was taking place in early summer, the weather was kind to us – rural OP work in midwinter would be absolutely no fun. I found the out-of-town, rural work just an extension of basic soldiering skills and really enjoyed occupying our well-concealed positions.

Occupation of OPs represented an important tactic in intelligence collection in their own right. But beyond this, they also played a pivotal role in mobile operations by providing the key 'trigger' for a mobile follow by observing and indicating when the target left an identified start point.

The key to successful rural observation was selection of the OP site. In the Province, extensive use of cameras covertly located to cover a specific arc of view, relaying back to a secondary manned location, was not uncommon when it was assessed as being too difficult or dangerous to get in close to a target location. We trained to observe the target directly from a manned OP. This required careful map and aerial photographic recce, confirmed by a boots on the ground look-see. Typically, if some sort of man-made cover could not be exploited, a patch of gorse or other thick vegetation was perfect. What was important was that the cover it could provide had to allow us to look out without any third party being able to easily look in.

Once site selection had been made, we went through the same procedure presaging any military operation. Construction of a plan and its reflection in a detailed set of orders to ensure all parties involved understood responsibilities and actions and reactions on all the different operational phases. In a longer-term OP, one of the key planning criteria involved re-supply of food, radios, batteries, film, other consumables and miscellaneous equipment, and extraction of rubbish, bagged excrement, logs and, now to a lesser extent with the advent of digital photography, used film.

There is a lot of equipment required for constructing and running a successful rural OP. This has to be carefully and systematically selected and packed. The deciding criteria was to take only what the team could physically carry on their backs. In a rural setting where no man-made cover exists, when it's time to deploy, the OP team, invariably a team of two, is transported to the pre-recced drop-off location some way away from the target, where they discreetly offload equipment and work their way tactically on foot to the OP site. Checking that all is quiet, the team then work their way into the natural cover prior to constructing the 'hide'. The route within the vegetation to the position we occupied would involve a dog-leg in order to deprive an interested party of an unobstructed view to the team – common sense, always consistently at the heart of covert tradecraft. The key factor inside the OP was to ensure we had a clear view of the target while maintaining sufficient cover to screen the observers and the lenses. The following morning, after the insertion, a daylight walk past would be conducted by a member of the team supporting the OP to confirm that it enjoyed sufficient cover and was not obvious to the target.

Getting into an operational rhythm was quick. There was a sense of contentment and satisfaction creating these micro-universes with the reassuring four-hour cadence of observe, eat, sleep, observe, eat, crap in the plastic bag, and sleep again. It was tough in the early hours of the morning to remain vigilant, and of course this is when the DS invariably inserted serials of target activity into the exercise play.

On completion of the task, the kit would be packed and the team and all equipment would be extracted and as much sign of occupation as possible disguised. The team would then move covertly to the pick-up point for the return to base.

Mobile surveillance was a whole new learning experience. I enjoyed the challenges of foot surveillance, especially in the heart of busy town centres, with all the cover and hindrance provided by oblivious shoppers and workers. It is not an easy skill to practise or develop, and I would certainly say that there is a certain natural aptitude to be identified in the really skilled operator, more so than in any other element of surveillance tradecraft.

We always deployed with secure and discreet comms. We retained our earpieces in situ when we redeployed to the surveillance cars to avoid the potential audible chatter of speaker comms. None of the Hollywood nonsense of talking into raised cuffs with coiled wires disappearing from ears into jacket collars. Good communications are, as I said, essential to effective surveillance operations and our equipment, pre-mobile phone era, was state of the art. I do actually have an old training pamphlet somewhere teaching the hand signals that foot teams used in pre-personal communications days. They would have been challenging times, but no doubt teams achieved results and successfully housed their targets.

The average-sized mobile surveillance team would consist of between eight and twelve operators. Again, common sense prevailed: anything smaller would not be robust enough to keep an aware, trained target under systematic and prolonged surveillance. A bigger team would lead to command, control and coordination problems. When on the road, conducting mobile surveillance, we did not work back to a fixed control room, as they did across the water. The operations officer leading and directing the team, the Surveillance Controller, or Sierra Charlie, would deploy as an integral part of the team – we took turns throughout the course assuming this key responsibility. He or she would control events from the front passenger seat of their car. This was the team's ops room. This gave the team the capability to operate over unlimited geographic areas working 'car to car', so long as they carried the appropriate pre-spotted map coverage, without the requirement for an extensive, and expensive, rebroadcast infrastructure.

Each surveillance vehicle, operated by a two-man crew, was fitted with communications kit, covert video and stills cameras. The ideal combination was a man/woman team – to any third-party observer this profile is the least obtrusive. There were five women on my course. The driver maintained focus on the target as they drove, while the front-seat passenger operated the radio net and navigated – good map-reading skills are an essential tool in the surveillance operator's skills repertoire.

Two operators per vehicle guaranteed the flexibility to react to targets moving from mobile transport to foot and back again. This was the ultimate test of the professional team, and meant that things got pretty busy and stressful when a busy, alert target was being surveilled – our exercise scenarios were peopled by hostile intelligence (HIS) targets, rather than terrorists, so all operational aims were intelligence focussed. With one's navigator deployed out of the vehicle on foot, the driver, now operating the vehicle single-handedly, had to manoeuvre the car, map read in unfamiliar areas, work the radio while continuing to keep an eye open for target related activity, and be in position, right place, right time, to pick up their teammate, or another member of the team, once the tactical situation required it, ready to move on to the next operational phase. Stressful and fun – the way we predominantly operated across the water in the FRU.

Mobile surveillance, I found, was rather tedious, despite this description of operating 'one up'. During exercises we would drive for hours and travel miles. When the target was under surveillance the five or six cars in the team, again the number predicated on command and control criteria, would support the one call sign controlling him or her. At tactically apposite points, the controlling car would hand over control to the vehicle directly in support. By chopping and changing the vehicle, or indeed foot operator – the tactical imperative remained the same – no one call sign remained behind the target for too long, thereby reducing exposure. When knowledge of the ground was not good, effective map reading was required to take supporting team members on parallel routes to reduce potential exposure to the target and increase flexibility anticipating the action of the target. It was not uncommon for the controlling call sign to follow the target from the front – taking it 'by the nose'. The key to a successful follow was mutual support, anticipation of the target's actions, and sound tradecraft when behind the target. Being in control of the target was the fun and rewarding aspect of the game.

For the rest of the time, unless one had become separated from the team and had to drive fast to get back into contact, I found it fairly dull. When looking back on my time in the Mill, I struggled to identify a balanced comparison. I sometimes found myself wishing that I had been able to take the course before Ireland, before I had been inducted into the agent-handling orbit, fully realising that I was being given another unparalled opportunity to learn the most exciting and relevant skills in the int business, but feeling fundamentally a sense of being underwhelmed by the whole experience.

In terms of widening and broadening my tradecraft skills as a covert operator, the course was absolutely invaluable and served me so well in the years to come. But in contrast to the challenges and potential intelligence value of agent operations, I began to feel increasingly, and with a sinking heart, that a two- or three-year tour as part of a surveillance team deployed around and about the plains of northern Germany was not what I wanted.

Surveillance as practised by 14 Coy in the Province would have been a totally different proposition, with their far wider operational remit and the attraction of operating covertly aginst the backdrop of the Troubles. But ultimately surveillance is a tactical tool, of course potentially valuable, but still fundamentally an intelligence tool; agent handling, on the other hand, is a discipline with tremendous potential impact right up at the highest strategic level. And to be really frank, I have to say that, with no previous experience, I found I was having to work really very hard just to keep up with the best on the course, and my performance was less strong than I personally demanded, and I think, less than the DS expected – I felt I was not a natural 'covert passive surveillance' operator.

I was not invisible and frankly I did not want to be invisible; I was not passive by character and wanted to take a more active, and demonstrative, personal role in my concept of intelligence collection. I much more enjoyed the challenge of trying to project my character, rather than striving to hide it, and working directly with people, with individuals, in the attempt to motivate and steer them into courses of action, not necessarily ones that they would have picked for themselves. What greater challenge than the attempt to turn a terrorist into supporting and working for the organsiation he is striving to attack. More and more, I realised that I just was not enjoying myself – and back yet again to my days next door in the Agent Handling Branch the year before, and the daily buzz I had felt as the course progressed, compounding my declining motivation.

One practical thing I found particularly distasteful with regard to the whole surveillance philosophy, which added to my disillusionment, was the manner in which daily operational debriefs were conducted. At the end of each day, as would be mirrored on real-life operations, the team would sit down together and jointly construct a narrative describing the actions of the target/targets, if we had shifted focus from one target to another, during that day's follow. The Ops Offr/Sierra Charlie would lead the process and build up a picture for the final surveillance report at the end of the operation. The debrief would commence with all operators giving a numerical self-assessment of their exposure to the target resulting from the day's follow. A One would mean you had probably packed your Klingon cloaking device, had switched it on, found it to be fully functional, and were doing really quite well – the target would have been very fortunate, or professional, to have noted your existence. At the other end of the spectrum, a Seven, Eight or Nine probably meant that you had had some horrible luck or committed a real tactical faux pas that would require some degree of appearance change the following day. A Ten meant being burnt to the target and a train ticket back to base.

This Maoist-style self-assessment exercise then led into the main part of the debrief. This inevitably became an 'I did, you did' post-mortem as the day was dissected in detail, and could descend into quite aggressive and pointed personal attacks on the operators with the higher 'scores' who had committed tactical errors or made other errors of judgement. I remember one such debrief where I became the target. The other target, the exercise target, had stopped outside a house in a densely populated urban neighbourhood, row upon row of houses. It was after dark so all vehicles engaged in the exercise had their lights on. I had control of the target and had pulled in unobtrusively further up the avenue, close enough to observe and report on the target but far enough away to maintain discretion. I remained in position until another call sign had moved into position to take over control of the target, now inside the house, and assume the 'trigger'.

At the debrief, once we had wrapped things up for the day, I was accused, after I had pulled in to maintain observation, of moving a number of times closer to the target's location, leapfrogging along the road. I had not and stated that I had not. Things got quite personal and frankly unnecessarily silly as they descended into a pantomime 'yes you did, no I didn't'. This approach underpinning operations was, I think, paradoxically a factor, despite surveillance being nothing if not the ultimate team-critical process, that created and nurtured a 'cult of the operator'. This nurtured a prima donna mentality, and an almost adversarial environment at times in some that was anathema to the handling world, and to me personally, and certainly to my perception of the way to get the job done.

As we began to spend more and more time on the road away from Ashford, I got to increase my knowledge dramatically, particularly of the Brighton and Portsmouth areas. I have always enjoyed the Sussex coast, pointedly in direct comparison to the run-down neglect of south-east Kent. If my life had unfolded in another direction and I had found myself commuting daily up to London, I think I would definitely have looked at Brighton as a potential home base.

In October, we happened to be in Brighton for a two-day exercise. After we had finished for the day and sat down to debrief, I popped out from the bed and breakfast that I and three of the other students on the team were staying in for something to eat and a leg stretch.

I was wandering just up from the seafront, enjoying the freedom and the crisp sea breeze, when I heard a commotion behind me. I turned around to see a lad of about 20 sprinting towards me. Behind him, a young beat bobby was lying on the ground, helmet rolling on the pavement, the scene illuminated by a street lamp overhead. It looked like he had tripped and fallen in pursuit of the other. The young lad raced past me. Instinctively, I gave chase. He was fast but I was faster. We had gone about 150 metres and rounded a street corner into some sort of darkened alleyway. I called to the 20-year-old, now just a few yards in front of me, but still intent on escape, that he should stop right now or it wouldn't be good when I caught up with him. To my surprise, he did stop! I grabbed him. As he doubled over to recover his breath, the young police constable sprinted up, complete with helmet, and proceeded to lay into him.

Eventually order was maintained and the lad was cuffed. A police van duly arrived and we all debussed at the main police station. After making a statement, and being thanked for my sense of civic duty, no further mention of any hint of police brutality, or attempts to resist arrest, I returned to bed. The next morning the story was out, and I was taken to task by the senior instructor for blowing my cover and sacrificing my grey man persona for engagement with the real world. Sorry, that did not conform to my sense of operational priorities or attitude to duty – balancing the considerations of an exercise against real life? I think I had heard the voice of one of the prima donnas.

We booked out of our 'digs' and headed back east towards home. The next day the news was bursting with the story that PIRA, overnight, had exploded a bomb in Brighton's Grand Hotel, targeting the Prime Minister and her Cabinet while they attended the Tory Party annual conference. Five people had been killed and thirty-one injured. A pretty big coincidence, but absolutely nothing to do with my exercise the night before, and nothing to do with any of our presences in the town that week. But I did wonder what the owners of our various bed and breakfasts had thought when they considered the very early check-outs the day before of the dozen and more scruffy and slightly suspicious individuals they had been hosting. The whole thing was a tremendous coincidence, and does serve to redress the balance in the debate about the existence of coincidence in this sort of real world situation. Could have been the basis for a great conspiracy theory, if nothing else.

The course finally finished. I had learned some very important lessons and expanded my professional knowledge exponentially. The most lasting of these lessons was the understanding of how a professional surveillance team operates, what its strengths are, and critically what weaknesses can be exploited by a professional target. As a professional intelligence officer, I now had a clear understanding of when surveillance could, and should, be tasked as part of a multi-asset collection plan, and what it, as a collection tool, can bring to the all-source party. Closer to home and more personal, I learnt how an intelligence officer can identify when he is the target of surveillance and how he can evade a team utilising knowledge of both overt and covert anti-surveillance drills. This became very practical and valuable knowledge when I was personally confronted by the Stasi surveillance teams who routinely followed BRIXMIS tours as we conducted our intelligence-gathering operations in the old DDR. When I returned on posting to the Manor as the Training Major in the early 1990s, I taught our Military Attaches how to spot and evade surveillance – those taking up their embassy posts conducting roles in less permissive countries, and with more pointed intelligence collection functions, hopefully found these lessons useful. By extension, I learnt how surveillance can be used as a tool to enhance the effectiveness of an agent handler. How it can be most efficiently used to support targeting operations, and how counter-surveillance techniques can enhance the security of both a working agent and his handler. This was invaluable experience that, frankly, few of my colleagues over the years to come had had the chance to benefit from, and which time and again contributed to making me a better and more productive HUMINT officer.

By now, however, I was completely certain in my own mind that surveillance, in the Int Corps context, as a full-time role was not for me. Quite simply, I did not want to be a member of 28, let alone its Operations Officer, engaged in the type of surveillance operations with which the unit was tasked. I sat down with the commanding officer of SIW and we discussed the situation. Robert was not a very well-liked member of the Corps, but was always open and friendly with me. He had been an MIO, liaising with the local Special Branch, working in County Down where he had met his wife, Fanny. It was reported on the rumour vine that he had accidentally killed a fellow road user in some sort of accident out on his patch. But he was best known for his enquiry at some officers' mess function, when, on entering one of the rooms, he had loudly enquired, "Has anyone seen my Fanny?"

As we talked, I explained the way I felt. When he talked it was readily apparent that we were discussing a balanced equation and a shared outlook. The trainers shared my doubts about my future in surveillance, but I did have a nagging suspicion that this assessment was also supported by some less objective factors and considerations centring on personalities and the realities of the posting plot – a friend and former colleague of some of the DS who was looking for a surveillance role. Regardless, this ultimately, if true, played to my advantage; I felt tired and disappointed that the experience had not been the positive one I had hoped for and been excited about, but overall a sense of relief. I did not enjoy the job, I did not want to do it for the next three years of my professional life, and I definitely could not see myself rushing to work every morning eagerly to jump into a surveillance car. The 'hybrid' and more dynamic nature of surveillance in Northern Ireland aside – a totally different box of frogs – I had witnessed an anal side that did not appeal to my temperament or personality. The highlight and success of following a target on foot or by car was to see where he or she went – to house them, in the jargon – or catch a glance at something they did. I knew from my limited experience already that the agent intelligence tableau was a much broader, colourful, complex and frankly more interesting and important picture than this. Scarily, I now knew that if I could not return to the FRU, with little interest in a conventional military intelligence career, I would reluctantly look for something else in my life. I was standing at a big wide-open crossroads looking at the clearly marked signposts, wondering in which direction I should take my first and next step.

At this point, Colonel Ford stepped in with a new and additional arrow, intervening once again to realign my destiny and keep me focussed on a career in the Corps. News, of course, travelled fast. We met later that same day and he rolled out his hastily amended plan on the table. Synchronicity was still an issue but not the insurmountable one that it had appeared to be. He proposed I head to BAOR for nine or ten months to bring me into line to take over from Duncan, still, of course, the current OC of S Det, after his decision to retire from the Army earlier than expected. I was elated and could not have expected more. It re-demonstrated how nothing is set in concrete and how, if one variable changes, the whole pond ripples. I was still 25, but by then I would be commanding a special duties unit at the age of 26 as a Regular officer. This was where I wanted to be – had the genie given me a blank sheet of paper and three wishes, I would not have had anything different. It was not very long before I realised how blessed I was at avoiding a posting to Herford, but still having had the opportunity to broaden my professional skills.

My nine or ten months in the wilderness was a small price to pay, even though it meant, as Colonel Tom explained, pining away in 14 Signals Regiment, the Army's electronic warfare unit based out towards the Inner German Border in Celle. The time would, I was confident, fly. It did, very slowly!*

* Before then, as a slightly tongue in cheek aside, after all the training I seemed to have undertaken in so short and concentrated a time, let me share with you the two lasting lessons of HUMINT tradecraft – agent handling and surveillance – that have always stuck in the forefront of my mind and could prove the most useful in everyday life.

If you want to engage in some nefarious act and it crucially involves a person or persons vacating a specific location, wait at least fifteen minutes, ideally twenty, once they have departed, before you commence whatever it is you must commence. There is always a chance that they have forgotten to turn off the cooker, switch off the bathroom light, or have left their mobile phone on the side. Do not move early, you will eventually be caught.

Secondly, perhaps less valuable in day-to-day life but useful and satisfying when watching spy dramas on TV, an operative, most likely a surveillance operator, or an intelligence officer conducting anti-surveillance drills to evade surveillance, attempting to vary his or her appearance by changing some of the clothes they are wearing, will potentially remain 'detectable' because almost certainly, especially if male, they will not change the shoes they are wearing.

14

THE REAL ARMY? NO THANK YOU!

Things got off to an inauspicious start. I arrived late in the evening after a sprint from Calais, across Belgium and the greater part of West Germany, through the industrial Ruhrgebiet, and around Hanover to the pretty little town of Celle. Somehow I ended up at the main gate of a small satellite location on the east of town in an unprepossessing place called Scheuen. I had missed finding the main Taunton Barracks, located in an imposing old imperial German Kaserne. I was tired and couldn't be bothered to go any further, so I bedded down for the night in a damp, grotty caravan that seemed to be there for no other reason than accommodating geographically embarrassed visitors. Welcome to the real Army and life on Germany's front line.

The next morning I pitched up at the right location, slightly dishevelled and not that rested, reported for duty, and checked into my room in the officers' mess, thankfully on the plus side, not in a portable building but in a typical example of stout, dependable teutonic architecture.

The role of 14 Signals Regiment represented an important strand of the NATO tripwire that would alert the Alliance to the shocking reality that the Soviet bear had begun its rapid race westwards towards the Channel ports. Unlike its brother, 13 Sigs, also stationed in Germany, the regiment tuned into tactical/operational level activity. As an electronic warfare unit, it targeted the Soviet divisions, brigades, regiments, battalions and other units deployed on the other side of the IGB whose mass constituted GSFG, the Group of Soviet Forces in Germany, later to be redesignated the Western Group of Forces. Doctrine dictated that prior to any move across the demarcation line, 14 Sigs would pick up the preparatory chatter, or alternatively, and more sinisterly, the deafening radio silence, that would herald the big push, and give NATO generals at least some warning to make ready. If the day ever came, the regiment would then have been one of the first mass casualties of the conflict, obliterated in the red blitzkrieg.

The unit was predominantly manned by the Royal Signals, with a smattering of Int Corps SIGINTers with their Russian language skills. We wore the same cap badge and were on the face of it members of the same Corps, but the reality was that the operational int boys, like me, were a completely different breed – we were effectively two different organisations. The Signals had the reputation of being focussed on 'out-infantrying' the infantry, by which they were regarded as striving to be fitter, more 'warry', and more soldierly than their teeth arm brothers – a factor highlighting an inherent inferiority complex rather than a sound professional imperative. I quickly appreciated that this was indeed no myth or playful putdown. The regiment was run without any humour or joie de vivre. The atmosphere was strict, tense and lacking completely in any sense of fun – not my Army, and actually not the spirit guiding the manner in which most infantry battalions were led, either.

I was made OC of one of the mobile EW troops, our intercept kit sitting in the backs of Land Rovers, and settled down to learn how the whole unit functioned. In contrast to the regiment as a whole, my troop were by and large good lads and were actually fun to command. There were a number of old sweats holding down the senior ranks but I think they welcomed the arrival of an outsider. I quickly immersed myself in the routine of training, alternating with a regular cyclical deployment forward to a fixed site near the historic town of Braunschweig, anglicised to Brunswick, closer to the border, in Langeleben, for some real-time intercepting. Here we were left alone, and it felt very much as it must have felt for a past generation serving during the Malayan campaign in an up-country jungle clearing, without the coconuts and monkeys.

I began to start ticking off the weeks. Then, without warning, I received a call that was to give me some welcome focus and a distracting sense of purpose while I gritted my teeth and played soldiers.

On the other end of the line was Pete Giddy. We speak glibly about 'dislocation of expectation' but I was certainly surprised by the call and had no idea what it would herald. After some brief small talk, Pete asked me if I was up for having lunch in Hanover, a forty-five-minute drive away, plus time for finding the restaurant he suggested. I naturally agreed to meet, my interest and curiosity definitely piqued, and genuinely looked forward with a sense of acute anticipation to meeting up – I did not see Pete as a frivolous person or a closet restaurant critic, so guessed we would be discussing something with a professional edge and intent.

I entered the restaurant on time, Bohemian cuisine and really good, and there were Pete and Tim. Tim had been a fellow student on the four-week German language course in Mulheim that I had attended at the end of my first year at university. Pete explained that he was now, on posting from Ashford, the OC of the counter-intelligence company in BAOR. His company, 2 Security Company, was the parent unit of a number of sections including 28, the bespoke surveillance unit. Tim was the OC of one of his sections. We talked as we ate. He explained that there were mutterings from unnamed sources suggesting that there was a security leak, potentially leading to Soviet intelligence, the KGB or GRU, within my current unit in Celle. The mutterings further speculated that the mole might be a commissioned officer. He named a couple of names that, of course, I recognised.

The purpose of lunch was to ask me if I would work on the inside and attempt to find some flesh to hang on the bare bones of these allegations. No prizes for guessing that I readily agreed without a moment's hesitation. For the rest of the meal we discussed ideas and approaches, and when finally Pete paid the bill and we said our farewells, I was ready to embark on some real work. But as an interesting point of tradecraft speculation, a moot, semantic question, would I be operating as an intelligence officer or was I henceforward an agent? In reality, my new-found role was highly irregular and probably fell outside of any strict, frankly irrelevant definition anyway – the point was, we were trying to do good.

We met a number of times before I left the regiment, sometimes with Pete and sometimes with Tim. I began to have stronger suspicions that pointed to one individual we had discussed on our initial meeting. I kept my eyes and ears open, hoping to pick up anything that could cue another collection source, and mounted some carefully controlled mini one-man operations inside the barracks to identify any substantive evidence – I did my best to manage and minimise the risk, very keenly aware that getting caught would precipitate, at best, some tricky-to-handle misunderstanding, and at worst some potentially more far-reaching ugliness. But the identity of any potential mole remained elusive and efforts revealed nothing substantive. I did, however, come across some interesting things that, had I been a KGB officer, I would definitely have used to pressure the individuals in question into compromising themselves further.

As a postscript, with the tearing down of the Wall, a whole tsunami of intelligence was unleashed identifying a whole raft of Eastern Bloc agents. I have not subsequently heard anything about a source in the military SIGINT community, so I can only surmise that the chunterings Pete had been fed were baseless. He was in my opinion, however, absolutely right to investigate them.

There was some official lighter relief during the nine months, and I did learn a lot about how the Army functioned in its conventional Cold War role. One has to remember that, at that moment in history, Germany was the real focus of our military effort with the East–West stand-off a very real and ever-present cold war, only a misstep away from a catastrophic descent into the most costly and devastating war of all time. We practised crashing out of barracks and deploying to monitor Soviet escalatory activities, and I was attached to a divisional HQ in the field, gaining an understanding of how the war would be waged if it became a hot one. I also got up to Belsen to visit this dismally depressing place. With BRIXMIS I would visit a number of other famous, even more soul-destroying concentration camps, then behind the Iron Curtain. And as a troop we mounted a border patrol along a section of the wire and guard towers of the IGB. It was fascinating to compare and contrast this with the divide in Berlin. It reinforced the certainty that this whole reality was madness.

A counter-balancing amusing story that appealed to me featured one of the less uptight Squadron OCs as the subject. He owned one of those bizarre Citroën 2 CV 'cars', and seemed quite proud of it. It had a fabric roof, so must have been a limited edition, and was probably worth an extra sixty quid as a consequence, pushing the total net worth up to around one hundred and fifty. He told the tale that he was bombing along on the Autobahn, probably near or at its top speed of 60mph, when there was a sudden, enormous report, like the sound of ripping fabric that an A-10's Gatling gun makes. He looked up and his fabric roof had ripped right down the middle and was completely shredded. His soft top had been effortlessly, and without any additional expense, been converted into a cabriolet. I don't remember if there was an additional punchline, or a happy or sad finale to the saga. But it appealed to my sense of humour and was a welcome and rare chance to laugh and relax my overly tight facial muscles.

What my time on the plains of Germany proved to me, if more evidence was required, was that I had zero empathy with, interest in, or connection to the green army. I promised myself that if ever the day came when I was posted into some 'ordinary' regimental or staff job, I would sign on the dotted line and go and do something else – and so this self-fulfilling prophecy came to pass, but thankfully not for another twenty years.

At last the clock ran down and I was formally dined out of the mess, one among several lucky individuals being posted out of the gulag. The CO made some sneery comment about my return to the Province where he felt I belonged, or some such double-forked throw-away, and that was that. Thanks for that, Colonel, high time indeed that I got back to some real soldiering and left you to your war games.

15

BACK IN THE MILL

I returned 'home' in October 1985. A different regimental pennant flew from Bessbrook Mill's guardroom's flagpole, identifying another ARB on the relentless treadmill of the arms plot. I noticed some new cars pulled up outside the rear entrance to the office complex, but clearly their age and condition showed that my concept of deploying tatty older cars, 'souped up' mechanically, to blend in better with south Armagh 'shabby chic', had not been adopted. Once inside, there were some new faces in the 'binner', but otherwise, reassuringly, nothing appeared radically changed. It felt absolutely wonderful to be back.

Duncan had run a tight ship. We had an easy handover/takeover. There were no surprises, no skeletons visible in any of the cupboards, but equally no dramatic new cases pumping out pre-emptive intelligence. I'm pretty sure my recollection of Duncan retiring and moving to one of the big airlines as a security professional is accurate.

As I sat at my desk in the office TC had occupied, what seemed like a century before, I spent a brief moment surveying the road that had led to the establishment of S Det as the Army's sole focus for agent operations targeting the disparate groupings that made up south Armagh PIRA. I was aware of the history of agent handling in the Province before the FRU's establishment, and I took a moment to pay silent homage to the vision of those who had brought this prescient and vital focus to the fight.

The FRU was the brainchild of General James Glover. He had seen how intelligence, particularly source handling, could empower conventional operations as a force multiplier during the Malayan emergency. During his tour of duty as Commander Land Forces in 1979–80, he witnessed at first hand the piecemeal approach to Army agent operations and contrasted it to the tightly coordinated approach Sir Gerald Templer had overseen on the peninsula.

Up to this point, teams of handlers had been 'attached' to the brigade staffs. Training was, if not ad hoc, at least less intensive, and equipment inadequate. I remember TC talking, perhaps apocryphally and tongue in cheek, about resprayed Army green minis still with the MOD-issued fire extinguishers visible inside. Glover sought to tighten up and 'professionalise' the discipline. The result was the creation of a centralised, dedicated unit. The FRU was born.* Until Hamish succeeded in re-subordinating the unit to the MOD in London, the FRU was a theatre unit sponsored by HQNI. Our anodyne and cryptic unit name was not classified, but linking it openly to our function was classified SECRET. The heavy lifting setting up the unit was carried out by an Int Corps officer who had served as a Desert Intelligence Officer in the Oman campaign. I regret very much that I have never had the opportunity to sit down and discuss these formative days with him – but Crispin is alive and well, so I guess there is still time. Utilising this experience, he shaped and fashioned the new unit and defined, rationalised and energised its approach to business. Cleverly adopting the symbol of the Roman retiarius gladiator, with its classical allusions to the age-old nature of human intelligence, with our nets and tridents, we became the 'net-men' – the fishers of men.

---

* In his book *The New Spymasters: Inside Espionage from the Cold War to Global Terror*, Stephen Grey describes the FRU as one of the most successful intelligence organisations ever. The FRU distinguished itself in the quality of the intelligence it produced, the method in that intelligence's collection, how that intelligence was disseminated, and in the way it interfaced in, and with, the process and infrastructure that exploited that intelligence.

We were a busy Det – that was something that had not changed, either. The levels of stress and pressure were high and unrelenting. The nature of the role, the persistent physical danger and the sheer operational pace of meeting existing assets and continuously attempting to identify and pursue new ones were unsympathetic taskmasters. Hours were long and irregular. It was not uncommon to perform a day's work in the office completing paperwork and ceaselessly trawling and researching new targets before deploying in the evening on a meet or a targeting or recruitment job. I certainly remember numerous late nights rolling into bed after 0100 hours, only to begin the new day in time to match the expectations of the nine-to-fivers in more regular jobs. For those operators with wives and kids, there was no alternative but for them to take a back seat. I have heard it said that the Intelligence Corps had, and maybe still has, the highest divorce rate in the Army. I would not be at all surprised if the FRU's record, based on the cumulative, corrosive cocktail of the long, uncertain, irregular hours, the sapping levels of stress, and the paradoxical counterbalancing narcotic-like addictive draw of the job, was even less statistically inspiring than that.

As the boss, running any unit, but especially a special duties unit, is a job with two very distinct and different faces. I found on day one that my time as a full-time operator was, of course, over – I bore no allusions that anything other than this would be the case. But I did everything I could to maintain an operational role – this was important for me personally and from my vision of the leadership perspective. I have always believed that a leader can only lead from the vantage point of one position. That is unequivocally from the front. Skills-wise, I have always worked hard to try to be the best, whether on the range, out on a run, or handling operational matters. This said, the life of an OC, as you will see, is not always *Boy's Own* stuff.

The glamorous and adrenalin-fuelled role, directing operations, and the excitement of handling secret intelligence day in and week out, is the face that draws most into the world in the first instance. But the beast has a very different and less glamorous face. As the boss, you have to keep the machine fuelled, trimmed and in good working order. This entails keeping on top of all the supporting, mundane but essential tasks. If the personnel and equipment side of the house – in Army-speak, the G1 and G4 issues – are neglected, operational momentum, the G3 stuff, will very, very quickly and assuredly grind to a very unhappy halt, and there will be nothing in the G2 – intelligence – cupboard. It must be like running a restaurant. The quality of the food on the tables is paramount, but if the raw ingredients are not ordered systematically, if the décor is not maintained, the mess not cleaned up, waiters and dish washers kept happy, one will very quickly find oneself on the other side of the desk having an unhappy and one-sided conversation with the bank manager.

In my career, I have always tried to delegate as much of the routine administration to my 2ICs as practicable. After all, delegation is the art of leadership, centralising operational matters in my hands. At the risk of sounding arrogant, I have always believed that this has played to my strengths. As an officer, and the officer in charge, there will always be some matters, however, that cannot, or should not, be 'off-loaded'.

Before looking at some of the key operational tests that we faced as a Det, I will briefly examine the sort of issues that play a supporting role to the operational output of any unit. In all things I will remain mindful of the continuing caveat regarding security while trying to provide a sense of how it was, there in Bessbrook in the mid-1980s, that we maintained our hawk-like focus down the road on the south of County Armagh.

Matters of discipline have the most potential to destabilise a unit. In a special duties team, disciplinary problems should be few and should be minor. That was thankfully my experience. We had too many car accidents, the majority minor and not the fault of our drivers – road conditions, especially on the back country lanes, were sometimes questionable, and the general skills level in these areas was certainly sub-advanced driver standard. But we did have, collectively as a unit, a number of more serious crashes due invariably to excess speed. We, in Bessbrook, had a star performer, who now, I clearly see from the privileged position of hindsight, I should have sacked several times over. But always the prospect of wielding the claymore rubbed up against the reality of the numbers game: too few volunteers, too few course passes, too many vacant posts. Illustrating this point graphically, the Research course run in early '85 was actually completely scrapped, as none of the students were assessed as having the required attributes. Our star totalled several cars without a scratch, including one incident in which he ploughed into a flock of sheep – on the road, not in a field, thankfully. He did end up in court, as the consequence of one particular demonstration of excessive professional immaturity, on a speeding charge that could not be quashed, despite my attempt to do so through the good offices of the local Special Branch office. These sorts of issues, thankfully, were handled, when things got messy and complicated, by the administrative unit, 12 Int and Sy Coy, that supported all Int Corps units in the Province.

I do, however, remember a couple of serious incidents within the wider unit that were handled expeditiously and by the letter of the law. In E Det, during a farewell do for one of the handlers, as the late night began to draw to a close, a Royal Marine handler inextricably took up his glass, smashed it on the corner of his table and plunged the remnants into the face of his erstwhile best friend and close teammate. He could easily have killed him, and almost did. What motivated this completely and seemingly unprovoked assault remained unfathomable – speculating, was it stress-related, something uncontrollably snapping; just too little sand left in the glass? Whatever, he left the unit in chains.

One of a few young officers, untrained and married in this instance, who had the good fortune to be attached to the unit on brief familiarisation jaunts had parked his covert car outside the Europa Hotel in Belfast – with its dubious, unwanted but well-merited reputation as Europe's most bombed hotel – while he spent the night inside with a girlfriend. This was a restricted area for non-operational tasks. Sometime during the night, the car was broken into and stolen. He left the unit in hood and chains. He returned to the mainland and became embroiled in an even bigger and more serious set of misdemeanours precipitated by his disgruntled wife, which led directly to his court martial. He was a pleasant lad but, ultimately, it was fortuitous that he did not remain in any capacity in a special duties environment. He was not personally or professionally ready.

I chose to handle all career course issues for the guys, but again had 12 Coy to sort out the nitty gritty. Beyond this, what was really important was to keep lobbying the HQ to steer handlers who had passed the course in our direction, and exert pressure to fill our support posts, collators and clerks, in a timely but non-aggressive way.

The most important part of my G1 role, the people-related issues, was to look after the welfare of my men. Whether this meant ensuring we had time for five-a-side football in the Mill's small gym at lunchtimes, making sure our TV and video player worked so we could catch *Neighbours* if we weren't footballing, pushing guys to take their annual leave, or working to resolve personal and family issues, this was vital to ensure that we remained happy, focussed and motivated on the job. Later in the tour, I found that dealing with a marital crisis that one of my handlers was going through took up an inordinate amount of my energy, but I made the time willingly because he was loyal to me and worked hard for the unit. Loyalty and teamwork are two-way streets – how I wish civilian corporate life shared this self-evident maxim.

At the far left of the 'hard to solve spectrum' I had to deal with an issue of personal hygiene concerning one of our collators whose bed space in his portable building up in Thiepval was filthy and whose sheets had remained unchanged for weeks.

On a more serious note towards the right extreme, I had a senior handler, co-running our most valuable source, whose constant moaning, complaining and gossiping eventually proved the catalyst for the dig on the chin that he wholeheartedly deserved. I should clarify the situation. Moaning is an accepted, necessary and age-old feature of Army life. The right to moan is a safety valve through which tension, pressure and general cursedness is released. However, there is a very clear line that this particular handler regularly crossed. His moans were not the 'collective' gripes that bond teams, but rather 'personal', focussed on 'self'. This type of whinging becomes very tiring for those that have to suffer it and very quickly becomes a polarising and negative influence. Behaviour has to be modified.

It happened, short and sharp, late one morning while the two protagonists happened to be alone in the 'binner'. Of course, as the boss I had to take action to mollify the 'victim's' sense of victimisation, while ensuring things did not escalate to the silly heights that would impact adversely on my 'vigilante's' career. It was a fine balancing act and all the more tricky because I personally thought this unofficial sanction well earned.

I made the decision to sack another senior handler whose professional judgement I and my FSC, Alistair, had begun to seriously doubt. I sent him up to Lisburn to be interviewed by the CO, expecting to receive feedback on when he would be shipping back to his parent unit. Imagine my surprise when only two hours later I heard that, instead of having received his flight ticket and a posting order, he had been given a new and important central targeting role based in the Headquarters. I am convinced to this day that this was not a lack of faith in my judgement, but rather the insidious hands of Freemasonry at work.

On another occasion, I found myself counselling one of my clerks, Kevin Taylor, straight out of training and away from home for the first time in his young life, concerning a family problem that was worrying him. I sent him away on some compassionate leave so he could be home while the problems were resolved. He was fatefully posted away from us after less than a year and went up to Londonderry.

To his credit, once there, he obviously continued to take care of his personal fitness and must have begun to integrate into his new working and social environment. He and some colleagues decided to travel down to Lisburn in a 'covert' Army minibus to participate in the annual Lisburn half-marathon. This was an event that a number of us in the Det usually took part in when we could. We managed to participate again this year.

They took the fateful decision to park in the main car park adjacent to the run's start and leave the minibus unattended while they ran. PIRA must have been surveying the area, knowing full well that members of the Army would be taking part, waiting to identify a suitable security force target. This would not have been have difficult. The bombing team would undoubtedly have been small, conceivably just a couple of terrorists. If I had been planning it I would have selected a man and a woman in order to draw the minimum of attention and briefed them to dress in sports gear. Prepared and ready, once they had confirmed their target, the male, with the woman mounting guard and watching for anyone innocently approaching, would simply have dropped to the ground with his small sports holdall, reached underneath the minibus, and placed the small compact under-car improvised explosive device adjacent to the van's rear axle. Briskly walking away to their getaway car, they would have drawn not an iota of attention.

Of course, if fate had decided otherwise, if an FRU or SB agent had been aware of the operation and reported in to their handler, things would have been very different. A surveillance team would have locked onto the team and taken the device and the bombers to the car park, triggering an arrest operation. The PIRA operatives would have been caught red-handed in possession of an explosive device, and perhaps with a handgun or two for close protection, and a classic covert operation would have achieved its primary mission of saving life.

But in the event, Kev and his friends returned to the vehicle, no doubt buoyed up and feeling good with the inject of post-run endorphins, looking forward expectantly to a quick pit stop for something to eat and a sleep on the long trip home. As they negotiated their way through the town centre back towards the motorway and home, the bomb exploded, killing everyone aboard. I was caught up in the traffic on my way home, equally unsuspecting and relaxed, as the shattered minibus, and the bodies trapped inside, burned. Kevin was, if I remember correctly, just 19. It was a sobering, chilling and senseless event, all the more so because it could just as easily have been one of our cars that PIRA had picked out and one of us lying burned and mutilated, blocking the early evening traffic.

On the G4 front, the equipment-related issues, I have always been most interested in equipment that supports the tradecraft that underpins operations – the tactics, behaviour and then the equipment scaling on the ground that contribute to an operation's security and effectiveness. Especially with Hamish in the chair,

I found a sounding board who listened and, when convinced, took action to make things better. I know he would have shared my enthusiasm for the tradecraft initiative revealed by a tale that Brigadier Jackson, the Brigade Commander, had told me referencing the early days of the 1970s. Apparently, patrols would routinely stop cars at a VCP. During the course of the documentation check and any other dialogue, if the occupants came back with a positive terrorist-related affiliation, a small tape recorder would be discreetly switched on by one of the patrol members and dropped surreptitiously into the vehicle. It would record all ensuing conversation. The car would then be stopped further down the route and the tape recorder equally discreetly recovered while the car's occupants were again checked at a second vehicle checkpoint. The recording would then be checked for incriminating or intelligence-related information – so simple, and although limited, there's no doubt that this was a free and zero-risk source.

Proposed enhancements that we brainstormed were usually potentially less cost neutral, usually requiring procurement of new equipment, which in turn required a written case to justify the expenditure. I was convinced that, especially in the tight, incestuous operating environment of south Armagh, we needed to alter and minimise our operational footprint. We had to look different, while remaining benign, to any third party who took note of us out on the patch. I was convinced that sets of red Irish Republic number plates, that we could quick-fit to our cars and vans, would generate substantial flexibility and exponentially increase our security on the ground. Unfortunately, this idea failed to fly – I think we encroached on politically sensitive turf with this one and it took on the appearance of a fight not worth provoking. But replacing the bigger Hi-ace/Transit-style vans with much smaller and more compact Lite-ace mini-type vans was supported. As these were not capable of carrying a dozen soldiers in the back, they would not appear as readily on the terrorist radar, again enhancing our security. Equally, I advocated deploying motorcycles, especially for conducting recces. A man on an innocuous Japanese mid-sized bike receives much less attention than a man in a car. A man on a bicycle is even less conspicuous, but pedalling down to Crossmaglen or Forkhill might have been considered by the lads as 'a bridge too far'. The added advantage on a motorbike is that an equally innocuous helmet hides the rider's identity. The only problem in the mid-1980s was adapting covert radio comms integrally into the helmet, so that the rider could communicate easily and freely with other call signs. We had to settle for a compromise in that the rider could only really communicate effectively in extremis with his helmet removed. In due course we received two Japanese urban sit-up-and-beg-style 500cc bikes. Perfect for the job. We did not use them regularly but they provided us with operational flexibility and were cheap, and were the catalyst for my lifelong love of biking.

We looked at a whole diverse and broad range of other ideas that might have enhanced our security out on the ground: from adding some degree of armour to our cars; built-in in-vehicle fitted pistol holsters; mobile talk-throughs to guarantee car-to-car comms without going through fixed masts, which always suffered from black spots, as our trip to see 'Slab' had demonstrated; I trialled a detection device built into my car that would indicate if a magnet had been attached to the vehicle – PIRA used powerful sea-searcher magnets to attach under-car IEDs; right through to better access and panic alarms for our safe houses outside the wire. We also responded to intelligence by commencing regular systematic electronic sweeps, LTIs or Limited Technical Inspections, the technical term for looking for electronic listening bugs. We routinely and systematically swept our office space, all our safe houses, and my home, as I would sometimes meet the lads at home after a late meet when we had exploitation issues to discuss.

Looking back now it's like reminiscing about the days before Kitty Hawk and the dawn of manned flight; I am referencing a clear memory of approaching the Top and putting out feelers regarding getting our hands on something called a 'word processor'. Laughable. This new technology would quantumly decrease, I argued, the turnaround on operational reporting, reduce the clerical workload, facilitate the production of standardised and formulaic returns, etc., etc. How did we ever cope before the widespread introduction of IT aids, and actually relatively low-tech office tools like photocopiers? I know the answer, of course, to all these questions – we used age-old solutions and moved consequently at a much slower pace. As a collection resource we were relatively low-tech then. We did not enjoy the panoply of technical solutions to revert to that today's agencies enjoy.

Continuing on a technical theme, we ran two sources who required support in securely recording the volume of detail that they were collecting. We went to another government agency to investigate and discuss some operational techniques to assist one of our agents. This increased the agent's, and our own, confidence dramatically in carrying out tasking.

Never a fan of DIY, I decided it was high time we rid ourselves of a decade of grime, sweat, tears – but as far as I knew, no blood – and revamp the office to maximise the potential of our given floor space. Soldiers adapt readily, and usually without too much complaint, to pretty dire living and working conditions. In the Mill, the general state of upkeep and repair was extremely run down and ill maintained, not least the FRU offices. I drew up plans to modernise and adjust the floor plan and submitted the case to secure funding. Not glamorous but necessary.

Perhaps one of the easiest G4 wins that unquestionably enhanced our security was also the easiest and cheapest to effect. In fact, it cost HMG nothing.

The unit had an agent who regularly, after being out and about conducting his business, would meet his handlers and pass on details of vehicles that had alerted his security-conscious mind. In these instances he was confident that he was identifying covert cars. He was invariably right. When the details of these vehicles were passed on to 14 Coy, they confirmed them to be surveillance vehicles and then had to go through the rigmarole of re-plating them or moving them to another Det. It got to the point that they became very anti this source and definitely did not anticipate his reporting positively.

I was pretty confident that one of the anomalies that he was latching on to concerned something very simple. Today we take it for granted that the vast majority of cars have number plates that display the vending garage's address – and website. Back in the golden days, garages had printed stickers that were affixed to the bottom of the rear windscreen. I had looked at our vehicles independently and recognised that their obvious absence on our fleet made us stand out to a sharp-eyed third party, whether disinterested or more sinister. So I went to a local garage on the outskirts of Newry, part of a big chain, and asked the salesman who scurried over to interest me in a new car for a couple of handfuls of their stickers. He handed them across to me, I am confident without a second thought. Thereon after, the absence of this little telltale negated any potential negative attention – if a car was compromised, it was for some other reason, probably down to our own conduct.

More operationally related, one of my key roles as OC, and a slightly more exciting one, was my position as front man and 'ambassador' for the Det. But where there is excitement, there is danger. No less the case when you are responsible for liaison with the most important players in the game. As such, I had to maintain good relations with a number of agencies and formations who needed to be aware of FRU intelligence to inform their strategy and their operations, and who in turn had access to information that, when shared, gave us a perspective and a greater understanding of the operational field upon which we played. I had, as did all the other Det commanders, to maintain my wits about me and temper everything against the backdrop of never forgetting that, although we were staunch allies, we were also engaged in a highly competitive existential, unending turf war. A sad reality, but one that had the potential, with the slightest incautious footfall, to turn round and remove your hand at a moment's notice.

Building and maintaining good personal relationships here was vital – as handlers, if we could not succeed in this then there would be a major problem. I was lucky. I genuinely liked nearly every character I had to interact with, and even more positively, I admired the majority's professional ability, dedication and motivation to provide what support they could to us. This was certainly true on the Army side. This aside, one unguarded or ill-thought-out remark could provoke an unprecedented reaction that ultimately had the scary potential to see one on the next ferry home. It really was a potential minefield. A misplaced word could gratuitously enlarge the circle of knowledge. But the real issue was not the spoken word itself but an agency choosing to act on that word out of self-interest, without taking heed of the imperative for the protection of our source.

Underlying this inherent tension and perpetual grinding of the tectonic plates was the pressure to succeed. All agencies wanted a significant tactical success, or a never-ending catalogue of high-grade reporting to show the world how professional they were. But it went beyond self-aggrandisement or hubris – against the reality of finite government spending and perpetually limited resources, it was fundamentally a dog-eat-dog, internecine cold war. Organisations needed success to bolster status to guarantee continued funding and manpower.

The most important of these liaison contacts was without debate the RUC's Special Branch. I maintained direct relations with the Regional Head of the Branch, up in Gough Barracks in Armagh city, periodically with his boss, the RHSB Rural, a difficult character called Harry Mc who, from May 1985, oversaw all SB activity outside of Belfast and Londonderry – he had lost a hand in earlier days investigating a PIRA weapons hide that had been booby-trapped, or so the story went. He was universally feared by his subordinates. I vividly remember the day news came through that his father-in-law had died. The Branch virtually closed down for the day as its members thrusted and pushed to be the first to pass on their condolences. More a scene from the feudal Dark Ages than a vision of contemporary policing. I also maintained relations with the offices in Armagh city and Newry. For some reason, maybe a lack of personal chemistry, professional jealousy or any other interpersonal itch, the relationship with the Newry boss, Frank G, was terrible. Despite him having a son in the Army, we just did not see eye to eye, to the extent where the FRU plaque hanging in his office, I guess presented by Duncan, was removed, and we were no longer invited to their Christmas dos. Sadly, I got reports from Tom the MIO that Frank would take every opportunity to rubbish the FRU.

He had spotted one of the lads in uniform, one day, on patrol in Newry with the local unit and went berserk, reporting us up the line to Gough. On another occasion, a handler had been in the town and had spotted a known traced PIRA activist, and used his initiative to 'bump' the individual and ask him if was interested in a new and exciting career change. The individual had not been cleared as a target for FRU recruitment and caused another howl of protest. We always received direct support from the Top, who had seen all these issues playing out before in other patches, but it was fatiguing and of course raised questions in the minds of other agencies who were either drawn into bad-mouthing sessions or made aware of the bad blood.

On a positive note, I did get on very well with Spencer F, a Superintendent in the Regional office, and with Derek B in the Armagh city office, whom I had first met when I was in the main police station on my infantry attachment two years previously. I would regularly brief Spencer directly by secure phone or in person on all our significant intelligence, usually driving up to Armagh to his office. We would often combine a meeting with lunch or sit in his office and talk about the challenges of operating in south Armagh.

I think that part of the problem vis-à-vis the Newry office was that Spencer expected me to feed him rather than briefing Frank, thereby avoiding relying on him to brief upwards. This expectation was founded on RUC, and especially Special Branch, culture. This required the senior man to be the most informed in the matrix, deciding who below him received a cut of this information, when and how much. The SB was essentially a network of personal neo-feudal fiefdoms reinforcing the maxim that knowledge is very much power. This was alien to the Army approach, but as the RUC ultimately called the shots, we were obliged to be mindful, and if not respect, at least acknowledge their way of doing business.

There was always another underlying tension, in that Spencer wished to minimise the passage of intelligence to the Brigade so that he could control operational responses. My perspective was an acknowledgement of RUC supremacy, a desire to support all efforts by the Tasking and Coordination Group, as the reactive operational dynamo, while recognising and respecting cultural bonds to support my parent organisation, the British Army, and the pragmatic recognition that it, in the incarnation of 39 Brigade, could and would also provide valuable logistical and operational support to S Det. It was always a highly charged and devilishly slippery balancing act.

Regular, routine, direct, usually daily contact with SB was through the MIO and his deputy, the FINCO. This was a rock-solid relationship with Tom, who was the MIO for most of my tour. It was founded on a frank, open two-way sharing of information based on trust and, from my perspective, genuine affection and friendship.

The second most frequent guest in my office was the LO from TCG. We needed to keep this relationship positive, and also discreet, because it was TCG who fused all source intelligence, the product keying covert exploitation operations. It was TCG who could task other covert resources to back up our operations and exploit our intelligence, whether it was 14 Coy, the SAS troop or a COP. Steve, an Army officer, was always good fun and provided enough background from his side to make me feel I had a handle on things beyond our own relatively narrow perspective. I remain unsure of just how pro-FRU he was, but any doubts on his part did not intervene openly in our relationship.

The relationship with the Brigade, sitting up in Lisburn, depended very much on the character of the Brigade Commander. He had a full-time job because his formation combined the two busiest, and arguably deadliest, PIRA groupings in the Province – south Armagh and Belfast. With the rebirth of rural 3 Brigade, he lost Bandit Country but still retained a pretty full plate. For most of my tour the Commander was Brigadier Tim Jackson. He would be my boss in BRIXMIS. I liked him very much – he was approachable, always personable, and treated subordinates with respect. I tried to call in on him weekly to update him at his Monday 'prayers'. I remember on a couple of occasions sitting down with him, informally at his behest, once actually in his home, to discuss the reality of operations in south Armagh. As the plan began to unfold to build the string of OP MAGISTRATE observation towers, he sat me down to elicit my opinion on how they would affect the situation along the border – from the FRU perspective they became a valuable source of pattern of life activity, as the large lenses within the towers could command an enormous field of view – they had the capability to read a car number plate 3km away. From PIRA's perspective, I opined that he was providing them with an endless opportunity to hit high-profile targets if they lacked any other – and so it panned out, but paradoxically increasing the potential for covert operations to catch PIRA in the act.

We also responded on several occasions to requests from the Brigade to report back on local opinion and their reaction to the towers, and to gauge border opinion so that the Brigade could re-shape patrolling levels. I was very happy to task our assets and take the time to respond to these requests. But the reality was that this senior officer was not too full of his own self-importance to sit down with a lowly captain and listen to his professional advice. To me that was so refreshing and a true mark of leadership.

More frequently I saw Justin, the Light Infantry Major who was the senior intelligence staff officer in the headquarters, the SO2 G2. He was a solid champion and played with the straightest of bats. This ensured that he was trusted by all the agencies he called in on, and because of this he had a far wider and more in-depth knowledge of what the covert agencies were doing than would otherwise have been the case. He was a very astute and professional staff officer and served his Brigadier with style. I liked and respected him very much.

Less frequently I would speak with, and swap information with, ASP, the Security Service officer sitting in HQNI. His relationship was closer, for obvious reasons with HQ FRU, but I had regular dealings with Oliver, Sally his assistant, and then Peter McLaren, a Korean War veteran. Given the hardship and privations, this is, unjustly, the forgotten war. He was a lovely man, sadly now no longer with us. Also on the list was the JIRO, the Defence Intelligence Staff rep seconded from the Old War Office in Whitehall – I had been at university with a later incarnation – and the Irish Joint Section in Stormont, a small operational unit of handlers from other agencies – all their agents coinciding with my time in S Det were ex-Army cases. We provided them, at their request, with a number of viable targets, and when they needed help, tasked our sources to keep an eye open and report on the movements of these targets, especially in the border counties of the Republic. I also met regularly with the Warrant Officer heading the 14 Coy int cell, and of course the local Army unit, the Armagh Roulement Battalion.

Relations with the ARB, the green army, were important not least because we were squatters in their home. They fed us and provided us with helicopter hours to get us in and out of the patch on patrol – this was always a fraught subject that took time and tenderness to make it work. Also fraught and very tedious was the enduring saga, unit to unit, of car parking. For us it was not just an issue of prestige or convenience to have secured, allocated spaces. It was much more an existential struggle to keep drivers who had no need to see our covert vehicles at arm's length.

On the operational side, the ARB provided us with useful eyes-and-ears information, particularly in support of our targeting efforts, and particularly from their forward base in XMG. I would usually attend the weekly int meeting hosted by the ARB IO, usually just a talking shop, but every now and again reporting something of relevance to us. I would always make it my business to get to know the ARB Commanding Officers, who were usually fully supportive and pleased to be on the receiving end of the odd snippet of inside juice. I did not take to all the COs but it was always extremely interesting to me how their leadership styles and personalities stamped themselves on their battalions, good and not so good. I remember several who later became generals, including General Charles Lovat of the Scots Guards, who was known to his men as the Great White Shark. So regimental mythology recounted, he had bayonetted two Argentinian soldiers in combat during the Falklands War. Recounting earlier escapades in his life, he was a charismatic officer. I greatly admired future General Abbot, a highland officer, and was sad to read that he was seen as the villain by many, especially in Scotland, after the fundamental and savage amalgamations of the infantry, particularly the Scottish Division. His battalion, The Black Watch, were arguably the most tactically innovative battalion that I saw operating on the patch. I will also never forget the obvious distress of the CO of one of the battalions who were badly hit and took a number of fatalities during their tour. He obviously really cared about his men and about these losses.

I always forged a good working relationship with the Company OC in Cross, as we were frequently on his turf; less so with his opposite number in Forkhill. I got to know Tim Spicer of Sandline fame well and found him to be a professional and competent officer. His and Sandline's involvement in Sierra Leone in 1998 pulled in my predecessor in the Military Intelligence Liaison Officers office in the DIS and caused him some professional grief.

I always maintained a passing relationship with the CO and IO of the County Armagh UDR battalion, 2 UDR. Latterly in my tour, once we had taken over responsibility for the Nationalist area around Castlewellan and the County Down coastline, I established good and positive relations with 3 UDR headquartered in Ballykinlar. Their IO was actually running a number of CASCONs, in contravention of protocol, which they eventually handed over to us at our request. They were very happy to pass on targeting information to us – I generally felt that the UDR, although a sensitive subject, was a potential resource that we consistently under-exploited.

As a unit, the FRU entertained a steady flow of high-profile visitors, including the Secretary of State for Northern Ireland, the Minister for the Armed Forces, the head of the Security Service, and other worthies. As the IO of the FRU, on returning once I had left S Det, I would be twisting with nerves as, ten minutes before some of these high-price briefings, Hamish would take a pause in the frenetic way he commanded the unit and start to think about what he was going to say to them. I always had to laugh at his apparent lack of concern. His briefings were always without fail spot on.

We, in the Det, had our own regular trail of visitors beating their way down to Bandit Country – a mix of civilian and military high-ups, everyone from CLF to the intelligence coordinator in Knock, the DCI, a post set up by Mrs Thatcher for Sir Maurice Oldfield, once he had retired as head of SIS. This always entailed a formal stand-up brief on the threat posed by PIRA, our assets, and our MO. The briefings invariably were well received and appreciated, and I actually found them fun to deliver – give a briefing enough times and you begin to feel like an actor in a long-running play. I do remember on one occasion a visit from our then Int Corps Director. We had had lunch in the mess in the Mill and we sat back down in my office afterwards to brief on the Det. After about three minutes he was sound asleep. What do you do as a young captain when a brigadier is sitting in front of you, eyes closed, head bowed, and jaw sagging? I carried on, effectively briefing myself and Hamish, who knew the pitch as well as I did. His power nap ended, he rejoined the proceedings seamlessly.

Depending on the seniority of the visitor, we would then give them a quick tour around the patch in our cars to reinforce the messages delivered in the briefing. This might sound dangerous, but because the visits were irregular and we deployed randomly, never to a set timetable, or to a set route, the risks were low. The psychological impact of this 'military tourism' more than outweighed any danger and left the impression that we were as professional as we actually were.

But in extremis, if things went wrong it could be extremely hazardous. One of the constables with the SB in Newry had been ambushed by PIRA. He had been mobile in his car and was gaining on a small truck driving in front of him. Suddenly, without any warning, the truck abruptly stopped, effectively blocking the road. The rear roller door of the truck flew up, opened from the inside, exposing two gunmen. They opened fire on our man's car, spraying it with bullets. He was hit but not badly wounded. The gunmen assumed they had killed their target and sped off without checking on his condition, luckily for him.

In April 1987, Lord Justice Gibson and his wife were killed by a massive remotely detonated bomb as they crossed into south Armagh on the main Dublin–Belfast road. We had received a non-specific warning that PIRA intended mounting an operation that day, but regrettably no more detailed than that.

However, in March 1989 the Province was shocked, and our minds collectively focussed, by the much more sinister deaths of Chief Superintendent Harry Breen, the RUC local Divisional Commander, and Superintendent Bob Buchanan. The subsequent investigation revealed that they had been across the border at a meeting with the Garda in Dundalk. On their return trip home they were ambushed by PIRA and both officers were shot dead. Chief Superintendent Breen, unlike his colleague driving, had survived the initial fusillade and had actually exited the car, wounded, and was waving his pocket handkerchief in surrender before being finished off by a shot to the back of the head.

The incident fully brought home the seriousness of operating in plain clothes in south Armagh. Subsequent inquiries speculated that a member of the Garda had tipped off the IRA about the liaison visit. Whatever the reality of that accusation, south Armagh PIRA had deployed up to forty volunteers to cover all the possible routes the two policemen could have used on their drive north. At the point of ambush they had professionally, and ruthlessly, deployed a killing group and cut-offs. Nothing could have saved the pair – they were effectively dead as soon as they drove out through the main gate of the Dundalk Garda station. Thank goodness they were not taken alive.

Every time we headed down onto the patch covertly in plainclothes, and every time I slipped off the main Belfast–Dublin road onto the numerous cross-country minor roads to Bessbrook to work, when I chose not to transit through Newry town centre, I found myself 'switching on', moving up a gear, in anticipation of running into some sort of an ambush. This undoubtedly and immutably subtly increased our cumulative stress loading. But as the clinical and savage murder of the two senior officers chillingly demonstrated, if, rather than opportunistically running into an ad hoc improvised illegal vehicle checkpoint, called an IVCP, we had somehow been deliberately targeted, we would not have survived the compromise.

Thankfully, I still had enough hours in the long working day to devote to operational matters. I split myself easily and comfortable into directing and managing operations, and taking as much of an active role as possible without encroaching on the bailiwick of my handlers.

All matters pertaining to the operations mounted by Det personnel, the G3 side of life, came across my desk. Operations did not happen without my, or the FSC's, sanction, when he deputised for me. It was absolutely essential that everything we did was based on taking all variables and factors into consideration – operational, political, inter-agency, and above all security related. The utmost coordination was imperative to avoid blunders that at best would embarrass the unit and at worst imperil life and limb. This included all matters relating to our bespoke patrol force supporting us, the Force Support Platoon, support from the ARB, and all other external relations.* Most decisions were preceded by open and sometimes forthright discussions, chaired by me, involving the handlers and invariably the FSC. Frequently I would run things past the HQ, and was never backward at coming forward in seeking advice or another angle on things. No one has a monopoly on good ideas, and everyone in the unit had enough experience and intelligence to add to the mixing pot. This may smack of over-control and micro-management, but I would always argue that, so long as this centralised approach – once our approaches were clear – was tempered by leaving the handlers to execute the task in hand and take credit for success within and without the Det, this was a balance that worked. It was effective, efficient and kept the team motivated, and above all, safe. I know that I had the reputation, throughout my career, of pushing my guys – and, for that matter, myself – hard. My view, particularly regarding FRU days, was that we enjoyed the kudos of belonging to a covert unit, we enjoyed more money,

* We had been allocated our own patrol multiple, initially provided by the Royal Military Police, which was designated the Force Support Platoon, to generate increased flexibility and responsiveness, and also to enhance the security of our targeting operations – we were now able to effectively restrict the circle of knowledge. They wore the cap badge of the current ARB, leaving their bright cherry-red berets back home, changing it when the unit rotated out, and conformed to the resident unit in every way in order to blend in. Their presence demonstrated direct support from the Brigade and was much appreciated by us. E Det in Belfast regularly relied on their opposite number in 14 Coy to support them on targeting and recruitment operations – to be able to call upon a professional surveillance capability was a significant force generator. Hamish would consider, but reject, establishing a dedicated organic FRU surveillance team of six operators to generate this function for the whole unit.

more professional and personal freedom, so there was an expectation and responsibility to repay this debt. The mechanism and exchange was simple: hard work and commitment to do everything in our power to protect innocent life and bring terrorists to justice, or at the very least contribute to the frustration of their plans, before they could execute them to kill their targets. I knew from Peter that Hamish regarded S Det as the best-running and most effective detachment within the unit, so I guess, collectively, we were deemed to be successfully paying our dues. I maintained an overview of all existing casework, and vetted and approved all targets and their exploitation.

After each and every source meet, the handlers would brief me on the intelligence gained. This would key decision-making on its dissemination. Intelligence that related to targeting or pre-emptively to forthcoming attacks would invariably be passed on verbally by secure green phone or at a face-to-face meeting; for example, with Spencer at Gough. This would usually follow a discussion with the FRU Ops Offr. More routine intelligence would be MISR'd without requirement for verbal onward transmission – I would decide at what level and give guidance on the wording if this was necessary. We would then discuss case-related issues if the case had developed in any way, positively or negatively, since the last meet. This discussion would focus on matters of access and motivation, significant welfare-related issues, and any new potential for pushing the case forward in a new direction. Naturally, security-related issues would always be top priority and probably generated the most strenuous mental exercise.

I would then become involved again once the handlers had completed the Contact Form and the subsequent MISR. This was not always a stage in the process that I looked forward to. Invariably I would have to rewrite Phil's CFs from start to finish. He was a natural instinctive handler but, without wishing to cause him offence, he was semi-literate. He had joined the Army to jump out of planes and had successfully completed SAS selection and training, before falling foul of alcohol when he decided to drive home the night of the end of the course celebration. He did not join up to craft masterpieces of prose. Doubly regrettably, he handled our best and most productive agent, which meant even more work for me. But Phil represented the most extreme scenario, and because he was a fiercely loyal team member he deserved whatever support and help I could give him. In most cases I just had to tighten up the handler's comments, and sharpen the focus regarding case development. It was time-consuming but I usually enjoyed the challenge and satisfaction of signing off on a good report.

I would always be briefed on the new targets the lads had identified and would write the formal letter to the RHSB requesting clearance for us, in due course, to mount a recruitment attempt. I was always involved in discussions at the planning stage when we began to focus on developing new targets and taking things forward. When we were ready to pitch them, we would sit around the table for, sometimes, protracted sessions to hone down our approach and vector in all the possible contingencies, imponderables and different scenarios that could affect success. This was always a welcome challenge and saw a collective increase in the heartbeat of the Det in anticipation of the prospect of success.

I would chair the regular reviews we held to assess progress in individual cases and inject a sense of urgency if a degree of inertia had set in vis-à-vis some targets. This really was arguably my most pressing task and the one that proved the most tiring. The target list I inherited was poor. For the rest of my tour I kept the pressure on each and every handler to keep searching for, and identifying, new targets to assess and pursue. At one stage, I instituted a six-week rotation whereby within that period each new target had to be ready for a recruitment pitch. Obviously this was not a hard and fast rule, but it did succeed in generating a sense of urgency and a sense of process that was vital. Deadlines are invariably a useful management tool. This approach tacitly acknowledged and exploited the inherent competitiveness between handlers that pushed them to seek success. It was accepted that not every handler coming to the unit from the course was a recruiter, but it did frustrate me when the weaker operators attempted to distract themselves, and me, pursuing targets with, at best, peripheral value.

There were some pep talks, not all of which were received in the spirit with which they were delivered. Once or twice I had to pressure handlers who I believed were not expending enough effort and drive in their targeting effects. This was certainly not a disciplinary issue and had to be accepted as a reality – we are not all born with equal measures of handling and recruiting talent, and do not all continue to develop professionally after training. More seriously, I had to take one handler by the nose and lead him away from the dangers of becoming too close to his female source. I read the riot act to an older handler and his co-handler, who had missed reporting an update before they overran their meet cut-off. This could always happen if they were in a comms dead spot and the source was a low-risk agent being met in a very safe area. However, when the team pulled up after the drop-off and checked in at the ops desk, it was obvious they had been drinking. This I would not pardon or overlook. Both received a stern warning – it did not happen again during my time on any other meet.

As the OC, I was responsible for drawing up any reports and responding to any written requests that came into the unit. On one occasion, the Top needed a paper written on the cross-border smuggling scams being run wholesale by PIRA and their supporters. I put together a number of papers on measures and equipment to enhance tradecraft. Another put forward ideas for improvements in the course back at SIW to take account of operational developments within the unit.

I would regularly deploy to provide cover on meet pick-ups and drop-offs, and would frequently man the ops desk during jobs. When I identified a window in the diary, I would accompany the lads on targeting jobs in green to get me out again and keep my knowledge of the patch updated. These were aspects, as far as I was concerned, of leading from the front.

On one of these days out in Cross, I was with a new handler, Billy J, who had been posted into the Det. I had allocated him to the team operating in the western half of our TAOR. He was still finding his feet and getting to know the key landmarks and a feel for the target population. We were in one of the estates off the notorious central town square when we were ambushed by a little yapping dog snapping away at our heels. Dogs were often a pain in the town – you could almost suspect they attended special classes to inculcate canine antipathy towards patrols. This little pest was definitely, however, a victim of Napoleon syndrome and suffered from self-image issues, regardless of any training. It would not leave us alone. As it danced in front of Billy, completely accidentally – as he steadfastly maintained – without breaking stride, he caught the 'doglet' in the midriff and it sailed up, literally, six feet in the air in a graceful descending parabola. It was one of those moments when everything reduced to slow motion. The dog returned to terra firma, its mini-muzzle bloodied, its barking reduced to a pathetic yelping, and its master, now firmly on hand, on the point of apoplexy. I really thought we were going to have a massive punch-up, with visions of half the town rushing to join in the fracas – the infamous 'Chihuahua Riot' of '87. Fortunately, peace was restored after some quick, firm, silky words and the making of some very solemn apologies. The whole brief interlude certainly contributed nothing to our 'hearts and minds' campaign. Billy worked again for me in Cyprus, ten years later, and after a few drinks we would still have to laugh about this whole surreal image.

Patrolling in the town also provided the opportunity to meet a visiting Page Three girl flown in to XMG base to cheer the boys up. Poor thing, I don't think she had been briefed on exactly what she was letting herself in for, if she had received that courtesy at all. The whole scene reminded me of those newsreel clips from the Vietnam War, with visiting artistes flown in to entertain the troops on whirlwind tours in up-country fire bases before dashing back to their helicopter to be whisked away to sanity and safety, or just the next jungle hellhole. I chatted with her afterwards. She seemed a bit shell-shocked, struggling to make sense of the doppelganger world she had found herself dropped into, the heavily fortified Army base bursting with its young, heavily armed soldiers. But she was not in Vietnam, she was still firmly in a part of the British Isles. Her courage and dedication to duty definitely deserved a medal – I guess it would not happen in this day and age. Shame – she brought some distraction and some sense of a future to a lot of young lads who were otherwise submerged in a pretty bleak and fearful existence.

I also provided the Det with lasting amusement when, after a hard day over the fields and through the streams and hedgerows, we returned to the base and I had a seat in the little XMG officers' mess, awaiting our aerial lift home, only to drop off to sleep. No one came to grab me, I am sure deliberately, when our chopper came in – and, of course, I missed it. I had to thumb a lift with a later flight. Probably showed that the lads were not out enough in the evenings if that provoked such mirth. As part of my leaving present, one wag procured a little wooden plinth and on it mounted a little metal model Wessex helicopter surrounded by a frame of all the cap badges of everyone in the Det. I still have it somewhere.

Rightly so, policy decreed that OCs should not routinely handle cases, even though all our Dets were undermanned. However, I got approval from HQ to co-handle our cases in the north of the patch. Frankly they were low-level eyes-and-ears assets – 'asset' was perhaps too strong a word, but they were extremely low maintenance. The handler I had deployed to run the cases was solid but one of the weaker ones in the Det, so I figured it could do no harm. I explained to him that my presence was no reflection on his ability, he had the lead, and he should relax, poor guy. From my perspective, it was good to have the chance again to work through the process of meeting and debriefing a source, developing rapport and attempting to steer the case to achieve greater things. I failed!

Preparing for a meet, one went through a personalised ritual to ensure that one was psychologically sharp, and that nothing required in support of the meet was left behind in what could sometimes be a busy, and constricted, period of time once orders had been delivered to the cover team and ops desk. Once we, as a unit, were working to optimum equipment scaling, thanks mainly to the pressure Hamish exerted on the system, we were equipped with the very latest covert, fully secure comms slaved to the system fitted in the cars. We would use a small, almost invisible, covert earpiece, identical to the ones back on the Surveillance course. During my time we did not deploy with any personal security 'gadgets' – I was, anyway, sceptical about their utility because we knew that PIRA's immediate action on taking an operator alive would be to strip him or her of all clothing and equipment – remember the desperate images of the two murdered corporals lying on the Belfast car park tarmac in their underwear – and move them rapidly to a secure location, in our patch, south of the border. Far more practical, and cheaper, would have been a SOE-style L pill; the ingestion of its poison would resolve any kidnap scenario in a rapid, painless and secure manner – I did have a brief and in vain conversation with Hamish on this subject. I'm sure he thought I was deranged but I have to say, accepted in the cold light of day and safety of my home, I would not have hesitated to take one if it was obvious I would be taken – the last bullet syndrome.

We all took supporting props for our meets, the majority carried in our meet grips, the most important of which was our protective hardware. We were then armed with 9mm Mk 2 Browning pistols with ambidextrous safety catches. Some handlers fitted rubber Pachmayr grips to the handle to enhance grip and control – I was a big fan and they were not expensive. We also retained some old Walther PPK automatics, Ian Fleming's weapon of choice, for their reduced bulk and easy concealment. Some female handlers preferred to carry them as their primary weapons because the handles were a more practical fit. In the Mill, we were an all-male team. I do not know whether this situation changed before the ceasefire but we had one practical operational reality that precluded female handlers – we had to work in green, and female soldiers, then, did not patrol. All our pistols were replaced by the Sig Sauer family of pistols, the 226 being the prime model, once they were introduced.*

For potentially higher-risk ops, in addition to carrying my pistol on my body – usually in a pancake holster on my belt, because of the difficulty of accessing it while driving with seat belt fitted – I favoured a second weapon tucked into the door storage compartment. This would be loaded with a twenty-round extended magazine, which protruded beyond the length of the handle, making it impractical to carry on one's person but ideal as a back-up weapon. The advantage of this, beyond ease of drawing the weapon while seated, was that in the unplanned event of having

* Just as a matter of interest, the US military pistol is now the Sig Sauer 320, an updated model made by the Swiss company, replacing the Beretta M9.

to exit the car rapidly, one still had a pistol regardless, if for some reason it remained in the vehicle.

Because of the issue of ease of access, most handlers armed with a single pistol, while in the car, routinely tucked their pistols under their thighs between flesh and seat. Best practice here was to use a small towel as a seat cover to obscure everything but the butt. I was never a fan of this – a cocked weapon, in my book, should always be properly secured. Wedged loose on the seat it was an accident waiting to happen, way too near one's nether regions.

We would then carry an additional support weapon. By this stage we had both MP5Ks and HK 53s. The smaller MP5 was more compact and concealable – it could easily and comfortably be worn in a shoulder rig under a winter coat – and no doubt represented a potent enhancement to the SAS's room-clearing capability, but I preferred the larger HK 53 and considered that it provided better flexibility in a rural setting. Its extendable stock turned it effectively into a full-sized assault rifle should that be required. Collapsed, it could still be used from within the car in the event of trouble. The Heckler Koch went comfortably into the meet bag sitting on the front passenger seat. To this arsenal we added smoke grenades to provide cover from view in the event of a static firefight. I also usually routinely carried a small defender baton, which was perfect for a situation where deadly force was not appropriate and, if used, might see one in the dock on the wrong side of the law. Perhaps forestalling a curious question, we did not wear any form of covert, lightweight body armour.

To round off my operational responsibilities, I also enthusiastically took a full part in our recruitment operations. These really were the most exciting peaks in the monthly diary and we probably did mount, on average, one recruitment attempt every four or five weeks as the culmination to however long we had been cultivating each target. On reflection, although the continual push for new assets did not consume the majority of our time – unsurprisingly, handling our standing cases was the most time-intensive of our roles – certainly from my perspective, recruitment operations did drain the largest reserve of my personal energy. As I have already said, I felt I had to constantly pressure the handlers into taking that extra step in going after those targets that would open the doors to intelligence nirvana. It was too easy to sit back and let the routine of daily tasks dominate the agenda. Beyond this, it was too cosy to keep busy running after mediocre targets who would never in a month of St Patrick's Days enhance our Det access.

With Hamish in the chair, he instituted monthly conferences, alternating from Det to Det – it rapidly became a competition to serve up the best lunch. These were not the standard talking shops that all units and organisations feel it necessary to stage. Hamish used them to refine strategy, policy and tactics. They were sharp and focussed, reflecting his character and leadership style. He kept them as open forums in which to explore the adoption of new technical solutions, new equipment, new admin procedures and capabilities, including less glamorous but entirely relevant supporting functions such as our own vehicle breakdown capability, and more secure and efficient action on RTAs, etc. He collated ideas to pass back to Ashford to update the Research course. There was nothing that could not be discussed, albeit some issues might be re-directed to a discussion once the conference was over.

Crucially, with regard to recruitment operations, he pushed us Det Commanders to raise our sights and really focus on going for targets with established high-level access. To underwrite this imperative, he promised that we would be able to access very substantial quantities of cash to satisfy the potential financial motivation of any high-level player.

A fresh spirit of innovation, drive and focus began to permeate the unit at all levels. Hamish pushed for more handlers and more administrative support staff to really raise the FRU to a new level of potency. He took the initiative to establish the Fermanagh office as the fourth detachment when West Det was born in early 1988.

A slightly more frivolous-sounding brainstorming session, but with serious underlying intent, was a consultation that Hamish arranged with a personal family contact of his. We sat down to discuss the issue of projecting influence, manipulating the psychology of colour and the implications of dress, hairstyle and other subjective personal variables with a view to maximising our impact in interpersonal situations, not least when attempting recruitments.

Sounds rather effete, but it was thought-provoking and I have certainly tried to harness some of these lessons over time. What this demonstrated was Hamish's attitude that there was nothing that should not be considered, even if quickly rejected, to maximise our punch.

We received clearance from SB to attempt a recruitment operation of a target traced as being on the fringes of PIRA. This was to be an enforced attempt without any prior cultivation or contact. We had tried to intercept him at home or on his way to work, but singularly failed to be able to put together an exploitable pattern-of-life profile. We were working in an operational vacuum with no other sources of information to harness and draw upon. I decided we would mount a 'false flag' approach. This, simply put, involves pretending to be someone or something else, rather than revealing one's own true identity and purpose, or simply, inadequately leaving the issue hanging in the air. It is a tried and tested approach in the intelligence game to ease suspicion, anxiety and fear in order to establish, at least, some form of exploitable initial contact. Running some cases, some agencies will never reveal their true face and they will continue to sail onwards, someone else's flag fluttering from the mainmast. This was not a long-term strategy that we ever pursued.

We did know that the target ran a successful music agency, so started to kick around ideas centred on this as the catalyst for contact. In the end, we settled on contacting him posing as music journalists, inviting him for an interview with our fictitious music magazine. It was a conventional wisdom that intelligence agencies invariably did not use any degree of journalistic cover so as not to potentially endanger bona-fide journalists as they conducted their form of information gathering. I don't remember but I must definitely have requested and received dispensation for our plan. We sent the target a professionally formatted letter from our editorial office based in Belfast, suggesting a convivial meeting at a well-known hotel in a safe and non-threatening area on the outskirts of a local town to the north, rather than pushing him to journey up to Belfast. Our stated interest was to produce a profile piece focussing on local Northern Irish talent breaking into the 'big time'. In these pre-Google days, it was far harder for an individual to check the credentials or background of any individual or commercial enterprise, so we assessed our ruse might survive initial scrutiny.

Recce confirmed that our chosen hotel was modern and the layout perfect for our clandestine needs. It was just the right setting for a convivial business meeting and ticked all the right boxes from a tradecraft, and security, standpoint. From this operational perspective, it was cosmopolitan enough to provide us with the 'visual' cover we needed for the cover team, while allowing us to stage manage things, maximising both physical security, from both our own and the target's perspective, and guaranteeing discretion should we be lucky enough to have the chance to sit down face to face with the target. Would the prospect of publicity and five minutes of fame tempt him?

On the day in question, we had received nothing back from the target by way of a confirmation or polite rejection of our invitation, but decided to deploy regardless. We went through our full routine of prior confirmatory recces of the hotel and surrounding area, orders, preparation and deployment. Despite our normal reticence to plan fixed-point meets, we took up our positions in and around the hotel. In these situations we were always able to retain the upper hand so we were able to effectively manage the risk. The target did not show up. The ultimate professional anticlimax. We aborted the job and returned to base.

He did, however, call the following day on the office line, with its Belfast number running into the E Det office, that we had had specially installed and included on our letter. His call indicated that, although he was suspicious, our approach had been halfway successful. Our hook had at least partially snagged a fold of his skin. He said that he was hesitant about meeting because he believed we might be 'dole spies' trying to entrap him for fraudulent DHSS claims. He was reassured. We too were reassured that, significantly, he did actually make the call. We pushed back our publishing deadline and agreed to meet in two weeks' time.

We deployed again. The cover team, including a female operator borrowed from E Det, again settled inside the hotel bar area ready to trigger the handler once the target appeared. We felt optimistic and the atmosphere within the team was a little more taut this time with the expectation that our man would show. It was a quiet evening and we had the bar to ourselves. But suddenly there was movement as two unidentified males entered, raising the cover team's hackles. Failing to be able to confirm the target as one of the pair, they resumed their vigil but maintained a watchful eye on them. They continued to drink unobtrusively in their corner and caused us no further anxiety.

At 2200 hours, our female handler, part of the boy/girl team at the bar, phoned the target from the pay phone in the hotel lobby. He picked up. He apologised that he had been unable to come himself but admitted that he had sent two 'associates' in his absence to meet with us. They must have been the unidentified corner pair. He apologised again and promised that he would definitely turn up in person the following Monday.

By this stage in the proceedings our approach did not look hopeful. The despatch of the pair of 'associates' was certainly an odd response but, with the Top's endorsement, I decided we would mount one last try, taking the target at his word.

We deployed yet again from the office in Drumadd Barracks and took up our positions. It felt as though we were becoming hotel regulars – actually, in security terms, a positive development because it reinforced the impression of our belonging. We were blending in effectively to our surroundings. We had upped our own threat assessment for the meet, and drawn in additional Det handlers to increase our own security, but in truth no one was feeling particularly optimistic. We had the car park covered and our male/female cover team positioned, again, unobtrusively like a pair on a date inside the bar area to trigger the target and call forward the handler who remained out of direct sight.

At 2000 hours, the same pair from the last abortive job entered the hotel bar area, followed by a third male. The cover team instantly came up on the net, confirming the call that had just announced visitors arriving in the hotel car park, and alerting the whole operation. A collective jolt of excitement coursed through the team and the tension dial spun to max. Everyone was instantly poised, pointing towards the prey like hunting dogs. It looked like we were on and the decision to persevere had been vindicated.

There was a pause. The net sprang to life again. The third of the trio resembled the target. Pause. This was looking good. The pause continued. The next call came. It was not the update we were waiting for. The code word for 'Abort', the signal instructing all operators to stand down and fold the operation. This was not good at all. This was their call, as the cover team, but surely it was premature. It looked like our target had shown, or what? The whole team lifted off and we returned to Drumadd.

On returning to base, we conducted a robust semi-Surveillance Branch-style debrief. It is never good practice to second guess or criticise the operator(s) on the ground – they are the guys who are there at the sharp end, and on this operation they had felt insecure. But it was clear that the rest of the team shared my unspoken view that the cover team had 'bottled it', and prematurely at that. The presence of the same two unidentified characters was certainly less than ideal, but their demeanour had not appeared to be overtly threatening on the previous occasion or on this, only an irritation. If the third man had indeed been the target, we should have been able to squeeze some contact out of the situation, reassure him of our credibility and sincerity, and at the very least have built a bridge for a further meet back fully on our terms. Maybe not so easy and requiring some ingenuity and creativity, but we were, after all, handlers. This was what we did; we were paid to deal with unconventional interpersonal situations.

Regardless, safety should always be the primary concern. The background to our last three deployments did now suggest an overly cautious target. We had already invested considerable time and effort and had nothing positive to show for it. Upon reflection the next morning, reluctantly, but I think rightly, I decided to drop the case and file it for reassessment at a future date. Pragmatically, we had other fish sizzling in the deep-fat fryer.

Once in a while, we would find ourselves behind a really exciting target that did tick all the boxes I wanted to see ticked before sanctioning an approach. Sometimes our ongoing trawl would reveal an old case, previously stood down, that had since blossomed with renewed potential access and vigour. These cases would often require as much effort to get back onto the books as a fresh recruitment.

One such really exciting target had an interesting historical pedigree, and initial contacts in green revealed a cagey acceptance to engage with Alistair, the handler. Relying on the pattern of life study we had assembled, we were able to mount a string of casual bumps, slowly but surely putting her increasingly at ease and steadily building rapport. In order to create the circumstances whereby we could engage in a protracted conversation, while progressively defining who we were, we put together a complicated operation involving running her into a vehicle checkpoint that we would then cordon off and isolate, leaving us free to spend as much time as she would allow us without threatening her security.

The plan involved the local unit, our dedicated patrol capability, the FSP, and most of the office deployed in green to set up the VCP on a route we knew the target frequently took on her way to work in the Republic. A small handling team would deploy onto the patch covertly in plain clothes. Once the target had driven into the VCP, the handlers would be called forward, passing through the cordon to join the target, inside the net.

Alistair and I deployed in plain clothes as the handling team, sequestered in the back of our small dark blue Ford Escort van. Phil drove us into a lay-up location close to the border, and only a few rapid minutes away from the projected VCP site. Our plan involved our position being covered by a green-uniformed multiple we had borrowed and tasked from the local ARB company. They had already patrolled into position, intent on guaranteeing Alistair's and my security.

Always a man of few words, Phil, with a quick "See you later", was out of the van and was whisked away by a cover car to await the end of the operation to escort Alistair and I back to Bessbrook.

We sat uncomfortably in the back of the van with our reading material, if my memory is not failing me; Alistair's magazine was more glossy and artistic. The minutes ticked by, and thirty minutes became forty-five, which slowly became an hour. We were pulled into the verge of our narrow country lane, bordered by thick, high hedgerows enclosing the small fields that made up this rolling rich green patchwork of farmland, unchanged for centuries. Ostensibly, to a casual passer-by, the van belonged to someone off in one of the fields. To someone less casual, and local, its purpose would require investigation.

We felt uncomfortably vulnerable. We were certainly exposed and very aware that we would not be able to defend ourselves effectively if things went wrong. But these were not the things you dwelt on. If you worried about every operation and about every situation where things could go wrong, you would soon be crippled by doubt and unease, and basically stressed into a state of uselessness. You would be unable to function as an operator. We had to believe in the value of our training and the hard edge it gave to our operational planning. But situations like this did require a conscious ostrich-like head-in-the-sand attitude, which, psychologically speaking, probably comes easier to the young with their innate sense of invulnerability and underdeveloped imagination. War is unquestionably a young man's business. These were also still the days when we were our own counsellors and bore sole responsibility for creating and managing our own individual coping mechanisms. Our personal lives were adversely affected to greater or lesser extents because of this. But here, ultimately, we knew we were safe in the knowledge that the Scots Guards patrol had eyes-down on us and would intervene if any third party decided to mess with us, and shoot to kill if this attention was born of evil and sought to do us evil.

In reality, however, we were sitting here waiting in a fool's paradise. The patrol had moved into the wrong position and we were indeed sitting in splendid isolation. The only things covering us were the scurrying clouds traversing the leaden sky above us. We were in a potentially extremely hazardous situation. When this was confirmed in measured and muted words over the net, Alistair and I had a quick whispered conversation and made the decision to remain where we were – the patrol would be adjusting their geographical embarrassment but we had no estimate as yet of how far off they were. They would be making for our position. If we moved, we would potentially be moving into a more dangerous position with no potential cover. We did not want to move early into the safety of our own cordon because then all our planning would have been for nought. These were the decisions one made in seconds but potentially regretted for years. But that was the job. With our training and experience, we had the confidence and skill to make the right decisions.

Even with my head in the sand, it was distinctly unnerving to contemplate the reality of being completely alone in the heart of Bandit Country, sitting like two fish in a barrel. I abandoned my reading material and focussed my body on remaining absolutely still, and my ears on picking up any hint of a person or vehicle approaching. All was quiet. My watch hands continued their sweep even more lazily as though struggling to push aside something other than the increasingly fetid air around us. I could see that Alistair, too, was more focussed on our surroundings now than on the photos resting on his lap. All remained quiet. I checked for the tenth time that my HK 53 was easily to hand in my open meet bag, and visually reconfirmed that it was cocked and ready. Alistair moved his bag a few inches closer.

I cocked my head to the side. Sounded like a car. Not close. I moved my head – but getting closer. Alistair looked at me. He had heard it too. He raised an eyebrow. I reached for my 53 and slipped off the safety. Alistair had his in hand, too. I raised and slowly lowered my left hand and made the universal hand sign: be calm. We were blind here in the back of the van, but we could now clearly hear that a slow-moving vehicle was continuing its cautious approach towards us. We strained to pick up any other sound. It was now nearly upon us. We clearly heard the driver change down into a lower gear and the engine revs slowed as the car slowed. This was getting a bit tense. I carefully shifted my sitting position, drawing my knees up a bit closer to my body. The car was slowed to a crawl and was now upon us. The moment of truth had arrived.

Don't stop, keep going, keep going, keep going – it kept going. The engine note quickened and it was away. I lowered the weapon and smiled at Alistair. He shook his head. I loved this van. Ford made a great covert van. My watch hit ninety minutes and our patience and stoicism were finally rewarded when the call eventually came into my earpiece from the VCP that our target had been spotted and had entered the 'trap'. Somehow the instant surge of adrenalin paradoxically served to bring me down to a more relaxed state, rather than the heightened level of expectation that had marked the last few minutes. It was time to go.

We moved rapidly, but in full control, one after another, slithering awkwardly from the back, through the well-disguised sliding bulkhead, into the front of the little van. I eased myself into the driver's seat, Alistair beside me, and turned the key that Phil had left, as per his orders, in the ignition. The Ford's engine turned with confidence and we set off. Nothing in the mirrors, nothing left and right, and clear to the front. No sign of our patrol either but we were OK. I increased speed. It was good to be moving and swimming out of the barrel. In reality, there was no rush now. The target was secure and she was not going anywhere quickly. We did not have far to travel and drove through our cordon, reassured to see friendly faces, and into the checkpoint to join our woman. The operation was progressing well and entirely to plan, I told myself with an inward ironic smile.

We had taken all this trouble to ensure that we met for the first time in plain clothes on her turf. Our sudden arrival projected enhanced drama and reinforced the psychological message we wanted to impart. We wanted to graphically demonstrate that, whatever she may have assumed from our initial contacts, we were not her average squaddies from the nearby base. Rather, we were confident in working in plain clothes in PIRA's backyard, we had the power and clout to mount what she must have recognised as a non-standard and well-coordinated operation, and by extension, if she agreed to meet with us away from home, she could do so with two demonstrably unobtrusive, very ordinary-looking, but professional covert soldiers. We knew she would know what this meant and that this little charade was imperative if we were to move to the next level in our relationship.

In the event, she refused to come north to meet covertly but agreed to talk to us whenever our paths 'crossed'. She did later agree to further 'organised' meets in green on the patch. Over the next weeks and months, she produced some fascinating technical IED-related intelligence. When Alistair was posted, HQ instructed me to assume the lead on the case. I bumped her several more times, before I too left the unit. I valued our meetings, her personal and 'professional' gravitas, her connection, and her take on the current terrorist-related situation in south Armagh. She was impressive.

Proving the concept that existing cases could always play a useful contributory role in spotting new talent, we began receiving, unwittingly, intelligence from an existing source that an old asset had resurfaced and was out and about on the patch. We confirmed from ARB sightings reports that this was indeed the case. I made the decision that we would recontact him and attempt to persuade him to recommence meeting in order to give us the opportunity to assess whether his level of access and motivation had developed in our favour.

A phone call was made and he agreed to meet covertly, north of Newry. In security terms, a recontact is arguably more potentially hazardous than the initial covert meet with a new target or source because, as handlers, we have no conception of what might have happened in the months or years since contact had last occurred. On the flip side, the potential recontact would be fully aware of how we operated and what to anticipate, privy to too many of our secrets. We had no idea where his loyalties now lay.

With this asset's pedigree, background and contacts, we faced a potentially even more hazardous recontact. It would be higher risk for the first few meetings until we got a definitive sense of how the land now lay. We reflected these realities in our mission planning and deliberately located the pick-up well inside the normally secure Loyalist heartland, midway between Newry and Belfast. We had a pre-planning sit down and talked through all the factors. The plan factored in a heavier covering presence at the pick-up and we inserted a simple counter-surveillance phase into the operation to check his tail once the source had crossed into the North. I instructed that we also request the battalion ARF to provide cover from the air. Relying on the unit was a good way to maintain liaison and make them feel needed and wanted. In practical terms, it would more importantly provide us with a valuable additional resource and enhance the security of the operation. We knew that PIRA were always suspicious of helicopters overhead during an operation, believing they might be under aerial surveillance. This would frequently lead to an operation being aborted, especially up in the west of the city in Belfast.

The 'surveillance' car confirmed that the source was alone as he drove north across the border towards Newry. His tail appeared to be clear. It remained clear. Running the ops desk, I received confirmation that the ARF, with one of the collators as an LO on board in case they were called in, was airborne and waiting to pick up our 'surveillance' car on the other, northern side of Newry – the LO was, of course, aware, but the individual ARF members were not briefed on the details of the agent's car in order to limit the circle of knowledge and protect his identity. Both vehicles cleared the town and speeded up towards Banbridge.

The handler and the two cover cars were already in position, awaiting the update that the source was en route and secure. Everything was starting to look good but it was too early to relax yet.

The 'surveillance' car confirmed the source remained clear of any apparent hostile surveillance and moved to his position, from where he could maintain vigilance and observe all traffic coming into the town from the south. The ARF now confirmed that they were on station over Banbridge, awaiting further orders.

The source followed his instructions to the letter. However, there was some excitement caused by his furtive behaviour and the fact that he was carrying a small bag, which was definitely not part of the plan. I acknowledged this update and relayed it to all call signs, to ensure that this point was logged and understood by all operators. I requested that the ARF remain on task above the town, just in case.

The source was eventually picked up without incident, and I called off our air cover.

This initial meeting went exactly according to plan in every other respect. The small bag, it transpired, had contained a bottle of home-made poteen as a gift for the handler. We were quickly able to confirm over the next two meets that any security concerns were unfounded, that our man was very happy to resume the relationship, and continue reporting, and that he had returned well and truly to the fold. More than this, he seemed motivated to talk far more openly about the PIRA contacts with whom he freely mixed than his file reflected was the case historically. This looked really good and positive.

We started to build some useful pictures around the activities of some of the top traced active PIRA members in the area, and he reported on conversations he was both privy to and overheard as he rubbed shoulders with them, on the face of it as a respected equal. There was no intelligence to the contrary, so we were able to accept his assertion that he played no part in terror but he was accepted by those who did. On several occasions he was able to pass intelligence giving warning of forthcoming PIRA attacks – this is intelligence we craved and disseminated immediately to TCG and the Branch hierarchy.

Another old source living on the Monaghan border, if not streetwise, was certainly well and truly connected, by both itchy feet, to Mother Earth. Early on in our new relationship, after recontacting him, he had explained that times were tough and to make ends meet he was having to consider moving away from the Republic to look for work on the Continent. Whether or not this was a bluff, we had to react seriously to his threat. In consequence, we were forced to increase his retainer to match his expectation of what he would make in full-time employment. There are, of course, two sides to every coin, and he had just provided us the leverage to pressure him to increase his reporting. Based on previous comments I have made concerning remuneration for sources, had we created a potential security problem by regularly handing across sums that his lifestyle could not cover? Rest easy, no. Our man had well-developed historic relations with the criminal fraternity and could cover this new source of income easily. On one occasion, when I stepped into a debrief – a so-called 'boss meet', useful when a source needed extra encouragement, praise for good work, or a wrap on the knuckles for bad – we were chatting away happily and having a laugh generally about life on the border and more specifically about local criminal activities. With a twinkle in his eye, he mischievously suggested that I pass him a couple of thousand pounds of my own money and by the end of the week, he assured me, he would have quadrupled it. That is what I called business and case development. We could have run the whole S Det operation at no cost to the Queen, just 'laundering' our Det float. I gave him serious consideration for about half a second and politely refused his kind offer. The case did, however, graphically demonstrate the value of maintaining an ever watchful eye on our historic caseload, just as much as focussing on completely new virgin potential.

Another previous recontact did not advance so positively. We had reconnected and begun re-meeting the ex-agent. Things had started well enough and his handlers were confident that the case was progressing well with positive potential for development. But, unfortunately, the source quickly decided that we were pressuring him too hard and disappointingly went to Provisional Sinn Fein, PIRA's political wing, to hand himself in and confess his sin.

To limit the damage this setback caused, we had to rotate two cars and a van out of the Det, respray a second van, and change the number plates of the remaining vehicles that had played a peripheral supporting role in running the case and which the now very ex-agent may have noted. The three handlers who had handled him were required to take cosmetic measures to alter their appearances – one of them had a much-needed haircut and a shave and looked ten years younger. We conducted a thorough review of the tradecraft that the source could have since compromised in order to ensure that we missed nothing that could impinge on the security of our other cases. I was satisfied that his potential to inflict harm on us had now been limited, and we briefed the Top accordingly. The file was closed and, I assessed, unlikely to be reopened during the duration of this campaign.

We changed the source line again, but maintained the number that this agent had used. In the absence of an exposé and the usual piece in *An Phoblacht*, we wondered whether PIRA had made the bold decision to attempt to capitalise on their apparent inside information. If this was to be the course of things, the source would call in on his usual number.

The decision was made that should PIRA indeed attempt aggressive exploitation, we would play their game and agree to meet the source as if we were responding to a routine request for a meet.

On this occasion the would-be ambushers would be ambushed by the SAS.

A call did come in on the old source line. We experienced a sudden burst of excitement and expectation. In the event it turned out to be a lame enquiry asking for the source's handler by the false Christian name that the source knew him by. The caller was told that he was not there but to leave a message for him. They, whoever they were, rang off. With PIRA's usual timidity in these operational circumstances, all scenarios for any kinetic exploitation on our side died the death when no further call was made. A great pity. This could have developed into a hard-hitting operation with substantive and deadly results. It would have brought kudos to the Det and the Unit and been good experience to be able to play a part in it. As usual in these cases of compromise, PIRA was left to ponder how many other cases remained unreported and continued to tap their lifeblood in an incessant drip, drip, drip of intelligence. Every exposé fanned the flames of paranoia lapping at, and progressively sapping, their confidence and will to fight on.

What Hamish did establish early on in his tenure, as I highlighted previously, was the assurance that a high-level target with operational access could be offered really large sums of cash to aid the motivation process. We considered one target and received tacit support to offer him £100,000 as a single golden hello. We were not able to take this case any further, however, for operational reasons. Examining another highly accessed target, we considered the approach of offering a large cash incentive for him to sit down with us for a single one-hour debrief and answer all our questions – a sort of rent-an-agent approach. Of course, once this single session was over we would not have settled for a complete break. This too came to nought.

Taking Hamish at his word, we began considering a highly placed target who appeared to enjoy hard, direct access. Secure and consistent points of contact remained elusive and hard to identify. I decided we would adopt a tactic from the Malayan campaign that had always appealed to me. We began regularly sending the target envelopes containing higher-denomination banknotes. We sought to balance the dramatic impact of opening the 'letters' against the potential security risk that the regular arrival of package-sized post, containing reams of small-denomination notes, would provoke. This movement of free money went on for some time – just cash, no explanatory note, nothing else. The guiding psychology was that the target would get used to the cash and would subtly begin to rely on it. After the second or third post, he would have guessed who was sending him these 'love letters'. It would then be revealing to see whether he made some public statement revealing our ruse.

In the event, when we decided the time was right, we sent him a letter, no cash, explaining what to do in order for the flow to recommence. Regrettably, and probably predictably, we received no response. Equally, however, we did not hear from any overt or covert source that he had declared these gifts to PIRA. A risky omission on his part that could have potentially been exploited ruthlessly by a black op on our side. So, failure; but it was worth the attempt. If this little scam had worked, the gain would have more than justified the speculative expense.

Tangentially, it is a fair question to raise if you ask, "What part did black operations play in the FRU play list?" It was always an issue, right from my first months in the unit, that had interested me. I vividly recall that there were two occasions in E Det when we could have waged an aggressive op against a well-known top Republican. With hindsight, it proved to be fortuitous that we refrained. This individual's political position in PSF, regardless of his history in PIRA, which he still to this day comically and consistently denies, was key to the peace that now prevails in the Province. But looking at the tight, seemingly impenetrable cohesiveness of the south Armagh groups, I am still convinced that we could have wrought tremendous damage, unsettling their self-confidence, and neutralising some of the key players by unfurling some well thought-out black jobs. Revealing a hardened terrorist's inclination to hide away a substantial stash of the Queen's treasure would have been a simple and unchallenging start. But we did not work like this and this type of operation was not part of our job spec.

Thinking laterally, we discussed the potential for recruiting a completely clean, untraced and unconnected target and bankrolling him to set up and run a small business, 'Four Square

Laundry'-style, either in Crossmaglen or one of the other 'strategic' towns or villages along the border. This could have proved to have been an absolutely invaluable source of intelligence, as the business allowed our businessman to mix with the local community, especially those on the other side of the law. Our brainstorming on this one died in utero. This was a great shame. A bold initiative on this scale could have made a real difference as a potential source of intelligence.

While we were not the sole agency that operated in south Armagh, we were the only one that routinely lived and breathed, day in and day out, on the ground. We were the only agency that regularly and routinely operated throughout the patch. The other agencies, both Army and police, dipped in and out of the mix on specific missions and tasks. They were essentially guest actors and not regular members of the cast – essential to the plot but not permanently under the bright lights illuminating the stage.

This guest list did include the signals intelligence unit, E Troop, who played a tremendously important role in consolidating our knowledge of how south Armagh PIRA operated, how they were configured, and in providing warning and corroboration of attacks and other operational activity critical in the support of operations as they unfolded. We worked closely with them to use our knowledge, experience, and the information that we gathered to generate a unique and enhanced dimension to their product.

Looking across the border, the Irish authorities did not play any sustained, effective or enduring role in the war against the IRA, despite the odd high-profile instance such as the running of Sean O'Callaghan – incidentally, another 'walk-in'. Whatever the political constraints, evidence suggested there was very little investment in any anti-terrorist effort. In 1985, the Garda's nationwide surveillance capability rested on the shoulders of sixteen operators – their main target was organised and so-called 'ordinary decent crime'. With leave, courses, sickness and rest days, this amounted to a single operational team deployable on any one day. There were meetings between the local SB and their Garda opposite numbers and I do remember occasional intelligence tip-offs from across the border, but true joint operations were very, very rare. I have to admit that I was sceptical regarding the loyalty and security stance of the Gardai and the Garda. On the occasions when Newry SB requested to pass on our reporting, I always refused permission. We would sometimes see the Irish army in the distance when we were down on the border but, despite their UN peace-keeping posture, I do not think they played any substantive or meaningful part in cross-border operations.

If PIRA had been privy to the all-source intelligence picture that our combined operational efforts was creating by the mid-1980s, they would have been horrified. Agent intelligence has always – rightly, in my view, and supported by the reporting of strategic level agents within the Republican groupings – been credited with advancing the peace process. PIRA's assessment of the level of penetration crown intelligence services had achieved, and the resultant demoralisation this provoked, were absolutely pivotal in the decision Adams and McGuinness made to slant the 'ballot and the Armalite' strategy exclusively to seeking a political outcome. Had the hard men of south Armagh realised how aggressively their operational prowess had been stripped of the protective layers they strived to maintain, they may likely have been the Pied Pipers of the peace movement even earlier. The intelligence war, especially as it was fought in south Armagh, was a graphic success story. It was a textbook case study in harnessing the whole spectrum of collection and operational assets and fusing the intelligence product into a single poignant collage for exploitation. I would attest that this was the high point of Britain's anti-terrorist, counter-revolutionary warfare history. We certainly lost this supreme honed cutting edge in the conflicts that were to follow in Iraq and Afghanistan. There, on the HUMINT side, we suffered from the severe and chronic disadvantage of having to operate in an alien language and against a political and social backdrop that we just did not understand. But the radical groups our next generation of intelligencers encountered were by no means as skilled and wily as our Republican foes, and their operations were not tempered by the overriding imperative to avoid compromise – the Islamist terrorist knows no self-restraint with regard to protecting his or others' lives.

We had a comprehensive overview of how PIRA were organised, who belonged to which team, or ASU, names, faces and roles for most of the key players, tactics and MOs for bomb and mortar operations, and sniping attacks. We could not kill or capture them because they were simply the best, and perhaps luck was more with them than with us. As a more accurate summation, paraphrasing the old adage encapsulates the situation perfectly – in mounting their operations, PIRA had to be lucky only once to score a practical and propaganda success; we, the Security Forces, had to be lucky every single day, weekdays and weekends, to forestall them.

I for one very much admired their professionalism. As 'soldiers', their operational skills were unmatched by any grouping on the planet. Their tactics were professional and directed by effective command and control discipline. In security terms, they were incredibly hard targets. They routinely engaged in effective anti-surveillance drilling, making it extremely difficult to impose effective surveillance on the fixed locations we had identified and on the ASUs when they began moving on the various operational phases of a planned attack. Above all, they were consistently ready to abort an operation the moment they even sensed something was not quite right. Their philosophy was always live to fight another day. And one key factor that isolated them from other groupings in the Province was that they, south Armagh PIRA, did not hit soft targets – they did not murder off-duty members of the RUC or UDR (there were very few of these in south Armagh anyway) and they did not indiscriminately target civilians in the same way that the Belfast Brigade did, setting off bombs in shopping areas and against other commercial targets. South Armagh PIRA targeted the Army and the RUC, when they could spot them, 'military' against military. They were terrorists and they wantonly committed murder, but they were soldiers and professional operators too. They certainly displayed a courage and a commitment to their cause that set them apart from every other terror grouping in the land. This, of course, was not the case, tragically, with the renegade south Armagh members of the various IRAs that succeeded PIRA, post-peace accords.

What did South Det FRU bring to the intelligence party? I am going to hold back more than I reveal, for obvious reasons. There is nothing that I highlight that can be used to identify any of our agents. Where I have needed to think things through and have remained unconvinced, I have decided not to include reporting, even where inclusion would have added spice. Even if the days of a bullet in the back of the head are over, and I would need persuading that south Armagh PIRA would forgive and forget, being identified as a tout will still demolish, in one decisive blow, any standing a former agent would enjoy in this tightly bound clannish society. What I will readily admit is that my time as OC was one of a constant and unrelenting flow of intelligence from the significant number of agents that we ran. Total numbers of assets did fluctuate, with some being stood down and new recruits taking their place, but the reality was that we could never have too many.

Most of our intelligence during my tenure as OC reported on either the movement of munitions in the border region, both north and south; threat warnings detailing forthcoming PIRA attacks, but never, regrettably in sufficient detail to allow TCG to plan a definitive Loughgall-style pre-emptive operation; and then a rich and diverse spread of miscellaneous 'craic' – a wonderful Irish expression. As I look back, it was quite a roller coaster. We experienced few handling issues, and certainly no dramas with the intensity and implications of the agent extraction back in TC's time, but such was the intensity of reporting, and the general dearth of corroborative intelligence from other agencies, that confidence in our best and most prolific agents inevitably rose and fell until supportive product brought vindication, or we just kept moving forward to the next challenge and challenging situation.

I think a number of factors were at play. Certainly, operations we reported on pre-emptively were aborted by PIRA for operational and security reasons – vehicles broke down, communications broke down, plans simply failed to come together, a few players had had too much to drink the night before another operation, on another a fire broke out in a van transporting an explosive device into position. And operators were spooked and called things off, on one occasion because the SAS troop left footprints at a target location. There were several instances of PIRA aborting attacks in response to observing overt action by the green army in Crossmaglen, who had been in receipt of the threat warnings and chose unilateral defensive action. Not helpful. Certainly, there were other instances when sources passed on information that was simply wrong or that they had misunderstood or misinterpreted. And there were occasions when agents tried just a little too hard to please their handlers and overtaxed their imaginations. No doubt that inter-agency rivalry and competition inspired scepticism and a reluctance to task assets to exploit some threat information, but I worked hard to keep our liaison partners fully informed of our intelligence and strove always to temper it with objective and meaningful analysis – that was one of my most important, and taxing, roles.

Throughout, I could not have wished for handlers, or collators or clerks, who were more devoted, who put in longer hours, or who faced physical adversity with such courage and sheer equanimity. But on occasion, regardless, they were forced to confront the worst of experiences. Really striving hard to push their agents to bring in the best intelligence they could, they were greeted by scepticism from either our own bosses or other agencies. Relations with the local SB could be fraught at times in this respect. Most tension was based on a lack of personal chemistry between individuals, and more petty criteria, no different from any other working relationship in any 'workplace' environment, rather than any institutional issues. The FRU's relationship with the Special Branch was based on mutual respect and a realisation that cooperation and mutual support was essential in the struggle against our common enemy. But there was undoubtedly at times an element of professional jealousy and pure sour grapes when it was apparent that their reporting did not match ours for quality and timeliness. That is a reality in the intelligence game anywhere in the world, and we remained objective, unemotional and active in our attempts to provide collateral information.

Our reporting that I am most proud of emerged out of the blue with no prior build-up or expectation. We received the intelligence from several sub-sources but it was still greeted with raised eyebrows and giant question marks. We were the first intelligence agency to substantively identify the presence of surface-to-air missiles on the island of Ireland. This was a potential quantum escalation in PIRA's capability and a potential game-changer in south Armagh, where the Army's overt operations would have been crippled should our heli-force have been grounded. The whole issue of whether our reporting was accurate and credible remained in question until the media reported the SIS-led operation to intercept and board the cargo ship *Eksund* in French waters in November 1987. Its illicit cargo included twenty SAMs and 2 tonnes of Semtex explosive. Subsequent reporting stated that five previous Libyan shipments had been landed on the shores of the Republic, including SAMs, and that they were already safely housed in PIRA weapons hides. We had clearly identified at least a part of one of these shipments, if not more, identifying other weaponry in addition to the SAMs, and subsequent movements into the North across the border, including a quantity of US Army hand grenades. This was duly confirmed by one of the agent's unconscious sub-sources. We discussed the implications if the Dublin government were informed of our reporting, as they had been in the high-level agent case that had been resettled, only to return to the Province to home and death. We began to consider an extraction. We began also to consider the implications if the source was pushed too hard and we could not get him out. Additional regular reporting of the movement of more 'conventional' weaponry, including rifles, pistols and ammunition, along the border, we assessed, originated from the same shipments.

For the bulk of my tour we were receiving almost weekly updates on planned PIRA operations targeting the OP MAGISTRATE observation posts, the main XMG base, and other security force targets. Interestingly, we MISR'd intelligence that linked into, and corroborated, intelligence that had been passed by the Garda on one of the rare occasions we received product from the south. We pre-emptively predicted two mortar attacks but without sufficient hard detail to persuade TCG to deploy ambushes. One of these reports represented the first time an attack in south Armagh had identified the day, target and location of the base plate. No action was taken. But regardless, this was an incredible achievement for the FRU and the Army generally.

We confirmed the identities of active PIRA players and identified new activists who had, to date, remained faceless. Several of these new identities were openly scoffed at by SB until, with due passage of time, sufficient collateral reporting had swept aside their scepticism. We naturally experienced a degree of satisfaction when this happened. Every new piece in the south Armagh puzzle was an important addition and increased the chances of identifying a chink in PIRA's armour that might lead to a significant operational success.

On one occasion, we had informed SB that we expected a weapons move to take place during the hours of darkness the following night. TCG had decided not to react to the tip-off. We later learned that the SAS troop, however, had been keen to deploy but were not tasked. It was my assessment that at this juncture in the running of the case it really was important that we received collateral information in order to continue developing an asset that we assessed to be sound. HQ FRU shared my view. I decided that if none of the covert agencies could provide the confirmation we sought, we did have another, admittedly speculative, option. I knew that I might be able to get a helicopter and stand-off with a powerful night-viewing device. As it turned out, I was lucky enough to be able to book one for the following night, to synchronise with our reporting. I was slightly nervous despite this, because I knew well enough how the system worked – a tasking request with a higher priority could see ours slip to number two. With such limited availability, number two guaranteed the same priority as number ten on the list. In this specific instance, we had only one single shot – miss this and we would have to think again.

At 2230 hours, bang on schedule, the heli landed on the pad at the Mill and I climbed on board into the main cabin. We had not been bumped. I had not been able to get a clear look at the darkened outside of the airframe, but had waved to the crew of two in the cockpit as I moved to climb aboard. If they had been surprised to be picking up a passenger in plain clothes, I got no sense of this. It was a dark night that suited our task, and flying conditions were perfect.

There is an indefinable odour pervading all military airframes. Maybe it's a blend of avgas, ozone, warm electronics, nervous soldiery, aircrew ego – but it is distinctive. Smell is a massively underrated and undervalued sense but has the power to evoke so much. This militaristic perfume never failed to create the sense of being operational, of being on a mission. I inhaled deeply with the ardour of a two-packs-a-day man. I had brought a marked map with me and briefed the pilot over the intercom on where I wanted to go and what I wanted to achieve. They knew what to do. The heli lifted up and away and flew fast and low towards the stand-off location we had decided upon.

Coming in from the north, 'up wind' of the target, the crew put the helicopter north of my target location. I felt bonded in place to our piece of deep dark space. I had lost all sense of movement and motion, but I could feel the throbbing power from the engine resonating up through the soles of my boots and sense the deep rhythm through the cups of my headphones. We remained hovering on station, taking advantage of the cover of darkness, altitude and distance. I had no idea whether the crew had to hold the heli in position manually or whether they had engaged an autopilot, but I could sense that man and machine were working perfectly in unison. Anyone on the ground in the area of our target would have been totally oblivious of our presence. Even if we failed in our mission, I was reassured there was no source protection angle to provoke our concern.

I watched intently through the eerie green of the viewfinder. All was quiet and all was still. I almost began to fear that somehow the picture had frozen. There was little chat between the aircrew. It reinforced the impression of their professionalism. Following suit, I remained equally tight-lipped. I began to find that I had to exert progressively more effort to maintain my focus. I glanced at my watch. We had been on station for just over an hour now. We still had plenty of flying time left. I knew that when things happened, if they happened, there would be no forewarning and the action would be swift and quickly over. I maintained my concentration.

And then – 'Bingo', there it was, movement. Exactly as the source had briefed us, exactly what he said would happen, happened. A lone figure had emerged and was moving along the outside of the building. Something visually so minor and so insignificant but totally exhilarating. At that time, in that location, there could have been no other explanation for the activity we had observed. I was ecstatic. We had our collateral.* I thanked the crew for their professional support and their focus, literally, and we headed home to the Mill. The next day I briefed a delighted HQ.

We maintained a frenetic operational pace. We lived on what seemed to be a perpetual adrenalin high as our best-placed agents were met and debriefed regularly, and we processed the intelligence they delivered. The excitement of these meets was frequently enhanced by supplementary phone calls to which we had to react. They were great days. By this time we no longer felt any sense of being overshadowed by the city boys in E Det, although they did still have Brian Nelson. Of course, relative to the prodigious reporting of the Unit's top agent, all our efforts in East, North, out West and in the Mill didn't really compete. But we had caught the Belfast boys up in terms of the impact of our operations and they no longer enjoyed a monopoly on success. I felt an immense feeling of pride in my team and what they were achieving.

We received intelligence identifying the bombers who were responsible for the bomb that took the lives of the XMG Royal Anglian Company Commander, an ex-MIO, and two RUC uniformed colleagues. Another agent passed on intelligence relating to PIRA's attempts to overcome our electronic countermeasures and that they were ready to recommence attacks against green patrols and reduce their reliance on mortars. Strategic-level

* Racing forwards to today, of course, we now inhabit a battlespace over which the drone rules supreme. In a generation, airborne observation and intelligence gathering has advanced beyond our wildest comprehension back on that night in south Armagh, but everything is relative and you can only work with what you have. Nevertheless, the technology I witnessed then was state of the art and it was both impressive and effective.

intelligence of this quality was absolutely vital in guiding government scientific development projects and impacted directly on Army operational tasking.

We reported on the location of a likely PIRA mortar assembly area. Regrettably, it appeared to be no longer in use, so would not trigger a reactive covert operation. Intelligence of more IRA uniforms, and an armoured truck north of the border, was eventually corroborated when it was later discovered by Gardai in the south. We had no indication as to PIRA's intent and this subsequently remained a mystery. Another report confirmed the close relationship between PIRA and Sinn Fein in the region – the politicos, interestingly, it was reported, were kept aware of impending attacks within their political constituency.

An agent reporting in Newry provided an overview of Republican activity, invariably INLA, in the town and the shifting relationships between the various factions on the estates, including the Official IRA, OIRA, or Stickies as they were known, otherwise a grouping that had all but disappeared from the political, and paramilitary, scene outside of the town. We reported the occasional presence of armed men but it was a reality that TCG was focussed on the bigger fish that swam much closer to the border.

The Det did pass on two specific close-quarter assassination threats regarding off-duty members of the RUC and UDR. Our first threat report was issued based on the source picking up that local Republican members were targeting an RUC officer who regularly visited his mother in the village. The second report was from an agent living on the coast. He had observed the movements and actions of two PIRA members known to him. Knowing the identity of the individual that they appeared to be watching, and knowing that he was a member of the UDR, he was able to conclude that the soldier was being targeted for assassination. Both cases illustrate the value of low-level eyes-and-ears sources. Neither source had associate, let alone any degree of direct access, but they were trained, motivated agents who took their role seriously. For most of their working lives their reporting furnished the mix of vegetables that bulk out the stew. But then once in a while they came up with the meat that makes the dish. When these cases produce exploitable intelligence, the added bonus is that it is easy to act upon with none of the complexities and nuances of source protection to vector into the equation. I have always fully supported the strategy of maintaining the broadest swathe of eyes-and-ears reporting in a layered approach to targeting intelligence collection. You just never know what you might get. In both instances maybe we saved some lives.

These few paragraphs undoubtedly come across as a little flat and perhaps even disappointingly sparse. In reality they represent, and are indicative of, the two and a half years of reporting during my time as OC, and represent hundreds and hundreds of hours of hard and dangerous graft, gallons of sweat and some tears, and hundreds of thousands of calories of expended nervous energy, as well as a few trees' worth of paper reports. But this is as much as I can say to represent what we did, what a FRU detachment did, and what an anti-terrorist agent handling team can do. The dozens and dozens and dozens of other reports and snippets of intelligence are meaningless outside of their immediate context in our corner of the Troubles in this specific and unique region of the Six Counties in the mid-1980s.

We had one gap in our operational capability that our reporting graphically emphasised and re-emphasised repeatedly. It had struck me during my time with TC. We consistently reported on persons, places and events south of the border. But to us this was another world very much through the looking glass, and on the other side. We had no way to bring life to this reporting. Even making reference to mapping was no easy feat. Sheets were woefully outdated and extremely expensive – thirty Irish Punt per sheet, thirty-five years ago, was a lot of money. To put it in perspective, that constituted the weekly rent for a three-bedroom bungalow within commuting distance of Belfast. When we met agents and debriefed on things south of the border, we unavoidably lost credibility on the one hand, and failed to maximise the information that was being brought to us, through our ignorance. We had no operational remit to operate in the Republic. When we extracted our compromised agent, we could not plan any contingency that involved us crossing the border. When we needed to verify information or simply talk with confidence about a pub, a street in Dundalk, a business, or whatever, we could not. Now, I was aware that in the past handlers had gone south on occasion to check on specific matters – indeed, I had too, and it was common practice for other agencies to stray in order to answer specific tasking – but this was strictly beyond the bounds of our operational remit, and compromise in these instances would have provoked awkward questions at the highest levels.

This hole was one thing that Hamish focussed in on and began lobbying CLF for support. We began putting together a potential SOP to provide the direction and scope governing cross-border incursions that would further reassure the General that risk would be managed professionally, and was, in reality, minimal. Looking back, it is glaringly obvious how this operational concept was limited and restricted by the primitive state of communications equipment. Operations were much less flexible and required a much more disciplined approach to communicating and responding to contingencies, and probably were in reality more dangerous because of this.

Phase one of our draft SOP required the operators to travel to Dublin from Belfast by train. They would travel without weapons, radios or military ID cards. Once in the Fair City, a car, or cars, would be hired using the operators' mainland driving licences. If possible, vehicles fitted with in-car telephones would be procured. To reinforce the cover, a hotel would be booked in Dublin and paid for using a mainland credit card and receipts kept. There would be no identifiable link to the Province in any of these transactions. A strict reporting-in schedule would be maintained via pay phone, or car phone, to the support/emergency reaction team based back across the border in Bessbrook. The next operational phase would see the cross-border team travelling to their operational target/recce location(s) along pre-briefed routes, maintaining the reporting-in schedule. Upon completion of the recce, the team would return to Dublin and catch the train back to Belfast.

The General proved a willing ally and he took the issue to the Foreign and Commonwealth Office on King Charles Street for ministerial approval. We got the sanction we required and the official mandate, at the risk of invoking at least seven years' of bad luck, to crack that mirror. In the event, our incursions were mounted no less carefully and selectively, but without the formality of the stipulations of our initial draft SOP with its requirement to travel via Dublin. It was unnerving to be 'naked' when we crossed the border but we never experienced a single problem. The enhanced 'vision' these ops generated was invaluable, and if nothing else considerably bolstered the handlers' confidence, and credibility, when discussing issues beyond the Six Counties.

At one point it looked as though PIRA in Crossmaglen had begun to have suspicions about the existence of a tout in their ranks. To safeguard their security and deter those ASU members who might turn and come to us, PIRA even procured a polygraph machine from the US. We briefly started to construct a plan to extract the agent we assessed to be most at threat should this be required. We assessed that this was operationally premature in the absence of a specific, clearly identifiable threat, and instead considered reinforcing the agent's credibility by requesting TCG to insert a COP that our source could then compromise and expose to PIRA.

In the event, this plan was overtaken by events and became unnecessary – it was always potentially dangerous to be forced into taking this sort of pre-emptive affirmative action, raising heads above metaphorical parapets without being able to completely control the narrative. But we had gone as far as getting airborne in a Gazelle helicopter to recce the ideal site for our 'dummy' OP position. While we were in the air, PIRA attacked one of the MAGISTRATE positions. Using the pilot's stabilised binoculars, we capitalised on our unplanned eagle-eyed view over the area. We were the first SF on the scene and proceeded to attempt to identify the ASU. We quickly found the burnt-out car used by the terrorists, but they had escaped and melted back into the secure embrace of their heartland.

The local company, of course, drew the false conclusion that we had advance knowledge of the attack and were on hand to witness its execution – no way, of course, would a threat be pre-emptively anticipated and no advance warning issued by us to our own side. Equally, if their suspicion had been justified, we would not compromise any operation to hit the terrorists by swanning about on the scene, whether in a helicopter or in an ocean-going yacht. What were we, Boy Scouts?

As trained intelligence collectors, we were also able to report our own de visu intelligence. We dedicated one of our source numbers, 6009, as the mode by which we disseminated this type of reporting – obviously no CFs were recorded, but periodically a 6009 MISR would do the rounds. We had already identified a PIRA player who had thus far not been named. While on another job the lads spotted him north of Newry, way out of his own habitat in what was considered safe country. He appeared to be involved in some activity that could have been linked to a barn complex. We reported the intelligence to SB but never received feedback as to whether he was engaged in personal, criminal, or terrorist-related activity. We would regularly observe prominent players in the Newry area. Of course, in reality the majority of sightings could be explained as ordinary and innocent. Even hardened ruthless terrorists need to restock the fridge, snag a new pair of wellies, or a new pair of flares for next Saturday night's ceilidh.

While providing cover for a source pick-up, one of the lads reported the appearance of a large articulated lorry that had approached the border from the north and stopped 50 metres inside British territory. A white transit van then crossed the border from the south and stopped beside it. The handler radioed this back to the ops desk before having to move to get into position for the pick-up. Later during the operation, he spotted the same white van in Newry. He passed on this sighting to the duty NCO, who immediately alerted the RUC. They were quick to react and foiled a massive smuggling operation that quite conceivably would have channelled yet more funding into PIRA's war chest.

Of course, consistent with Clausewitzian logic, our agents were run in support of and to inform government policy. We did not exist inside the vacuum of a military/law enforcement bubble. The direct consequence of this reality was that the fate of an agent could depend on political expediency. In my time this impacted us forcefully, harshly and with the utmost permanence on North Det FRU. Any of us could have found ourselves in the same boat. North had recruited a very high-level agent. Through their skilled case development, he had become the PIRA Northern Command quartermaster, a dream position for an agent-handling organisation. His access provided the FRU with an unparalleled oversight of PIRA's logistical tail, particularly with regard to the massive arms shipments that had entered the Republic en route from Mu'ammar Qaddafi's Libya. Unfortunately for the agent, and for the long-term exploitation of the case, this operational gold mine had burst open as the Hillsborough accord sat on the table below the raised pens of the two respective government leaders, Margaret Thatcher and Garret Fitzgerald. In order to seal the deal, the case was laid open and those hides that were under our agent's control, in the south, were raided in the full realisation that the source's security could not be maintained. He was pulled out by the Det and moved to safety into the care of the Liaison Branch at Specialist Intelligence Wing in Ashford to start a new life.

I was briefed at the end of January 1986. By May, he had fatefully been in direct telephone contact with PIRA on at least a number of separate occasions. Martin McGuinness had personally, and with insuperable and cynical guile, persuaded him that his safe return to Ireland could be negotiated. Inextricably, he completely failed to recognise this preposterous assertion and agreed to return home. His body was dumped by the roadside on the border.

I remember the new Operations Warrant Officer being posted into the FRU HQ up in HQNI in Lisburn. Johnny E was an old hand and a thoroughly good guy for whom I would develop a great deal of time and fondness. He was scheduled to come to the Mill to gain a perspective on our operational profile and re-familiarise himself with the patch, since he had not been back since the late 1970s.

Sitting down in my office during one of our several brainstorming, and lamp-swinging, sessions, Johnny talked about his time on the border. It was fascinating how, in just those relatively few years, the whole operational scene had changed from an almost 'make it up as you go along' approach to the highly structured and disciplined approach that guided our operations.

Johnny's appearance reminded me of the utmost admiration and respect that I had always powerfully felt for Robert Nairac's courage, commitment and contribution. His lasting legacy for me was translated, in a living blend of positive and negative emotion, into the brooding, sinister image of south Armagh that his abduction and murder imposed on the land – I was never able to shake this sense of pervading background darkness all the time I operated on the border. I think this was a personal thing linked to my own reaction to his fate, perhaps rarely something that none of the other lads in the Det thought about, but I never discussed the subject with anyone, maybe to some extent out of a superstitious desire not to tempt the fates, until I sat down with Johnny. But it was always there, ever present, in the background, shaping the sense of respect I felt for the very real threat we faced down there, guiding and reminding that there were limits and constraints as to how far we could push and how daring we could be in our operations.

I had already been able to assemble a framework picture of the way he had operated during his brief time in south Armagh. I vividly remembered hearing on the news reports of his disappearance, his suspected abduction and murder, and the chilling effect this had had on me, as a youth of 17 intent on joining military intelligence. When I had eventually made it to Sandhurst on my pre-university course as a young cadetship officer a year later, I had been walking down one of the warren of corridors in my college when, suddenly, there before me was a photograph of him sitting, bearskin on knee, in his ceremonial uniform, a proud, dashing, handsome young officer, so full of hope and optimism for a long distinguished career ahead of him. It was a moment, so strong in terms of its impact, that I have never forgotten. I had hoped that Johnny might be able to add some substantive detail, or if not, then at least some superficial texture to enhance my own picture, but unfortunately he could not.

I had already found an old document written by Nairac. It was short, encapsulating his personal views on building relationships in the wider south Armagh community, but it was a sound piece of work. It demonstrated a clear understanding of the art from someone who was not actually a trained agent handler.* It appeared

* It has already been published in Toby Harnden's truly excellent book *Bandit Country*, in my opinion one of the best-informed works on the Troubles, and I reproduce it in Annex B.

that Nairac had effectively 'free-lanced' out of the Mill, following an operational remit of his own creation, as a complete romantic, regularly going out on patrol armed with a Wingmaster shotgun. It equally appeared that on numerous occasions he had entered pubs along the border on his own, regularly ending the evening singing traditional and Republican songs, always with the finale of 'The Soldiers' Song', before his last fateful 'performance' in the 'Three Steps'.

After that fateful night of his disappearance in Drumintee, the immediate spontaneous reaction of those who had found his bed unslept in the following morning was to assume, erroneously, that his absence was the consequence of his 'doing a runner' and going south following some fanciful notion to join the rebel cause.

Everything I had been able to uncover supported the evidence that Robert Nairac had been a complicated but gifted maverick.** His unconventionality was a throwback to another time and another era of military operations, more akin to Kipling's *Kim* and The Great Game, but for me his operational persona was founded on nothing if not staggering courage. Captain Bob had walked the thin line between hero and madman and fatally taken just one step too many.

During the latter stage of my posting, in November 1987, I was tasked by the CO to stand in as the Ops Offr while Peter was away for two weeks. I was the youngest of the Det Commanders and the junior in terms of life and wider Corps experience. I was very flattered and excited at the prospect of sitting at the operational helm of the unit at the desk across which everything of note flowed. I had no idea then that I would be back, longer term, sitting in the HQ the following year. It became clear that this had been a trial to assess the wisdom of this plan.

My trial 'attachment' got off to a roaring start. My works car wouldn't start, so I had to drive into Thiepval on day one in my own personal vehicle.

I very rapidly realised that, yes, we were busy in the Dets and we unquestionably squeezed the juice out of every minute, but here,

** Read *Blood Knots: Of Fathers, Friendship and Fishing* by Luke Jennings for an easy page-turner looking back at Nairac's earlier years.

up on the ship's bridge, the level of intensity was raised to a super charged level. We were navigating a supertanker. Being the boss in the Mill was akin to being the player-manager of a top Premier League side. Accessing the Ops Offr's filing cabinet was, in comparison, like managing the syndicated rights for world heavyweight boxing, Twenty20 cricket, and the Rugby World Cup.

By 0830 hours I had already received update briefs from all four Dets – excluding the team who were still busy processing the product from the latest meet of our most prodigious asset – since Peter would last have talked to them before the weekend prior to his departure. At 0845 hours I went over to the senior intelligence staff officer's office, ACOS G2, the assistant chief of staff for intelligence, in the main HQNI building, to take part in his all-source update in preparation for his update to CLF. All the covert agencies attended.

We had received intelligence on PIRA technical modifications to increase the effectiveness of their IEDs. This critically revealed that our electronic countermeasures had put PIRA on the technical back foot. They perceived that they now had to find a quick fix or we, the security forces, had negated their most important weapon. I was able to feed in some intelligence relating to some covert technical attacks on fixed targets and a critical source protection-related report.

It was the Ops Offr's responsibility to pass on any high-level FRU intelligence to SB headquarters. This gave me the opportunity to start to build some relationships that I would continue on my return. We were scrupulous in informing SB on everything that was important and that they needed to know. I also briefed up to Harry Mc in his capacity as RHSB Rural to ensure that he was aware of the implications of our IED-related update.

I was briefed that the seizure of the *Eksund* had probably frustrated PIRA's intention to escalate the level of violence in the Province, and in doing so had undoubtedly saved untold lives. It was interesting to interact at this higher level with a few of the liaison contacts I maintained in Bessbrook. I think it certainly increased my credibility when I returned to the Mill and resumed my 'normal' level of exchange.

That first evening I left for home at 1930 hours, poised for out-of-hours contact at any time, and expecting it to come.

As the week progressed, int continued to come in from the Dets as they worked through their meet programmes. N Det passed information on a PIRA own-goal that claimed the lives of three volunteers when the device they were working on exploded, and personalities at the subsequent funeral. E Det reported on a PIRA sniper attack on Springfield Road RUC station in the west of the city. I slipped back to Bessbrook on the Thursday of my first week to meet our number one target to continue the 'romancing' process.

ACOS grabbed me and asked me to write up a consolidated report on all our intelligence relating to arms moves in the border area, following the revelations that there had been five possible arms shipments into the Republic pre-*Eksund*.

On Sunday, 8 November, PIRA exploded a device at the Enniskillen Poppy Day parade. One of our agents called reporting that PIRA would be claiming the bomb – it was supposed to explode fifteen minutes later than it did. Hamish's mother was due to attend the parade but on the day was bedded down sick. As the details of this outrageous attack unfolded, I continued to work on the paper for ACOS. In the end, I completed it five minutes before he needed it in order to brief a conference that Monday evening. I had had the HQ collators slaving all afternoon on the detailed annexes. But, just in time is on time.

Back in the Mill, and back relegated to my lowly position as the Det Commander, on a lighter note, four of us from the Det decided it would be a good idea to participate in the Mourne Mountain Marathon – after all, it was on our back doorstep. It was a tough but satisfying test, two days of up hill and down dale, but we completed it without drama.

More fun was Hamish's initiative to form an FRU rugby team. Rather cheekily, we purchased a consignment of white-motifed Fijian Rugby Union shirts. I am sure opposing teams were puzzled by the significance of the palm tree logo – our three-letter initials would, however, have aroused little attention or interest. I played during the 1987–88 season out on the wing. We played other military sides in the Province and a few civilian teams. It was tremendous fun and special to be able to come together as a unit outside the strict confines of our separate working lives.

I have frequently rustled up an image in my mind that I have never forgotten, one that, without fail, always brings a smile to my face. It will serve as my only comment on the nature of true love.

I was parked late one night in Belfast just to the north of the city centre. It was a dark night, and as I sat in the car keeping an eye on the activity in the general area around me, a young couple came out of the pub on the other side of the small piece of waste ground just across the road from where I was parked. It was clear that they had been drinking but were still fit enough to walk with a reasonable degree of control, mutually supporting each other on their journey to I know not where. For whatever reason, they decided to break it and sat down heavily, still in supportive mode, on a low wall at the plot's edge. Naturally enough, perhaps, they began locking lips and supporting each other even more firmly. With little else to engage my interest, I watched on in mild curiosity. Deciding to surface for air, the young woman struggled to break the engagement, succeeded, half turned her upper body to one side and vomited copiously onto the rough broken surface of the waste ground. Involuntarily I braced myself, straightening my sitting position, in anticipation of the couple's follow-up to this rather unpleasant, unscripted development. I could have remained relaxed. She turned back in to her partner, and almost in the same flowing motion, the two resumed their vigorous and passionate embrace with absolutely no loss of momentum. After observing that moment of unparalleled intimacy, I felt cheated not to have subsequently been invited to the wedding.

I began recording these words with PIRA's mortaring of our base of operations in the normally peaceful – helicopters apart – little village of Bessbrook. Once the dust had settled, I recalled that we had received intelligence at the beginning of March that PIRA had aborted an operation in mid-flow that had all the hallmarks of a mortar attack. The assessment at the time had been that the target was most likely to be one of the two RUC stations in Newry. With hindsight, the PIRA team had probably been en route to deliver their mortars to us, and the problems they had encountered then had led them to return in mid-April. PIRA had deployed players from one of the Crossmaglen groups and from the Camlough team, about eleven men in total. Is it a coincidence that Liam Campbell, found guilty in the civil trial of orchestrating the Omagh bombing that took the lives of twenty-nine people in August 1998, was spotted in Bessbrook by one of our sources days before the attack? Another reported that immediately after the mortaring he appeared to have gone 'on the run', probably to his native Dundalk. The driver of the tractor towing the mortar trailer had been picked up by a car and was indeed driven away to safety once he had positioned his potentially deadly load. Of the sixteen mortars fired, thirteen were identified in the Mill compound. Despite there being some minor injuries, incredibly there were no fatalities. We had been uncannily fortunate. One could speculate that had the attack been launched those six weeks before, we might not have been so lucky. Again, the perverse hand of fate. What was heartening for us were the calls we received from a number of our sources phoning in to check that we were OK. We must have been doing more than a few things right. I guess these calls represented handler–source relationships that were strong, genuine and ultimately human.

As I approached the planned halfway point of my tour, my mind naturally began to wander and seek focus on what might lay ahead. It was clear to me that if the Army had it in mind to broaden my professional horizons and bring me back in line for the balanced career of the generalist and the commensurate promotion and advancement that having been a Cadetship officer had indicated, I was definitely not interested. I wanted resolutely to remain in the special duties world. I loved the challenges and excitement of the world of agent handling and I knew that I was fortunate enough to enjoy a natural aptitude. I revelled in the processes, both mental and physical: the adrenalin buzz of operations both in and out of plain clothes, the psychology, the requirement for unconventional and lateral thinking, and frankly this no-nonsense world with its lack of red tape and bullshit. Agent handling was something that flowed and swirled comfortably around, and I believed through, me. The whole discipline felt natural. I considered it an art form. It was just something I could 'do'. I imagined, as a completely non-musical individual, that it was like a gifted pianist who felt the music he played and could listen to a piece and instinctively find the right keys to play back the experience.

When I looked around and identified postings I thought I would enjoy and that would be challenging, I quickly saw that life could even more quickly become difficult. Not only would I have to be in sync for positions becoming vacant, but there would be other candidates with similar aspirations. I began to wonder if, despite my gratitude at my good fortune to date, the future that would bring me the most personal happiness and satisfaction, and allow me to contribute the most, might lie outside the military with a civilian agency. I had a number of very focussed conversations with Oliver the ASP and began to think about options with the Security Service or SIS. Oliver organised for me to travel to London to meet the MI5 recruiters.

I was impressed, and the guaranteed prospect of spending the rest of my working life in agent operations was enormously attractive – of course, post-9/11 the focus would have hardened even more with renewed emphasis generated by the commitment to the war on terror. An alternative option appeared to be to contract for a five-year period in the Province running agents out of the IJS. With a foot in the door, this appeared to be an initial step into a longer-term relationship once one had proved oneself. However, Oliver's successor Peter actually counselled me to wait and remain in the Corps. The postings machine started grinding away. First to pop out of the end was the flattering option of going to Sandhurst as the Int Corp's instructor, effectively the face of the Corps as far as cadet officers were concerned. Then came the option of remaining in the Province, either working with the MIO/FINCO HQ team, or as the MIO Border, a new post to be set up once the Third Army Brigade, 3 Bde, was established covering the whole rural TAOR. But once the CO in SIW in Ashford, Ian, a lovely man, and my original boss in the FRU when I arrived in S Det, pitched in asking me to come to the handling branch, I cast aside my fears and doubts and realised that my continued future and loyalty did lie with the Corps. I did not for another moment regret this decision.

Hamish was keen to prompt SIW to update and realign training.* They had now introduced a pre-selection week to objectively screen applicants and minimise wastage on the course. The pre-select tested practical skills, handling aptitude, personal motivation and commitment. The OP MAXIMISE recruiting campaign, mirroring 14 Coy's own, had begun to increase the number of volunteers coming forward, now that we were recruiting from all three services, so we could now afford the luxury of turning away those who were patently unsuitable rather than potentially losing a training place on the Research course – there were to be no more repeats of the 1985 course cancellation.

We wanted operators to be able to routinely incorporate anti- and counter-surveillance drills to enhance our operational security, both for agents and for handlers. The requirement for constant anti-surveillance awareness was graphically underlined by a tale from Belfast, a tale as tragic as it was unpardonable. A Special Branch handler had been observed meeting a source, and at meet's end dropped off the asset to return to his office. Unbeknown to him, the agent had been spotted and recognised, by chance, by a fellow PIRA member. Showing some initiative, the terrorist decided, out of curiosity, to follow the unknown 'acquaintance' of his comrade, in equal measure to feed his curiosity and to allay his suspicions. Perhaps to his surprise, he was led to a police station in the city and the fate of the agent was sealed. Had the handler been more alert – or any cover team supporting him, if there was one – or conducted even the most elementary anti-surveillance drills, his tail might have been lost or more actively shaken off and the agent might have survived a security team interrogation with a simple but effective cover story. Very, very sad.

---

* We considered enhancing our CQB training to adopt some of the drills that 14 Coy included in their training package – for instance, quick reaction aggressive drills to free an operator in the immediate aftermath of his or her capture – but rejected it. We very much relied on our tradecraft to mitigate these risks and were fortunate to be able to control our operational environment more readily than they could.

(Just to clarify the terminology, as there are even intelligence professionals who confuse the two concepts. Anti-surveillance drills provide an operator with the skills to identify hostile surveillance and to overtly or covertly defeat it if he is required to. Counter-surveillance drills provide the good guys with the capability to identify hostile surveillance on one of their own assets.)

Working in conjunction with SIW, we scheduled our first Advanced Agent Handling Course to identify and trial key surveillance-related lessons. Those of us in the unit who attended would be the first trial 'students'.

About a dozen of us travelled back to the Manor and spent the next week 'playing' with Surveillance Branch, sharpening our skills and practising melding surveillance-related serials onto our own tactical routines. We concentrated on identifying the most effective counter-surveillance tricks, and which anti-surveillance techniques would most effectively identify hostile surveillance and defeat it.

For the final exercise, Hamish nominated me to plan and lead our consolidatory operation and final agent meeting. I had an hour to plan and write my orders before briefing the team. This was a pretty tight deadline. I felt more under pressure than at any time on any course past or future. As a Det Commander performing under the full scrutiny of my Commanding Officer, another Det Commander, a couple of handfuls of handlers from the unit, plus the surveillance team members, this had to go well, if not perfectly.

In the event, I planned for a dummy handler's car to leave our exercise start location in advance of the real handling team. The surveillance team took the bait. This left the real handler to deploy for the agent pick-up with a totally clean tail, which he was able to confirm with some simple but definitive anti-surveillance drills. The rest of the run went equally to plan. We totally defeated the surveillance team tasked against us and were able to stage our meet securely without compromise. If we could defeat trained surveillance professionals, then we could counter any operation PIRA might mount against us.

Hamish's vision was not only to grow our access, enhance our tactics, supplement our equipment holdings and provide new capability, he was intent on growing the unit. Once 'ownership' of the FRU changed and the central MOD took responsibility for our mission, we began to enjoy better resourcing. The number of handlers in the unit rose to fifty, with a commensurate supporting staff. Hamish also envisioned increasing the size of the headquarters element. And this effectively took care of my immediate destiny. Peter had dropped a cryptic comment about remaining with the unit after my time in Bessbrook was up, but I did not really pay too much attention to his words. When Hamish announced that he was creating an Intelligence Officer post in the HQ and that he wanted me to be the inaugural incumbent, I jumped at the opportunity. I knew it could only be for one year, because, for career reasons, I needed to complete a staff post as a captain, my SO3 slot, to secure my promotion to major. Nevertheless, I decided to risk this unknown part of the equation for another breath of special duties air. In the event, it was entirely the right course to take because I was to go to BRIXMIS as a staff officer, even though all operational posts in the unit were staff appointments, and following my three years there I got my opportunity to work in SIW, going there as the Training Officer, running all three branches, including a six-month tour in Bosnia. When I pan forwards and add commanding the HUMINT unit in Cyprus and then globe-trotting as a trouble shooter as a Military Intelligence Liaison Officer – including operational deployments to the conflict in Kosovo, the emergency in Sierra Leone, and reporting on the wars in Angola and Sri Lanka – when I look back I am amazed at just how lucky I was, and how I really do not think I could have planned things so well with a pen and a blank piece of paper.

I handed over to George Moore in the spring of 1988 with the less than inspiring but unavoidable formality of first completing my Junior Division of Staff College (JDSC) career course at Warminster, the heart of Army country, before I could return. George was a lovely guy and tragically yet another of those who perished in a helicopter crash. I knew his wife and his young son, which made it all the harder to reconcile.

I felt a really searching feeling of grief and sadness at leaving S Det. They had been marvellous years bursting full of sheer hard work and commitment, bolstered by a sense of achievement against very real and enduring odds. I felt tired, but not the limb-numbing sense of exhaustion that drains one's will, faith and hope. I felt I had matured into a professional leader and operator with much more to offer, and felt buoyed by the energy and resolve that the appreciation of success and our collective achievement had generated. I maintained the strong belief that agent handling, while certainly not providing any silver bullets, was the greatest weapon we had to hit the terrorists hard, and if we just continued pushing, probing and continuing to build our reporting base we would continue to inflict life-threatening damage to the mind and body of our enemy. I had ridden my good fortune and not for one moment was oblivious of the good luck I had encountered in the job along the way. But I had worked hard to hone my skills and develop the personal credibility to command my men and hold my own with those in the unit who had been older, more experienced and probably, at heart, resentful of a young Regular officer intruding into a world that they thought was their own. It was the prospect of ending this interaction, especially leaving the lads who I considered as my team – even though, by this stage, none of the original faces on my arrival were still serving – that I regretted most. But the knowledge that I would be back, only just up the road, in a mere three months eased my passage.

16

THE 3IC

Despite my lack of anticipation, I actually enjoyed my time on JDSC fighting with, and against, the staff handbooks, and embracing the fanciful exercises against the Soviet menace, which of course was still the prime focus of the rest of our, and our allies', armed forces.

The DS were generally fair-minded and represented good role models for us, the younger generation of up-and-comers. And it was nice to know a few other officers on the course, including Dick, the Royal Marines officer who had been my opposite number with S Det 14 Coy.

The first part of the course dealt with tactics and logistics. The appeal of tackling these tactical issues was that it was all largely new to me at the elevated level we were studying. I enjoyed the intellectual challenge even though I found the practical lessons largely irrelevant. The teaching was slick and professional. One thing the military can never be faulted for is its preparation when it comes to delivering a message. Everything was polished and rehearsed. There was no packing or waffling or lack of focus. I particularly enjoyed the module on counter-revolutionary warfare and wrote a short paper on the issue of Internment in the Province during the early 1970s.

My exposure to logistics was the catalyst for the sincere appreciation and utmost professional respect that I feel towards these unsung heroes of our military: the professional logisticians. The reality of any conflict is that if the fighting troops are not supplied, and not re-supplied, in a timely way with the right scaling of munitions and equipment, not even a race of armed supermen will prevail. The Falklands was the classic example of this, and had our supply of artillery shells run out, as it so nearly did, there may not have been a Union Flag fluttering above Port Stanley to this day. That said, I hated having to work through the logistical lessons we were mandated to learn, still less to practise them. Let there remain horses for courses.

The second half of the course was an introduction to military technology. It was not as punchy or quite as well run, but thankfully it passed without too much stress or ennui. I did struggle to demonstrate the required enthusiasm when we were discussing various artillery-related issues, communications theory, the volume under armour concepts governing main battle tank design, but I did get a ride in a Chieftain, which was fun, and a US CH-53 Jolly Green Giant helicopter.

I was back almost before I knew it. I have to say that on the negative side, my brief interlude of schooling was soon forgotten. Positively, recalling the even briefer time I had spent standing in for Peter had allowed me to realistically recalibrate my sights, and I feared no surprises or tasks from left field as I occupied my new office.

The hours were as relentless and unceasing as I expected. In my whole career I have never experienced the levels of stress that I did then as IO FRU. I seemed to bounce from one call to another, from one complementary task to another, and from one meeting to another. There was rarely a moment to pause and contemplate my navel or anything else. I would come in on Saturdays, and if it was a quiet day, manage to slip away at lunchtime. If not, then it could be late. It was not uncommon to be in on Sundays too. It was all analogous to boxing. A boxer soaks up so much punishment – takes, and gives, so many blows – that in the end he feels nothing and recalls nothing. The last time I was in the ring at Sandhurst, I had to move up a weight from light heavy as we had no fighter in that category, eating to put on weight. The bout was a real slugging match and really gruelling. At the final bell I had a ticking nerve in my upper lip for the next two months but absolutely no memory of the fight whatsoever – not a single blow. Working in HQ FRU was a bit like this, without the tick. Looking back, the whole experience is a bit of a blur and I am struggling to pick out dialogue, detail and decisions.

Against this level of activity, I also had to study for my promotion exams to major and complete the regular assignments. I tried pointing out to the staff running the programme – it felt as though they were as remote, disconnected and disinterested as a team occupying some call centre in outer Reading – that I could not always meet the deadlines because I was kind of busy on an operational special duties tour in Northern Ireland, but this got the predictable response. Basically, so what. I probably just came across as arrogant. It would have been nice to be home at 1700 hours every evening and have Wednesday afternoons off as sports afternoons, but I am absolutely positive that the novelty would have worn off completely by the following Tuesday. I thought it was poor, though, and completely representative of the green army/14 Sigs/BAOR attitude to reality. But take the rough with the smooth – would I have wanted that tame existence in some far-flung German outback, like a Langeleben?

The greater part of my day was spent in conversation with the Dets, very much in receive mode as they briefed on the latest agent meets. As I had done before, I distilled the salient highlights into less-heavy briefs for the CO and Peter – it was an unrelenting barrage of reporting. The most intense 'downloads' were from the regular debriefs of our most prodigious source. The volume, quality and consistency of the intelligence was phenomenal. So too was the quality of the source's two handlers, Mark D and Gary F. They had an amazing grip on the product and were invaluable in providing big-picture context for the reporting, as well as teasing out all the minute implications of this and that. I cannot praise that whole team enough.

The days slipped by. I still got the chance to get out to the Dets but not so frequently. I continued attending the weekly update briefs for ACOS, but my treat for good behaviour was my regular run to Knock, spearheading our liaison, to sit down with the SB leadership. They were always welcoming; a visitor is always a source of interest, and I liked to think that my forthrightness and easy manner was, if not a positive aid to maintaining the link, perhaps at least an interesting novelty. But I always detected a palpable atmosphere of underlying coolness counterbalancing the smiles, handshakes and good wishes.

At this level there was definitely a broader focus and perspective. It was not just about driving operations and ensuring intelligence was used in the most effective way possible to damage the terrorists. The reality beyond this operational aim was strategic. Of greater existential priority was maintaining supremacy in the battle for resources and political kudos. The RUC were top dogs and they had to maintain this position. Against this mindset, my presence represented and served as a reminder of the potential threat to this supremacy that we were seen to pose – our demonstrable contribution as a committed ally mattered less. I think that, fundamentally, they reflected their own ways of doing business on us and believed that we were not sharing all our intelligence with them – somehow, for some reason, we were always holding something back. Certainly in my experience this was absolutely not the case. We had no empire to build and we were firmly and fully committed to our Military Aid to the Civil Authority, MACA, role, which we understood and supported. But ultimately you see the world from where you stand.

What we also began doing ourselves, excitingly, as a Headquarters, was more systematic targeting of players in the higher echelons within PIRA. We mounted a few jobs as the Headquarters team with backup from E Det when we needed it. One particular high-calibre target was Brendan 'Darkie' Hughes, a well-known senior player who had fallen out with the Adams faction.

'Darkie's' PIRA CV is an impressive testament to his commitment to the Republican movement. He had served as the Belfast Brigade OC and he led the 1980 Hunger Strike. As the Brigade OC, he was instrumental in the Bloody Friday attack of July 1972, which remained the biggest single bombing attack during the whole campaign. He was interned along with Gerry Adams the following year, and as one of the original hunger strikers he lasted fifty-three days without food before Bobby Sands took over the lead of the second wave that ended after the death of ten of them. 'The Dark' was released from prison in 1986 and returned to Belfast. He grew progressively more and more disillusioned with the political direction in which Adams was leading the Republican movement, and for the last eight years, until his death in 2008, he remained estranged from the struggle and from Adams, his former close personal friend and IRA comrade.

When we decided to target him, Hughes was traced as working with the IRA's internal security unit, their counter-intelligence unit tasked to investigate failed operations and hunt down the touts who PIRA knew were destroying its operational capability. Direct access into this team would provide us with invaluable intelligence. We knew it was a long shot and at best speculative, but we knew that the destabilising effects of a failed approach would still create benefit – the usual win–win for us.

We sent him an invitation to meet in the city centre and deployed a large team just in case he showed. We took his absence at the pick-up point on the first attempt as just a case of bad manners and tried again. I remember parking behind the Europa Hotel waiting for the report over the net that he had been sighted. But he remained a stranger and we abandoned the attempt.*

It was great to deploy together and go through the process as the ultimate FRO. It meant we could all keep our professional hands in, and beyond this, I also think it set a positive example and sent a positive message to the Dets. We were actively targeting high-grade players in an attempt to improve the unit's access, even though, as they knew, we had our own massive work burden leading and directing the unit – we were not just a talking shop but operators too.

Complementing our systematic targeting efforts, we stumbled across a fascinating individual. He was a 'walk-in' – more aptly

* I have to say that even the most cursory reading of the first part of Ed Moloney's *Voices from the Grave* makes it pretty clear that there was absolutely no way that 'Darkie' would have sold his soul to the devil, even given his disillusionment with the Provisionals, but it was worth a try.

stumbling across us, rather than a target we had identified and pursued. In this scenario we assumed the initial passive role. There are always three possible scenarios waiting to play out with this type of case. The first is the attempt by one's adversary to get inside your organisation, dangling a carrot when in reality they are pushing a double agent. This was a tactic that PIRA did not seem to have attempted to exploit. The second potential ending is the happiest – the volunteer is genuine, his or her motivation is true, and their intelligence accurate, and ideally valuable. The third potential play features the intelligence nuisance. They are the Walter Mitty-like characters who seek to peddle stories and have absolutely no value, except as perverse stand-up comedians. The int nuisance is the bane of the business – they suck in resources and eat up valuable time before they are fully identified for what they are. Identifying their motivation is never straightforward and not necessarily relevant. It could be financial, it could be the manifestation of a psychological issue, or a mix. The important thing is to identify the nuisance as rapidly as possible and cut all ties.

It is particularly difficult to deal with an int nuisance because institutionally we look at every case from the perspective of wanting it to be genuine. This inevitably tends to string out the process of eventually cutting ties, because we give the Walt more than a fair crack of the whip to prove themselves. Every newly recruited agent is rigorously scrutinised to ensure that their intelligence is genuine. This process never ceases for the duration of a case – no single piece of intelligence is taken at face value or recorded without scepticism. But eventually, in the case of an int nuisance, patience runs out and the wool-pulling is over. In Pat's case it was easier, because his tales were so uncredible – a tighter weave of fact and fiction would have been far harder to discount. A credible Walt can make a unit look very silly until they are exposed.

I remember that in this case he had woven in some story with a Gibraltarian angle hinting at involvement with the abortive PIRA bomb attack there the year previously, in 1988. It took several meetings to unequivocally conclude that he was fabricating a whole volume of nonsense. He became known as 'Pat the Twat', christened by the always witty Ben K, who led the handling effort, with me as the co-handler. Ben's claim to fame, apart from being a good operator, was to have inherited an engineering business from his prematurely deceased brother, probably worth more than most of his fellow handlers would earn in the entirety of their military careers. We cut Pat loose. Strange psychology but a good learning experience.

A personal highlight for me was being called mysteriously into Hamish's office first thing one morning to be told that I had been awarded an MBE in the Operational Honours list for my time in Bessbrook. It was a complete surprise, but a pleasant and satisfying one. The joke about these orders is that the MBE is awarded for 'My Bloody Efforts', while the OBE is for 'Other Buggers' Efforts' – without doubt I would not have received the award without the hard work of my buggers in S Det. Hamish generously handed me a good bottle of champagne, which like an idiot I put down on the floor beside my desk. Mid-afternoon there was an almighty explosion as the bottle, too near the radiator, exploded. What a waste. I'm pleased to say that no one on the corridor dashed to take cover.

I want to touch on the 'feeding frenzy' that continues to periodically swirl around the well-publicised FRU agent Brian Nelson. He is highlighted for criticism as an individual and as a representative of UK plc's wider strategy to fight terrorism. While it is not my purpose to present an academic paper on the broader issues underpinning agent operations in a modern liberal democracy, I will make several points from the perspective that working for the Top brought to me.

The first is that whatever moral and legalistic objections are raised against the employment of agents against the backdrop of fighting terror, the strategy is both operationally effective, cost-effective, and arguably represents the only collection platform that can get right inside the terrorists' thoughts and decision-making processes. Human sources expose the guts of a terrorist organisation. With the right level of access, agents can take us an additional quantum step forward and actually influence the strategy and operational objectives of an organisation. This is critical and unique.

But, as my second broad generic observation attests to, what we cannot escape is the fundamental, key, pivotal, unavoidable reality that for an agent to have the access we require to support effective counterterrorist operations, that agent has ultimately to be an active, trusted member of that terrorist organisation. He or she has to be a terrorist and has to either have direct knowledge of unlawful activity or, if not directly breaking the law themselves, be close enough as a conspirator or accomplice.

My third point is that human sources are by no means perfect. I have heard it argued that to place oneself in the position of being recruited as an agent in the first instance reveals a flawed personality. Agents are human beings, and as such, in keeping with the rest of humanity, they are imperfect and fallible. As agent handlers, we motivate them and frankly exploit their weaknesses and character foibles. But they make mistakes, they get things wrong, on occasion they lie, and they can fabricate. This is because they, like the rest of us, have their own interests and motivators. The greatest of these will always be the drive for self-preservation. Agents operating at the higher levels face commensurately higher pressures. They are exposed to higher levels of security scrutiny, there is far less room to make forced or unforced errors in judgement, and they are subject to far higher levels of operational and psychological stress. It is no surprise to me that on occasion a top-flight agent may knowingly mislead his or her handlers to preserve, or reinforce, their own security. They are experienced and streetwise enough to realise that, on occasion, passing a certain piece of intelligence will potentially place them in an exceedingly difficult and invidious position. They know that if we exploit their intelligence, it will be their backs feeling the lash. If they report to us in good faith, they will implicate and incriminate themselves in criminal activity – they are terrorists. Knowing how the system works, can we be surprised that an agent may, on occasion, be selective in telling our handlers certain things? If an agent chooses to withhold information, can we then blame the handlers and hold them responsible for this situation? If we do not know something, we, as an agent handling organisation, cannot report it.

This is what I think occurred in the Brian Nelson case. Nelson had been a British Army soldier. He had been recruited as an agent on his return to the Province on leaving the military.

Subsequently, in due course he had moved to Germany in search of work. I remember Hamish planning to recontact him and bring him back to Belfast to continue working for us. This duly happened and he rocketed up within the ranks of the UDA to become its chief Intelligence Officer, directing the organisation's targeting operations.

This put him, and us, in a unique position. He was able to provide the FRU with unparalleled access into the terror group and an unparalleled overview of its operational priorities. But then the cart came off the rails. Nelson was subsequently arrested by the RUC for his UDA activities, no doubt based on information supplied by other agents within the UDA working for the Special Branch. The Loyalist groups were even more critically compromised by agent penetration than their Republican cousins. He was charged with murder. The FRU then became embroiled in the inquiry, which John Stevens headed, then the Chief Constable of Norfolk and Suffolk.

During his subsequent trial, the prosecution alleged that Nelson had withheld intelligence from his handlers and aided and abetted in the murder of Republicans. The thrust of the Stevens investigation was to investigate allegations that the FRU had knowingly colluded in at least some of these murders.

I want to record my views on this matter – I stress that they are my personal views but they are certainly not, at the risk of sounding arrogant, uninformed. By the time Nelson was at the peak of his 'career' as the UDA intelligence supremo, I was sitting in the Headquarters at my IO's desk. My key responsibility was to act as the focal point for all intelligence that the Dets reported up to the HQ. After I had briefed the Ops Offr and CO on the most important reports, I was then to ensure that Special Branch Headquarters in Knock was briefed. I would regularly travel to Knock, as I mentioned earlier, to brief the hierarchy in person. My point is that there was no evidence of any conspiracy by the FRU leadership to collude illegally with any of our agents in the commission of criminal activity. Put simply, I would have been directly aware of this information or been in a position to identify the red flags that indicated something was seriously amiss. The Security

Service's ASP would likewise have spotted that something was not as it should be. Not a single item of intelligence came across my desk to indicate anything of the sort. Nor did I pick up the barrack-room whispers that would have been fuelled by breaches of this magnitude. The FRU was a small and incestuous organisation that kept few internal secrets for long. Any such conspiracy would have had to have involved the CO, the Ops Offr within the HQ, and the OC of E Det, almost certainly the FSC, and Nelson's handling team. This could have been a good plot in a racy novel but just did not hold even a drop of water with regard to a high-calibre covert organisation led by equally high-calibre officers.

At Nelson's trial, it was stated that he had in fact reported to his handlers somewhere in the region of 200 UDA death threats, including, ironically, one against Gerry Adams. I repeat the point that it is not, in my opinion, possible to run so protracted and large-scale an illegal operation without details of it leaking out in so small and so tightly controlled a unit as the FRU. Further, the premise that the FRU, acting alone or in direct response to tasking from the government, would use Loyalist terror groups to target PIRA is based on a complete lack of understanding of the factors at play. Neither the UDA or the UFF or the UVF had the professional reach or prowess to liquidate significant numbers of PIRA or PSF activists. If this was a policy aspiration, such a strategy would be doomed to fail. Supporting Loyalist gangs to continue what they did have a pedigree in doing, murdering ordinary innocent members of the Nationalist community, brought absolutely no strategic benefit and would have received no buy-in from any member of the security forces, and certainly not from the highly trained, motivated and, frankly, above-average intelligence covert operators of the FRU. Who would willingly take such a professional and personal risk in the full knowledge that compromise would result in a lengthy sentence behind bars? Generally no one in their right mind, and specifically no one I knew in the FRU.

Frankly and crucially, regardless of this sanction, we were more aware than any agency in the Province that PIRA was feeling itself more and more weakened by our, and SB's, contribution to the intelligence war, and that they had lost all confidence by the late 1980s that they could score any sort of military victory. There was simply no strategic imperative to break the law to break PIRA. The damage our agents had wrought had already broken the organisation.

This is not to say that I believe E Det FRU was not without its problems as a Detachment – there was a general view within the unit in the late 1980s that it was not being led in the most robust way, and that there was an element of 'operator power' at work within the office whereby some handlers exercised a disproportionate influence within the Det. But it was not a rogue unit acting independently. I knew the OC, and I had worked with and knew Nelson's handlers. No one in the unit would have countenanced the illegal activity we were accused of. It just did not make any sense. It just was not credible.

Just to note, these accusations escalated to a risible level when it was claimed that a fire in the Stevens team offices within Carrickfergus RUC station was started by FRU arsonists in an attempt to destroy evidence. To break into a manned police station with the means to create a fire severe enough to destroy metal filing cabinets, etc., and then to leave undetected, would be a high-risk and complex operation. Destroying documentation, notes, notebooks, reports, signed testimony, etc., would slow down an investigation but it would certainly not derail it. To do that, conspirators would be required to either kill or intimidate both investigators and witnesses so that there was no case to answer. I think it an unlikely scenario on all counts. Again, good fiction but lacking credibility in the real world. But I never fail to be amazed at the preposterous nature of some conspiracy theories. I personally consider this whole panoply of assertions to be a conspiracy theory that sadly and cynically attempts, but fails, to damage and discredit a dedicated, professional and vital cog in the UK government's fight against terrorism, and by implication every member of the unit. Post-Stevens, the FRU did lose its name when, for 'branding' reasons, it was changed to the Joint Support Group. What a pity, but after all, if we're honest, what's really in a name?

As a unit, across the Dets, we maintained a high level of personal fitness and religiously maintained our weapons proficiency with regular range days keeping our skills honed, instinctive and effective. We did not just shoot our full range of weaponry, but also practised our anti-ambush drills. One thing I had always felt we lacked, however, was continuation training and confirmation of our unarmed combat skills. I received Hamish's blessing to set something up to correct this potential life-threatening deficiency.

I had got to know a Royal Marine SNCO who had taught the skill to Commando recruits at Lympstone – he actually later joined the FRU as a handler. We talked and he agreed to set up an initial course for handlers currently serving in the Province. He roped in an old friend and colleague of his, a former RM instructor who now ran restraint training for the Met Police, and put together a package that we ran down in Ballykinler. We opened the course up to all the Dets and managed to put a good dozen or more of the lads through it. Blending traditional commando techniques with some police skills, it complemented and broadened the training we had all gone through at SIW. The ethos remained the deployment of simple explosive skills that were primarily effective, but just as importantly did not require technique that had to be practised regularly. It worked well.

Again, running the concept past Hamish and receiving his OK, we took the process one important step forward and followed up with a course to 'train the trainer'. Now we would have the capability to train within the Dets and maintain the sharpened edge we needed.

This time we returned to Ashford with a smaller of volunteer handlers, representing all Detachments, committed to conduct our own in-house training, and some representation from the Manor. We used the same trainers but this time spent a little more time. We were away for three or four days. The course was superb and provided us with exactly what we needed. We were able to plug a capability gap that should have been addressed a long time before.

But as a postscript, the ability to defend oneself effectively does not always lead to scar-free encounters when a situation unravels.

I had returned to Ashford, to SIW, as the Training Officer and 2IC in 1992, after my three years with BRIXMIS and JIS. Ashford was always a pretty hard, tough town, and it was not difficult to court trouble during an evening out; intentionally, if that was one's want, or unintentionally if one misjudged or misguided a word or glance. I had a Belgian friend visiting, Frank, married to a friend of my girlfriend's family. We decided to head out to my favourite Indian restaurant on the edge of south Ashford, adjacent to the old railway engine works. I had been here many times before and knew the owner and staff, all Bangladeshis from Sylhet, the town that was home to all the original Indian restaurant owners in Britain.

We were comfortably settled at a small table. I had my back to the wall and was wedged in quite tightly but comfortably. We had already ordered, a quick-fire procedure as I was well aware of what was good and not quite so hot. Sitting in the corner by the kitchen door, the subtle, soothing notes soared from the strings of Shankar's sitar, blending seamlessly with the heavily spiced air creating a sense of contentment and anticipation.

It was still early and the restaurant was quiet, with only two other tables occupied, until there was a commotion outside with the arrival of two American-style, large-cab pickup trucks. They rapidly disgorged a dozen young men in through the front door. Our sense of peace and tranquillity fractured as readily as a poppadum as the noisy, boisterous and excitable group pushed and jostled their way inside. A highly charged mood neutered and subsumed the blessings of the sitar. But good business for the restaurant, as the waiters pulled a number of tables together to accommodate the gang.

They ordered drinks, but instead of settling to study their menus the noise level continued to rise. Before long it had become the sole source of sensory stimulation in the small restricted space the restaurant occupied. It was irritating, distracting, and detracting from any feeling of enjoyment of a simple evening out. To his credit, the owner – a little, rounded gentle fellow – intervened, requesting the party to moderate things.

I had already had a good look at the bunch. The eldest was around 40, short, squat, puggish, with heavy features and untidy sandy blond hair, with a couple of youngsters in their mid-teens. The rest aged from late teens into their twenties. They were obviously Irish itinerants or travellers, what most people incorrectly call gypsies. Kent has always attracted a sizeable population because of its less-restrictive policies towards them and their caravan sites. I knew that the groups littered around the outlying areas of Ashford were generally well-known to the local police. I guessed this was an extended family outing and that their voluble and pumped manner was probably due to an altercation they had already been involved in.

In response to the owner's request to quieten down, one of the group turned and focussed his attention on me and called out whether I, 'mate', minded the noise. With hindsight probably not the most politic response, but I have always spoken my mind plainly and, when necessary, without overly dressing it in typically English discretion and nuance. I called back that actually it would be really rather nice if they quietened down – and I've never responded positively to being addressed as 'mate'. Well, that marked the end of the evening, for everyone, without even a mouthful of chicken chat as we sat waiting for our food.

The older guy and a couple of others pushed back their chairs and approached our table. A small gaggle exited the restaurant and quickly returned with four steel baseball bats. Everything then took on its own momentum and rhythm. As I covered up, protecting the sides of my head, with my elbows tucked into my flanks, I could feel the bats pounding into my ribs but thankfully not my head – that would have been serious. As it was, it was just like being in the ring, albeit being totally outclassed and out-hit by my four or five 'opponents'. After half a dozen or so blows, the baseballers decided that they, or I, had had enough and laid off, while their leader markedly stood in front of me and, as we locked in unblinking eye contact, punched me hard square in the face, breaking my nose, and caught me under the eye with a signet ring he was wearing with another straight. I remember consciously weighing up whether I should counter-punch, but, rightly I am sure, made the decision that retaliation from the group returning would leave me in a far worse condition – it never fails to surprise me how lucid, quick-thinking and calculating we remain during times of extreme stress. They were then all out of the place like the film of an avalanche in rewind, revving engines and roaring off at speed. I was pleased they had not eaten either.

An unnatural peace returned to the scene as Ravi played on. My Belgian friend had disappeared and I did not see him for the rest of the evening. I did not hold it against him. I was still firmly and unequivocally wedged in behind my table and still up on my feet, having risen I'm not quite sure why. The staff told me later, as I waited for the ambulance they had called and the police, that they were really impressed that I had remained standing despite the onslaught of blows. I had to laugh to myself – I could not have gone down even if I had wanted to. I wasn't in any great pain or discomfort, yet, and kept mobile as I circled around the open space in the middle of the restaurant floor, chatting distractedly to the waiters and owner. They promised me that when I returned, dinner would be on the house – I was not able to return that night, but I claimed my prize two weeks later.

The ambulance took me up to the William Harvey hospital – coincidentally the hospital that treated the UK's first case of mad cow disease – feeling every bump and jolt in the most uncomfortable ride I had had in a very long time. I sat in casualty for four hours waiting, frightening women and children with my bloodied face and shirt, but otherwise feeling in pretty good, post-incident shape. Finally, I was seen by the doc and told what I already suspected. Probably three broken ribs and nose, and some facial lacerations. I was amused to see the clear imprints of some of the baseball shots on my upper body.

I smiled a little less over the next ten days as I was forced to lie in bed as my ribs slowly began mending. I have had broken ribs on two further occasions and they are extremely painful as every half-move, cough, sneeze or chuckle sends arrows of pain shooting through one's torso. News travels fast. I received plenty of calls enquiring on my condition and wishing me well, I'm sure some more genuine than others, the less sincere probably amused that "One of those wankers from the Manor got sorted out, then – thought they did all that unarmed combat stuff." I was also visited by one of my guys, a hard Royal Marine, who had canvassed a few of the lads and was keen to get my permission to pay a visit to the Pikies' caravan site, the location of which, apparently, he was well aware of. I firmly rejected his offer but very much appreciated, and was touched by, the sentiment.

The police treated my case as a serious aggravated assault and were quick to raid the site that they suspected housed the gang. The main culprits, they reported, had already fled the area. Subsequently, they brought in a couple of the younger lads and set up an identity parade to establish whether I could pick out anyone for charging. As I passed down the line, I guess it must have been about a fortnight or so later, I recognised two of the youngsters who had been in the Indian. They betrayed themselves by looking seriously nervous and worried about their predicament. But, as they had not been involved in the 'fight' – 'bigging up' the one-way rain of blows – I walked on by, but did let them know out of the corner of my mouth that I knew who they were.

So that was that. The incident graphically showed that I had broken the first rule and allowed myself to be drawn into a situation rather than avoiding it. I had undoubtedly provoked things rather than proactively seeking to minimise my exposure. What it did more positively demonstrate, however, was that once the situation had deteriorated to the point where violence erupted and I was embroiled in it with no recourse to remove myself, my training provided me with the ability to assess things and implement the decision, rather than fight back and deploy aggressive skills against the threats, to cover up and defend myself, and, in so doing, not provoke matters further and minimise damage to myself.

No one was ever charged, but I did receive a kind gift of £2,000 from the criminal injuries establishment.

So again the fateful clock wound down and my year's reprieve ended. My time had come to an end, this time with that sombre sense of finality that brooks no hope for compromise. There was no way this time that I would ever return for anything longer than short updates. I would visit the Province again, wearing my SIW training hat, after I had completed three amazing years in eastern Germany with the Mission and the unit that succeeded it, incidentally commanded by Hamish, but I would never again serve here.

Frankly, with the advent of peace, I would not have wished to. There is nothing worse than the bore who continually alludes to the 'old days', never tiring of commenting on how this or that was done, and of course by implication, done better.

A new generation of peacetime operators came to inhabit the unit, as JSG, until it was finally disestablished a few short years later, its job done. The peace ensured there was no continuing useful role for a unit with its skills, capabilities and mindset – in a way, we were part victims of our own success, which is, if we are honest, no bad epitaph.

I have often said that I would love to return to the island as a tourist and revisit some of the starring locations in these pages – Belfast, of course, Newry, Bessbrook, and definitely places like Cross, Forkhill, and over the border to Dundalk and beyond. If you were to ask me to name one thing I would like to do on this visit, how special would it be to sit down around the table with some of those key names we juggled with, day in and day out, the key players in south Armagh PIRA, a Murphys in hand, to swap stories about those wild, unforgotten, defining days?

But frivolous and unrealistic thoughts aside, I think it is appropriate to end on a more serious note.

FRU days were deadly serious days, fully stocked with serious business, their legacy an enduring impact on the drawing to a close of a bloody, painful and supremely tragic period of this United Kingdom's history. The fight we fought as a unit was a deadly one in its pursuit of the deadly intelligence that we hoped could – and, we now know, did – make a difference. I am immensely proud to have served in the unit as a professional soldier and an intelligence officer, and I am immensely proud as a human being that I was a part of a force for good that succeeded in doing good, and contributed in no small way to bringing about a peaceful ending to a dark period of our history.

But more than this, I salute the courage, sacrifice and dedication of our agents who made the greater contribution. I hope that they too feel pride in what they did and have been able to reconcile any enduring, lingering doubts that they might have betrayed their heritage, history and community. Surely they did not, because their heroism has served greater gods, vital in bringing a return to normality so that these cornerstones of normal life can continue to flourish and evolve in peace. The peace they contributed to so emphatically has been robust and enduring enough to watch over and protect the newest generation, including the lives, welfare and hope of their children and grandchildren.

They are the unsung heroes.

POSTSCRIPT

So that is the tale of my days in Northern Ireland with the Force Research Unit (NI).

I have enjoyed recording these pages far more than I ever imagined I would. So many times in my life, writing has been an irksome chore, usually put off until whatever deadline has been about to expire, but this has been tremendous fun, day in and day out reminiscing, squeezing out distant recollections and memories, pulling together thoughts, saving some, discarding others, and teasing them into some sort of coherent order. Perhaps we use the term 'cathartic' too readily, but this has without doubt been a period of intense and largely positive introspection, and a time of considerable self-examination and analysis. Writing has forced me to look hard at myself, not just my actions, but my thoughts and ideas on the trek I have made as a person and a professional. I certainly understand more about myself and appreciate how these early experiences have influenced my views on people and life, and shaped the way I approach it – again, good and bad. The result has been a positive experience, so much so that it has encouraged me to complete similar exercises detailing my time in the British Mission in the old East Germany and on later HUMINT collection missions, including Bosnia, liaising with the UCK during the war in Kosovo, the UK's intervention in Sierra Leone, conflicts in

Angola, Sri Lanka, the Great Lakes region of Central Africa and other assignments on four continents.

What has surprised me has been the degree to which I have felt myself transported back to those days. I have recalled faces and places, events and meetings, operational ups and downs, emotions, frustrations and moments of supreme satisfaction – that is to the good. The reverse side of the coin has been the remembered sense of perpetual stress and pressure – not healthy.

But writing every day, I've been unavoidably transported back to days of purpose, energy and excitement – in stark contrast to the anodyne mediocrity and superficiality of life in the 'crunch-less' slow lane of today's 'new normal' – I increasingly feel the urge to increasingly take longer and longer backward glances at times passed. I have felt a constant sense of anticipation and the taut confidence of doing something, if not useful, then at least reinforcing perceptions of meaning. Once again, I've experienced that long-lost sense of instant wakefulness each morning; an impatience to get a start on the day – there are few sensations as good. When not sitting in front of my keyboard, out running or mountain-biking, words and ideas have pulsed through my brain, tumbling into sentences and paragraphs so that I have had to rush in upon getting home, struggling to keep them ordered, and get them down on paper before losing them.

But as I re-read these words, I am torn by two prevailing emotions, perhaps uncomfortable bedfellows but nonetheless palpable.

I feel a great sense of personal pride, and a great sense of institutional pride, for what we, collectively, as the Security Forces, achieved, and especially the contribution we, as agent handlers in the Force Research Unit, made to restoring peace in Ulster. Our practical successes and the psychological pressure that our very existence contributed to bringing PIRA to the peace table is impossible to underestimate.

But increasingly, with the onset of family and the sensitivity and understanding that inevitably comes with the passing of years, I feel a tremendous sense of sadness as I contemplate the waste of it all. It saddens me even more when I realise that this is now probably the prevalent sensation, and that it progressively blunts those feelings of achievement and accomplishment.

The reality of the loss of life is stark. The reality of the sheer scale of physical, psychological and emotional injury is numbing. I think, ultimately, very few who were brought up there, and very few of us who soldiered in the Province, especially 'undercover', escaped unmarked. A staggering 3,635 people lost their lives during 'The Troubles' in this tiny corner of Europe. Prior to the Good Friday Agreement of 1998, it is estimated that in excess of a staggering 100,000 suffered some form of personal injury, a great many of them damaged forever, just for the fluke of destiny that they had been born, lived or worked in the troubled counties of Northern Ireland. That equates to approximately 6.5 per cent of the Province's population. Extrapolate this figure to the population of the UK as whole, and a conflict of similar proportions would have exacted 3.5 million casualties – that is half of the people living in London at the time. These are weighty figures, but translating them into the weight of personal loss they become almost unbearable. If you doubt my words, take a browse through David McKittrick's *Lost Lives*. It is a supremely moving and intensely depressing catalogue of suffering.

I think back to the deaths of some of those whom I knew personally, others whom I might have met, who lost their lives in south Armagh and beyond, that as a much less mature and experienced young man I glided over, largely untouched, at the time, and failed to take the time and the emotional resources to confront and acknowledge. But I do vividly recall the seemingly regular and unquenchable rhythm as bodies were dumped on the border, blindfolded and hands tied, and contemplate the terror of their last hours. The bodies of those who were identified as agents and those who were murdered mistakenly for something that they did not do. Tragic. Indeed, lost lives.

But would I do it again? Without even a momentary pause to question the question, unreservedly, "Yes!" Would I let my children do it? Unreservedly, "No!"

There certainly was a price to pay in doing what we did, for my generation and the one that followed, that I would not want them to have to pay. Should they join the military, there will be no FRU, and quite likely life in the cyber-focussed armed forces of tomorrow will be healthier and less dangerous. But I would not stop them if this was their considered wish. Every generation faces its own challenges and must earn its own successes. Rather, though, join a large multinational and rise up its slippery pole to financial sufficiency and an early retirement. Or invent something useful that will somehow seduce our society away from its headlong descent into a social media-dependent mire!

The world will continue to change. Whatever comes to pass, regardless, I hope that soldiers will never again have to patrol the streets, lanes and fields of Ireland in uniform, or out of it, in response to the scourge of either Republican or, perhaps more realistically, Loyalist terrorism.

We will see.

APPENDICES

Appendix A: Military Glossary

ARB	Armagh Roulement Battalion. The four-month emergency tour battalion headquartered in Bessbrook Mill.
ARF	Airborne Reaction Force. Heli-borne force to react to incidents.
ASUs	Active Service Units. The small operational terror units of PIRA and INLA.
ATO	Ammunition Technical Officer. Royal Army Ordnance Corps bomb disposal specialists.
B Div	RUC divisional area covering the most violent areas of west Belfast.
BAOR	British Army of the Rhine. The British Army units based in Germany.
BRIXMIS	British Commanders'-in-Chief Mission to the Soviet Forces in Germany. Military liaison mission operating in DDR until end of the Cold War.
CASCON	Casual Contact. A human source but not under full control.

CF	Contact Form. Classified report detailing all aspects of an agent meet.
CHIS	Covert Human Intelligence Source. The RIPA phraseology for an agent.
CLF	Commander Land Forces. The Major General running overall operations in NI.
CO	Commanding Officer.
COP	Close Observation Platoon. Non-SF discreet observation capability.
CQB	Close Quarter Battle. Practical shooting skills and weapons training.
DCI	Director and Coordinator of Intelligence. The intelligence supremo in the Province.
Det	Detachment. FRU latterly was comprised of four: N, S, E and W.
DDR	Deutsche Demokratische Republik. Former communist East Germany.
DINT	Director Intelligence Corps. Brigadier directing the Corps.
DMSU	Divisional Mobile Support Unit. RUC Land-Rover-borne quick reaction force.
DS	Directing Staff. The teaching staff on military courses.
ECM	Electronic Countermeasures. Technical protective measures to negate technical attacks, typically in NI against IEDs.
E2	Non-Int Corps personnel in the FRU.
E4A	RUC covert surveillance unit. The equivalent of the Army's 14 Coy.
FINCO	Field Intelligence NCO. In NI they supported the MIO in his SB liaison duties.
FRG	Federal Riot Gun. Fires non-lethal plastic anti-riot bullets and tear gas rounds.
FRO	Forward Research Office. A forward handling team run from a Det located elsewhere. Before the creation of S Det and W Det, the FRU operated five FROs.

FRU	Force Research Unit. Latterly an MOD-sponsored unit. Recruitment operation referred to as OP MAXIMISE.
FSC	Field Source Controller. An old SIS term denoting the 2IC of a FRU Det.
FSP	Force Support Platoon. S Det FRU's dedicated patrol multiple, originally manned by Royal Military Police.
GCHQ	Government Communications Headquarters. SIGINT agency based in Cheltenham.
GRU	Soviet Military Intelligence.
GSFG/WGF	Group of Soviet Forces in Germany/Western Group of Forces. Soviet military contingent based in DDR until end of the Cold War.
G1, G2, G3, G4	Army staff branches dealing with Admin, Intelligence, Operations, and Logistics.
HIS	Hostile Intelligence Service. A foreign enemy intelligence organisation, e.g. KGB.
HK	Heckler & Koch. German armaments company. Maker of MP5 and HK 53.
HQNI	Headquarters Northern Ireland. Located in Thiepval Barracks, Lisburn, Co. Down.
HUMINT	Human Intelligence. Generic term for all intelligence derived from interpersonal contact. Sources are exclusively human rather than technical, e.g. IMINT, MASINT SIGINT.
HMSU	Headquarters Mobile Support Unit. Highly trained RUC unit akin to SAS.
HQ	Headquarters.
IED	Improvised Explosive Device. Formal nomenclature for a terrorist bomb.
IGB	Inner German Border. The Cold War fortified border between DDR and West Germany.
IJS	Irish Joint Section
INLA	Irish National Liberation Army.
Int Corps	Intelligence Corps. Never referred to as I Corps.

IO	Intelligence Officer. Interchangeable term used to refer to both terrorist and Army personnel.
IRA	Irish Republican Army. Refers to the organisation before the 1969 schism.
ISC	Intermediate Search Centre. Secure location to search vehicles and engineer target meets.
IVCP	Illegal Vehicle Check Point. A terrorist-operated VCP.
JIRO	Defence Intelligence Staff officer deployed to the Northern Ireland Office in Knock.
JSIO	Joint Service Interrogation Organisation. Interrogation unit based in Templer Barracks, Ashford.
KGB	Soviet intelligence service.
LO	Liaison Officer.
LTI	Limited Technical Sweep. Debugging action.
MILO	Military Intelligence Liaison Officer. Based in DIS with a worldwide troubleshooter role.
MIO	Military Intelligence Officer. Army liaison officers working with RUC SB.
MISR	Military Intelligence Source Reports. Used to disseminate FRU intelligence.
MOD	Ministry of Defence.
NATO	North Atlantic Treaty Organisation. The alliance facing off against the Warsaw Pact.
NCO	Non-Commissioned Officer. Military ranks from Lance Corporal to WO1.
ND	Negligent discharge. Unintentional discharge of a weapon, invariably the result of poor weapon handling drills.
NI	Northern Ireland.
OC	Officer Commanding. Sub unit command function supporting the CO.
OFCON	Official Contact. Not relevant in FRU context.
OIRA	Official IRA. Also known as 'stickies'. IRA split in 1969, creating OIRA and PIRA.

OP	Observation Post. Covert position in urban or rural environment.
Ops Offr	Operations Officer. Directs all operational aspects.
Ops WO	Operations Warrant Officer. Supports Ops Offr.
PIRA	Provisional IRA. The militant organisation emerging from the IRA split.
PSF	Provisional Sein Fein. Political wing of PIRA.
PX	US military shopping centre. Great prices and great selection of goods, from cars to chocolate bars. NATO servicemen enjoy access.
QRF	Quick Reaction Force.
RHF	Royal Highland Fusiliers. Scottish battalion recruiting from Glasgow.
RHSB	Regional Head of Special Branch. There were three RHSBs.
RIPA	Regulation of Investigatory Powers Act. Law introduced in 2000 to regulate powers of investigative and intelligence agencies.
RIRAC	I was never aware of what the acronym stands for, but it was an int report from the civilian int agencies in the Province.
RM	Royal Marines. In my opinion the most professional infantry unit in the British Military.
RTA	Road Traffic Accident. A vehicle crash.
RUC	Royal Ulster Constabulary.
RV	Rendezvous.
RVH	The Royal Victoria Hospital. Just off the Falls Road in west Belfast.
SA 80	Replacement for the FN SLR as the infantry rifle. Original version was loathed.
SAS	Special Air Service. Referred to as the Regiment. Individual members were referred to as Flatheads, but not usually to their faces.
SB	Special Branch.
SF	Special Forces. Comprised SAS, SBS and 14 Coy. Commanded by Director Special Forces.

SIGINT	Signals intelligence. Refers to all int derived from communications interception.
SIS	Secret Intelligence Service. Also known as MI6 and Box 850.
SITREP	Situation Report. Any report providing an update on a situation.
SIW	Specialist Intelligence Wing. The Army's covert intelligence school based in Templer Barracks, Ashford. Now located in Joint Intelligence Training Group (formerly Defence Intelligence and Security Centre), Chicksands, since 1997.
SLR	Self-Loading Rifle. Made in Belgium by Fabrique National. Superceded by SA 80.
SNCO	Senior NCO. Refers to all ranks from Sergeant to WO1.
SNONI	Senior Naval Officer Northern Ireland. Commander of all RN and RM forces in NI.
SOE	Special Operations Executive. Second World War intelligence, sabotage and recce organisation.
SOP	Standard Operational Procedure. An established approach to dealing with an issue.
SOXMIS	Soviet Military Mission. Russian organisation working in British zone of West Germany until end of the Cold War.
SVR	The Russian Foreign Intelligence Service. Successor to the KGB 1st Chief Dir in 1991.
SO2 G2	The officer with the rank of Major fulfilling intelligence staff duties in a HQ.
TAOR	Tactical Area of Responsibility. The area for which a unit has military operational responsibility.
TCF	Telephone Contact Form. Records all contact with an agent by telephone.
TCG	Tasking and Coordination Group. The joint Army/RUC fusion cell directing covert operations. There were three in the Province.

UCK	Kosovo Liberation Army (*Ushtria Çlirimtare e Kosovës*).
UDA	Ulster Defence Association. The largest Loyalist paramilitary group.
UDR	Ulster Defence Regiment. Locally recruited British Army regiment consisting of full-time and part-time members.
UFF	Ulster Freedom Fighters. Loyalist terror group.
USAF	United States Air Force.
UVF	Ulster Volunteer Force. Loyalist terror group.
VCP	Vehicle Check Point. Usually refers to one mounted by police or Army.
VRN	Vehicle Registration Number. All vehicles registered in NI were recorded on the OP VENGEFUL data base and accessible by troops on the ground.
WO1	Warrant Officer Class One. The most senior non-commissioned rank.
WO2	Warrant Officer Class Two. One rank junior to a WO1. Incumbents referred to as Sergeant Major.
XMG	Crossmaglen.
2IC	Second-in-command
14 Coy/Gp NI/JCUNI	All names used to refer to the Army's surveillance unit in the Province. Unit directed by Director Special Forces.

Appendix B:
Talking to People in South Armagh
by Captain Robert Nairac

1. Just as it is important to regard everyone with serious suspicion, it is also important to regard any local as a possible source of information. Most people (possibly 80%) are sick of the violence and would like to see the Troubles end. Some would go as far as to do something about it, if approached in the right way. Among fringe PIRA (or even active terrorists) there are those who might be 'turned' by the right approach. Generally speaking, four factors prevent this:

   a. Fear of PIRA
   b. Fear and mistrust of the Army
   c. Genuine sympathy for the 'Republican' cause
   d. Tradition

2. Most of the points in this paper are applicable to the RC communities throughout NI.

Aim

3. The aim of this paper is to suggest how best to overcome these four difficulties.

Fear of PIRA

4. Fear is the most important factor in keeping people's mouths shut. They look at everyone – fathers, mothers, sons, neighbours – as possible dangers. To have been seen to talking to soldiers may mean a 'visit' and some sharp questioning. All too often a friendly nod from a local has resulted in uniformed soldiers openly halting or greeting them. If this goes on, a beating or a knee or head job is the end result. Therefore, if you wish to talk to someone, follow these points carefully:

   a. Do not single them out for attention. If you visit their home, visit at least four or five others, before and after. Try to make your visit to your subject as normal as possible.
   b. Make sure that your subject realises that your he/she is not being singled out – even if they are.

c. Give them an excuse for your visit. They will certainly be asked why the 'Brits' visited. Find a plausible excuse and tell them straight away e.g. 'We are calling on all the houses around here because...' Obviously, use the same story for all the visits on the operation.

d. If, after the interview, they appear at all friendly, give them the opportunity to ask you back, e.g. 'We often check the houses around here so we will see you again if that's okay?' This gives them the chance to say how they would like you to come, e.g. 'Fine, but come after dark', or 'when the kids are out'. If you get this then you have a contact.

5. If you can convince your subject that you are totally discreet and will not put them on the spot, many will help.

Mistrust of the Army

6. Many innocent people fear and mistrust the Army. Some, no doubt, have excellent reason to do so. The Army is, inevitably, a 'Brit' instrument, and harmless people suffer inconvenience, or worse, after an incident. Furthermore, we are seen as outsiders and interlopers. When faced with sincere complaints, blind denial is worse than useless. One is merely calling your 'plaintiff' a liar! They may well be, but a far better line is to switch to the attack, e.g. 'I agree it is bad, but when you have seen your friends blown to bits...'. Also try the 'young eighteen soldier line'. Any soldier who has been killed must be either eighteen years old, fresh from home, or married with a new baby. It is possible to gain sympathy and genuine emotion from these very emotional people. Nonetheless, the best way is to avoid giving useless offence. Admittedly, if a totally committed PROVO gets a beating, it may not do any harm. However, it creates a bad impression. In any case, it is difficult to tell who are Provos, and many innocent people have traces. It is always worth mentioning that some who are openly anti-SF (security forces) in public, are probably putting on an act to impress the real terrorists.

Genuine Republicanism

7. At heart, all Catholic men and women in south Armagh have some sympathy for the Provo cause. It is a complete waste of time, and totally unproductive, to heap abuse and pour scorn on PIRA. Remember that you are an outsider and are probably talking about their son, neighbour, etc., 'misguided and misled' is a much better line of attraction than 'foul bastards'. Then once again attack their sympathy. Try the 'young soldier' line. Be wary of using accidents – south Armagh PIRA have a good record of not causing civilian casualties. If that does not succeed, move onto 'Kingsmills' or the 'Tullyvallen Orange Hall Massacre'. You could suggest to them that these two incidents were unlikely to win over Protestants. It is useful to use these three lines of attack for different age groups:

a. The Young (14–25 years). These days this age group is very up on history so know your facts. The best line of approach is to try and share their convictions. Attack PIRA propaganda and use all the Provo nastiness you can think of. Some of them have consciences, if so they will have some doubts. One good line from you could shake them out of their attitudes. Try and get them to argue politics with you. The hard facts of Protestant determination and military power always shakes them, e.g. 'If we pull out, do you think anyone can control the Prot paramilitaries' or 'If 20,000 British soldiers are pushed to defeat the Provos, who the hell is going to control over 20,000 UVF men?' Ask them for their solutions – but know your facts; they will know theirs.

b. The 26–38 year olds. All the above arguments can work well for this age group. If they are newly married or have young kids try 'is this a fit place to bring up kids?' Also, this age group is also very financially aware. The advantage of British social security, etc., can be used: be careful not to patronise. Try talking very much 'man to man', or indeed 'man to woman'. You will often get a favourable reaction by talking about 'wild tearaway kids'.

c. The parents (40s…) In this age group you probably have the greatest chance of success. Undoubtedly the emotional 'eighten-year-old soldier – just like your Danny' line can work well. Also try the 'Evil men leading young lads astray' line. Above all with this generation play on their parental worries, use the picture of sinister, hard men pushing young Republicans getting irretrievably enmeshed in an organisation which lost its decency. Ask if they worry about their kids. A great deal of success will come to you with experience. If you are very sure of your ground, hint darkly that you saw young Pat in dubious company. Finally and most powerfully, ask them if they would like the evil and hard men of the PIRA to rule their lives if we pulled out.

Tradition

8. South Armagh is traditionally a lawless and independent area. It is resentful of authority of any kind. Furthermore, certain things are taboo. It is said that if you raped your next door neighbour it will soon be forgotten: if your grandfather had been an 'INFORMER' you would be an outcast. It follows that there are certain deep-rooted things that will shut up people like a clam. Never use words like INFORM, INFORMATION, WITNESS or INTIMIDATE. Never write anything down; it smacks of police work. Never offer money for 'INFORMATION'. (It may come to that after months of cultivation, but to offer it is fatal.) There are ways around these taboos. 'May I call for a chat?' Avoid the direct question, hint, suggest and work round the subject. If you wish to say 'It is high time the bad men were locked up' try to get them to say it for you. Ask their advice, opinion, in very general terms.

Security

9. Finally be very wary of giving away any more than you get. Always consult 'Int' to see whose name you may mention. Do not ever use information from MISRs or 'P' Cards directly. You could be talking to the local PIRA IO!

Useful Euphemisms

10. No	Yes
'Can you give me information?	'Will our visit lead to intimidation?'
'Perhaps you might be able to help.'	'We don't want to embarrass you.'
'The PROVOs are stupid murderers.'	'We will come to see you.'
'Some of the boys have gone too far.'	'We are calling on all the houses around here because…'
'Your son is a terrorist.'	'We want to ask you some questions.'
'Your son is taking up with a bad crowd.'	'We've just come for a chat.'
'Did you see that shooting/ bombing?'	'How can we see you without fingering you?'
'Terrible business that bomb, it must have given you a fright.'	'We'll call again but we won't embarrass you.'

Useful Lines to Take

11.a. That a young soldier was killed – only eighteen and a half – just arrived – left a mother and baby, etc.

b. There are some evil men working on the lads and leading them on, etc.

c. THE WOMEN FOR PEACE – Would you like your lives to be run by the PROVOS? 25,000 marchers attended the peace march in Belfast – 400 people were at the Provo rally in Camlough.

d. Every bomb that goes off and every shot that is fired puts peace another ten years further off.
e. The Provos are the worst Republicans we have ever seen.
f. The Easter proclamation: 'Let no rapine cowardice or inhumanity dishonour our cause.'
g. Cite various Provo murders of policemen off duty in front of their wives/kids, etc.
h. When genuine complaints are made: 'Well I agree, but when you have seen a young boy (like that soldier etc.) blown apart…What if it was Danny/Pat etc. etc.'

Some Answers

12. Question:

'Who are the Army protecting in XMG?'

Answer:

'Well I agree; but face it if the boys stopped shooting and bombing we could go.' OR: 'I agree but shooting and bombing for six years has meant more soldiers/SAS/searches/VCPs.' OR: 'Yes, but do you want those PIRA boys running your lives.' OR: 'Yes, but how long would an unarmed policeman last in XMG – you must have some law.'

Conclusion

13. Throughout South Armagh there are many people who have vital bits of information. With skill and professionalism it is possible to extract life-saving titbits. If approached the right way, the fence-sitters (probably 60% of the community) will come down on our side. When that happens we have won.

RL NAIRAC
Captain
SAS LO

Appendix C:
Military Source Grading Matrix

	Rating	Description
A	Reliable	No doubt about the source's authenticity, trustworthiness, or competency. Record of complete reliability.
B	Usually reliable	Minor doubts. Record of mostly valid information.
C	Fairly reliable	Doubts. Provided valid information in the past.
D	Not usually reliable	Significant doubts. Provided some valid information in the past.
E	Unreliable	Lacks authenticity, trustworthiness, and competency. History of invalid information.
F	Reliability unknown	Insufficient information to evaluate reliability. May or may not be reliable.

Information Grading Matrix

	Rating	Description
1	Confirmed by independent sources	Logical. Consistent with other relevant information and corroborated by independent sources.
2	Probably true	Logical. Corroborated by other relevant information but not confirmed.
3	Possibly true	Reasonably logical. Agrees with other relevant information, not confirmed.

4	Doubtful	Not logical but possible. No other information on the subject, not confirmed.
5	Improbable	Not logical. Contradicted by other relevant information.
6	Untested	The validity of the information cannot be determined.

Appendix D: Civilian Agency Agent Intelligence Grading

Sources
F1: Regular
F2: Casual
F3: New source on trial

Access
A1: Direct Access
A2: Quoting well-placed informant
A3: Dubious access
A4: Quoting unconscious informant

Reliability
R1: Reliable
R2: Reliability not assessed
R3: Reliability unassessable

INDEX

Note: the suffix 'n' indicates a note